CRITICAL SURVEY OF POETRY

Russian Poets

Editor

Rosemary M. Canfield Reisman

Charleston Southern University

SALEM PRESS

A Division of EBSCO Publishing, Ipswich, Massachusetts

Cover photo:
Boris Pasternak (© Lebrecht Authors/Lebrecht Music & Arts/Corbis)

ISBN: 978-1-42983-665-4

CONTENTS

CONTRIBUTORS

David Bromige
Sonoma State University

Mitzi M. Brunsdale
Mayville State College

Julian W. Connolly
University of Virginia

Desiree Dreeuws
Sunland, California

K Edgington
Towson University

Margot K. Frank
*Randolph-Macon Women's
College*

Tracy Irons-Georges
Glendale, California

Sarah Hilbert
Pasadena, California

Maura Ives
Texas A&M University

Gerald Janecek
University of Kentucky

Irma M. Kashuba
Chestnut Hill College

Rebecca Kuzins
Pasadena, California

Vasa D. Mihailovich
University of North Carolina

Jane Ann Miller
*University of Massachusetts,
Dartmouth*

John P. Pauls
Cincinnati, Ohio

La Verne Pauls
Cincinnati, Ohio

Rado Pribic
Lafayette College

Stephanie Sandler
Amherst College

Jonathan Thorndike
Belmont University

Janet G. Tucker
University of Arkansas

RUSSIAN POETRY

For Russians, Aleksandr Solzhenitsyn says, "Poetry is born from the torment of the soul." Russia is a vast land, bordered on the north and south by the Baltic and the Black Seas, on the west by the Carpathian Mountains, and on the east by the mighty Volga River. In the thousand-year history of Russian literature, no natural barrier has preserved the Russian people from the agony of invasion, and Russian poetry has become unbreakably forged to their historical suffering.

The poetry of Russia's youth

The earliest ancestors of the modern Russians, the agricultural East Slavs, settled the inland plateau of the thirteen-hundred-mile Dnieper River and were preyed on during the ninth century by the Varangians, piratical Scandinavian merchants who founded petty principalities around Kiev. Under Grand Prince Vladimir of Kiev, their loose confederation was converted to Byzantine Christianity in 988 C.E., an immense religio-cultural invasion that consolidated its position in Russia by introducing the Old Church Slavonic alphabet based on the spoken dialect, importing Byzantine Greek forms as literary models, and assimilating native pagan elements into religious ritual. Although Old Church Slavonic served as the chief vehicle of Russian literature from the eleventh to the eighteenth centuries, it choked off exposure to the classical Humanistic heritage of the West and rigidly identified church with state, fortifying the autocracy of Russian rulers.

Russia's earliest poetic form was the vernacular and formulaic *bylina* (plural *byliny*; literally, things-that-have-been). These oral epics celebrated mythological figures and, more frequently, human heroes in groupings that resembled the Arthurian cycles. In the Kievan *byliny* cycle centered on Grand Prince Vladimir, the hero Ilya becomes "a symbol of the self-consciousness of the people," according to Felix J. Oinas in *Heroic Epic and Saga* (1978). Novgorod, a northern city belonging to the Hanseatic League, had a *byliny* cycle whose central figure was Aleksandr Nevsky, prince and saint, who repelled the Livonian and Teutonic knights. The Galician-Volhynian *byliny* cycle records the strife between this area and its western neighbors in the thirteenth and fourteenth centuries. As Oinas remarks, the *byliny* of patriarchal Russia "captivated and thrilled people of all walks of life until the nineteenth century," inspiring later poets with traditional Russian ideals.

During the twelfth century, the disintegration of feudal Russia set the bitter groundwork for the Mongol invasion of 1237 to 1240 and the imposition of the "Tartar yoke." *Slovo o polku Igoreve* (c. 1187; *The Tale of the Armament of Igor*, 1915) is Russia's first written poetic achievement, a stirring blend of the aristocratic warrior spirit and a call to self-sacrifice in defense of the Land of Rus. The poem poignantly and accurately predicts the great defeat to come: "O, how the Russian land moans, remembering her early years and princes!/ . . . in discord their pennons flutter apart." Based on the Novgorod Prince Igor's unsuccessful attempt in 1185 to dislodge Turkish Polovtsian usurpers from the lands near the Don, and startlingly modern in its complex imagery, allusion, and symbolism, *The Tale of the Armament of Igor* has sometimes been considered an imposture since its discovery in the early 1790's. Alexander Pushkin claimed, however, that not enough poetry existed in the eighteenth century for anyone then to have written it, and more recent scholars concur.

Until 1480, the Mongol tribute was paid by a Russia brutally severed from the West and struggling to unite itself sufficiently to cast off the hated Tartar yoke. Little national strength was left for poetry. Looking back from 1827, the religious philosopher Pyotr Chaadayev observed, "At first, brutal barbarism, then crude superstition, then fierce and humiliating bondage whose spirit was passed on to our own sovereigns—such is the history of our youth."

From Dark Age to Golden Age

Kiev was destroyed in Russia's literary Dark Age under the Tartars, and Russian culture was dominated by the Grand Duchy of Moscow, whose ruler Dmitri won a victory over the Tartars at Kulikovo, memorialized in the fifteenth century Cossack epic *Zadónščina* (beyond the river Don). Ivan II at last drove the Tartars from a unified Russia in 1480, less than a generation after the Turkish conquest of Constantinople, and Moscow became the "third Rome." Imperial power was inseparable from Orthodox belief, and Ivan II, wed to a Byzantine princess, regarded himself as the sole genuine defender of the Orthodox faith. His grandson and namesake, Ivan IV, popularly known in the West as Ivan the Terrible (more accurately, the Awesome), a talented political polemicist, practiced heinous excesses in the name of personal absolutism. After Ivan murdered his oldest son, his line died out, and for the next generation civil disorder was exacerbated by crop failures, famine, and plague. Finally, in 1613, delegates from all the Russias elected Mikhail, the first of the Romanov czars.

During the post-Ivan Time of Troubles, literature in Russia was confined to Old Church Slavonic, though the people clung to folktales and Russianized Western romances. Under the first Romanovs, every Western form of literature except theology began to be translated and widely promulgated with the advent of Russian printing in 1564. In 1678, Simeon Polotsky, tutor to Czar Alexei's children, introduced a syllabic verse system, solemn and even pompous, that dominated Russian poetry for a century.

Westernization accelerated under Peter the Great, who during his reign from 1682 to 1725 reformed every aspect of Russian civilization. The czar personally directed this mammoth invasion of Western thought, but he enforced its adoption by ruthless, even barbaric means. Peter's unprecedented debasement of the Church removed schools and literature from religious control, and from 1708, all nonreligious texts were published in a simplified Russian alphabet rather than in Old Church Slavonic. West Russian syllabic verse, originally panegyric or didactic, became fashionable among Peter's courtiers as an instrument of amatory and pastoral poetry, in imitation of French and German models. Peter's reformations were implemented at enormous cultural cost. The secularization of literature contributed to the dangerous rift opening between the general population and Peter's sophisticated nobility, who largely abandoned the language and the folklore of the exploited populace.

In the thirty-seven years of political upheaval that followed Peter's death in 1725, the first four greats of Russian literature imposed French classical standards on Peter's simplified Russian language. All writers imported Western literary forms and theories while employing at the same time traditional Russian materials.

Prince Antioch Kantemir (1708-1744) is widely considered the first Russian writer to "blend life and poetry in his works." Kantemir served as Russian ambassador to London and Paris, and as a confirmed neoclassicist concurred with Nicolas Boileau-Despréaux that the highest of literary forms were the ode and the satire, which he used to attack reactionary Russian political and social elements. Kantemir's language is realistic, but his satires are framed in the imported syllabic verse dependent on fixed accents, a form of versification unnatural to the Russian language. Kantemir's less talented and nonnoble contemporary Vasily Trediakov sky (1703-1769) freed Russian poetry from these unnatural constraints by introducing a syllabo-tonic system based on equal bisyllabic metrical feet, a rhythm found in the Russian popular ballad.

Mikhail Lomonosov (1711-1765), a peasant poet, achieved scientific fame abroad and returned to found the University of Moscow in 1756. Lomonosov's *Pismo o pravilakh rossiyskogo stikhotvorstva* (1739; letter concerning the rules of Russian prosody) set stylistic criteria for poetry: a "Noble Style," employing Old Church Slavonic elements, used for heroic poetry and tragedy; a "Middle Style," for ordinary drama; and a colloquial "Low Style," for correspondence, farce, and everyday usage. Lomonosov's syllabotonic odes exhibit conventional patriotic themes, but as Marc Slonim has noted, Lomonosov's meditations are "still living poetry." With Lomonosov, the aristocratic poet Aleksandr Petrovich Sumarokov (1718-1777) established the principles of Boileau and Voltaire as paramount in Russian letters.

Russia's most famous empress, Catherine the Great, who ruled from 1762 to 1796, ranked herself with Peter the Great and consciously patterned her dazzling reign upon his. After the abortive Cossack uprising (1773-1775) under Emelian Pugachev and the sobering example of the French Revolution in 1789, Catherine tempered enlightenment with political conservatism. She extended education into the middle class and encouraged a fivefold increase in published translations from the major European languages. She also imported many foreign artists and sponsored secular music.

Catherine, who wrote widely herself, indelibly marked Russian literature by naming Gavrila Derzhavin (1743-1816) as her poet laureate. Nikolai Gogol called Derzhavin "the poet of greatness" who dominated Russian literature for more than thirty years. Alexander Pushkin (1799-1837), however, accused Derzhavin of thinking "in Tartar," a pungent assessment of Derzhavin's sacrifice of Russian syntax in favor of voicing his deistic and epicurean love of the sublime. Derzhavin's stylistic duality presaged the dismemberment of the Russian classical order; he pioneered Russian civic poetry, which burgeoned in the nineteenth century with Kondraty Rylevyev and Nikolai Nekrasov, and he left a sensually concrete language to the flamboyant oratorical poets of the twentieth century, his legacy as well to his immediate followers, who taught Pushkin.

The harsh fate of the prose writer Aleksandr Radishchev (1749-1802), however, indicates that Catherine did not practice what her humanistic love of letters preached. On calling for the empress to amend Russian social sins, especially serfdom, Radishchev was exiled to Siberia and later committed suicide. Despite heavy risks in a censored land, Radishchev, whom Pushkin called the "foe of slavery," was widely read by youthful poets well into the nineteenth century.

By 1800, historical research in Russia was uncovering folk literature, and young Russian poets were intensely discussing the unification of aesthetic principle with cultural heritage. Though rapidly Westernized under Peter and then Catherine, Russian literature now was straitjacketed by state, not Church, censorship, and the democratic ideals that emanated from the West were difficult to implement in Russian poetry. Into this complex literary milieu loomed the shadow of yet another invader: Napoleon Bonaparte.

Prior to the disastrous Napoleonic invasion in 1812, the country had passed through the lunatic reign of Catherine's son, Paul I, who despised revolutionary ideas and attempted to beat them out of his people. After Paul was strangled in 1801 with the scarf of a palace guards officer, Paul's son Alexander I, whom Napoleon called "the cunning Byzantine," liberalized government, education, and literature, and writers began to hope for emancipation from the state.

Just as the novelist and historian Nikolai Karamzin had begun to use sentimentalism in prose, launching the pre-Romantic movement in Russian literature between 1791 and 1802, the poet and translator Vasily Zhukovsky (1783-1852) sounded the first poetic notes of the Golden Age. Zhukovsky believed that "translators of prose are the slaves of their original text, whereas the translators of the poets are the rivals of the poets themselves." Zhukovsky thus established a tradition that has ensured the excellence of Russia's poetic translations, such as the Russian *Iliad* of Zhukovsky's contemporary, Nikolai Gnedich (1784-1833), described by Slonim as "probably the best in the world." Zhukovsky's original poetry is highly subjective. He identified poetry with his virtue, and his lyric melancholy caused one of his contemporaries to observe, "Happiness would break his lyre's most beautiful string!" Later, under the influence of German Romantics such as Friedrich von Schlegel, Zhukovsky celebrated human sentiment in melodic diction and transitory impressions that introduced the enchantment of Romantic idealism to Russian verse. The young Pushkin praised Zhukovsky's captivating sweetness, and twentieth century Symbolists such as Aleksandr Blok revered Zhukovsky as their predecessor.

At the same time, however, bureaucratic Russian conservatives were furiously striving to preserve the Noble Style in Russian poetry and stamp out all vestiges of "that vile and foul word—Revolution!" As Slonim has noted, "A literary problem was, as is always the case in Russia, assuming the character of an ideological clash." Complicating the literary scene, the profound strain of classicism so eloquently displayed in Gnedich's *Iliad* dominated the poetry of Konstantin Batiushkov (1787-1855), who called himself "The bard of earthly happiness." Batiushkov was a modernist in form and diction, but he reveled in the mere joy of being, claiming that perfect happiness is attainable only by youth, physically capable of experiencing the heights of ecstasy. Batiushkov's delicate Latinate sweetness inflamed the youthful Pushkin, who rejoiced at his mingling of classical themes with sensual delights.

Pushkin's early poetic mentors, Zhukovsky and Batiushkov, soon fell from Russia's literary firmament—Zhukovsky abandoning poetry for the court of Alexander I, and Batiushkov, his closest friend, dying mad after serving as a Russian officer between 1812 and 1815. This period was marked by an internal struggle between Russia's conservatives, allied against the "infernal sophistication of French enlightenment," and the liberals, who believed that the victory against Napoleon had been won by the Russian people, not their leaders.

ALEXANDER PUSHKIN

Growing up during this crisis, Pushkin became, as Thaïs Lindstrom says, the Russians' "comrade in life . . . whose stanzas, recited with universal familiarity and pleasure, crystallize Russian life in the language of the people." Pushkin took pride in both his ancient Russian aristocratic family and his descent from "Peter the Great's negro," the Abyssianian engineer General Abram Hannibal. Pushkin's earliest poems date from 1811, and while he was still attending the new lyceum in Tsarskoe Selo, the established poets Zhukovsky and Batiushkov came to consider him their poetic equal. Pushkin steeped himself in Russian and French literature, and at his lyceum graduation in 1817, he swept into the glittering debauchery of St. Petersburg, savoring wine, women, gambling, and dueling.

Because Alexander I had outgrown his youthful liberalism even before 1812, the Russian Army, sadly not for the last time, had been greeted by brutal government police as it returned victorious from the West in 1815. After the czar had become hypnotized by "exalted prophetesses," the uneducated General Arakcheyev, whom Pushkin called a "brutal and treacherous hangman of freedom," dominated Russia for a period characterized, in Alexander Herzen's words, by "servility, coercion, injustice everywhere . . . serfdom solid as a rock, military despotism, silence and whips."

Russia's youth, many of whom had been exposed to Western revolutionary ideals during the Napoleonic Wars, responded with what Slonim describes as "a revolt of words in a country where silence was compulsory." In 1817, a group of young Imperial Guards officers formed a secret Union of Salvation, the True Sons of the Fatherland. Their efforts culminated eight years later, on December 14, 1825, in the ill-fated Decembrist uprising. "Even if we fail," wrote the poet Kondraty Ryleyev, "our failure will serve as a lesson for others."

Remembering the Decembrists, Herzen recalled, "The cannons on Senate Place awakened a whole generation." Pushkin and his contemporaries were secretly familiar with the long historical poems of Ryleyev (1795-1826), who sacrificed family and life to the Decembrist cause. Ryleyev cited the democratic ideals of the Cossacks and the ancient Slavs, writing, "I know that death awaits those who are the first to fight the despots, yet self sacrifice is the price of freedom."

Such youthful idealism permeates *Ruslan i Lyudmila* (1820; *Ruslan and Liudmila*, 1936), Pushkin's first long poem, a romantic epic written under the sign of Byron. It captivated an immense audience, and Pushkin received a portrait of Zhukovsky inscribed, "To a victorious pupil from a vanquished master." Alexander I was less enthused about Pushkin's revolutionary epigrams, however, and the poet was exiled to the South for four years, a period inspiring his Caucasian verse tales. In these works, Pushkin moved from the stereotyped Byronic hero to a three-dimensional protagonist, the conception of which formed the nucleus of his monumental novel in verse, *Evgeny Onegin* (1825-1832, 1833; *Eugene Onegin*, 1881), begun in 1823.

After an unfortunate love affair that resulted in his expulsion from the Russian Civil Service, Pushkin spent a period under house arrest at his mother's estate, Mikhailovskoe. During this time he fell under the spell of William Shakespeare, after whose chronicle plays Pushkin patterned his *Boris Godunov* (1831; English translation, 1918), a towering attempt to banish French classicism from Russian literature. Lindstrom believes that *Boris Godunov* "recognizes and stresses the power of a faceless, formless mass of common people to alter the course of history."

Even Pushkin, a most uncommon man, found himself restricted severely by the Russian government. His poems had been found in the Decembrists' possession, and although he was allowed to live in Moscow again in 1826, censors reviewed all of his work before publication and secret police constantly monitored his words and actions. He continued work on *Eugene Onegin*, completing it in 1833. Regarded as his masterpiece, it is widely considered to be the greatest single work in Russian poetry, and generations of Russians have memorized passages from it.

Pushkin became infatuated with sixteen-year-old Natalie Goncharova and married her in 1831, after which he was constantly short of money. Their opulent St. Petersburg lifestyle detracted seriously from his writing, but Pushkin still produced remarkable lyric poetry and prose novellas in his last period, as well as the great dramatic poem

Medniy vsadnik (1841; *The Bronze Horseman*, 1936), in which he accurately predicted Russia's eventual enslavement by totalitarianism. He died in a duel involving his lovely but vapid wife.

Pushkin's works, which Russians claim to be untranslatable, have influenced all the Russian arts—music, ballet, sculpture, and painting. Pushkin left Russian literature its modern language, a profound fusion of popular idiom and elegant expression that sublimely weds sound to meaning. He bequeathed to world literature one of its most magnificent apologiae for the dignity of humanity, making poetry a living instrument of humanistic values. Gogol called him "an astounding and perhaps a unique phenomenon of the Russian spirit," embodying "what the Russian may become two hundred years hence." Pushkin's most fitting memorial, however, appears in his own rendition of Horace's "Exegi monumentum":

> I shall long be loved by the people
> Because I awakened their goodness with my lyre
> And in my cruel country celebrated freedom
> And appealed for mercy for the downtrodden.

For the multitude of other brilliant writers of Russia's Golden Age, Pushkin's creativity was, in Gogol's metaphor, "a fire tossed out of the sky, from which lesser poets of his day, like candles, become alight."

OTHER GOLDEN AGE POETS

Evgeny Baratynsky (1800-1844), an intellectual and classicist, lacked Pushkin's *sprezzatura*, that attribute of genius which makes the most difficult achievement appear effortless. A poet with a strong metaphysical bent, Baratynsky decried the decay of human vitality that accompanies industrialism. Nikolai Yazykov (1803-1846) contributed intoxicating rhythms to traditional Russian poetic recitation. Alexei Koltsov (1809-1842) based his Burnsian lyrics on Russian folk life, while more progressive poets of the 1830's, notably Aleksandr Poleshayev (1805-1848) and Prince Aleksandr Odoyevsky (1802-1839), rejected Pushkin's classicism completely and stressed the emotional impact of poetry. Odoyevsky, who died as a private soldier in the Caucasus, is chiefly remembered because Mikhail Lermontov, the most widely recognized heir to Pushkin, wrote an elegy for Odoyevsky that is often cited as the most beautiful in the Russian language.

MIKHAIL LERMONTOV

A Eugene Onegin with a touch of the demon, Mikhail Lermontov (1814-1841) was demoted and exiled in 1837 for circulating manuscript copies of a poem on Pushkin's death, attacking "base lovers of corruption" who dared to "strangle freedom, genius, glory, and hide within the shelter of the law." Lermontov had an unhappy early life. His mother had died young, and he was separated from his father by his wealthy grand-mother, an unhealthy situation reflected in several of his poems. A precociously talented child, Lermontov matured into an unappealing young man who admired Lord Byron deeply, seeing in the English poet a reflection of his own passionate revolt and *Weltschmerz*. Lermontov nevertheless realized their essential difference: "No. I am not Byron; like him I am a persecuted wanderer, but mine is a Russian soul."

While attending Moscow University, Lermontov was influenced deeply by secretly obtained works of the revolutionary Decembrist Ryleyev. At that time, Lermontov wrote an uncanny prediction of Russia's future: "The dark day of Russia will come when the crown of the Czars will fall, when the mob, oblivious of its former allegiance, will spread death and blood far and wide." Such musings continued to obsess him even after he joined the Imperial Guard Hussars in 1832, though he abandoned himself to the dissipation of St. Petersburg. Just as eagerly, he welcomed his exhausting, dangerous Caucasian exile, where he began his most successful novel, *Geroy nashego vremeni* (1840; *A Hero of Our Time*, 1854). Lermontov's patriotic historical epics, influenced by the contemporary popularity of *byliny* collections, and his romantic monologue "Mtsyri" ("The Novice"), the tale of a religious novice who prefers freedom to the futile safety of the monastery, were all written in the Caucasus.

Almost all of Lermontov's important poetry was produced in the last four years of his life. He was pardoned in 1839 and became a celebrity in St. Petersburg. The novelist Ivan Turgenev remarked, "There was something fatal and tragic about Lermontov . . . grim and evil force, passion, pensiveness, and disdain." Lermontov's fury at the vacuousness of society appears in biting satire, as in "Smert Poeta" ("The Death of a Poet"), where, Coriolanus-like, he spurns the mob, and the powerful "New Year's Night," where he contrasts his early vision, "the creation of my dream, with eyes full of an azure fire," with his present disillusionment. Again he was exiled, and after a brief fling in the capital, he wrote as he left for the South, "unwashed Russia, land of slaves, of slaveholders, of blue uniforms and of the people whom they rule." Not long after, Lermontov dueled with a fellow officer over a woman and was killed at the first shot.

Like Pushkin, Lermontov shed his romantic postures early and adopted a vivid realism. Lermontov's style, unlike Pushkin's chiseled classicism, resembles "verbal masses molten into indistinguishable concrete," according to D. S. Mirsky, who sees Lermontov's "Valerik," "a letter in verse," as "a link between *The Bronze Horseman* and the military scenes of *War and Peace*." Nicholas I is said to have commented on Lermontov's end, "A dog's death befits a dog," but later critics rank Lermontov as one of Russia's greatest poets. Lermontov gloried in his "proud enmity against God," as "the Cain of Russian letters," and a melancholy rebellion lies at the heart of his finest works. He wrote, "There are words whose sense is obscure or trivial—yet one cannot listen to them without tremor," a quality of poetic expression used by the Symbolists at the turn of the century.

Perhaps Lermontov's greatest work is his long narrative poem *Demon* (1841; *The Demon*, 1875), composed between 1829 and 1839; his appeal to his countrymen lies above all in his "strange love" for Russia, as seen in "My Native Land," a peculiarly Russian response to "the cold silence of her steppes, her poor villages, the songs and dances of her peasants." For outsiders, the enigmatic life and abrupt death of this talented and tormented young poet seem to sum up the brief glory and the eloquent sunset of Russia's poetry in the first half of its Golden Age.

Slavophiles versus Westernizers

Although the glow of Pushkin's literary gold, subtly blending Romantic and classic elements, lingered through the 1840's, prose realism soon became the literary ideal in the harsh atmosphere inflicted on Russia by Nicholas I, determined to stamp out revolutionary liberalism at home. Discipline worthy of Ivan the Terrible was imposed on the Russian army, whose common soldiers served twenty-five-year terms. The czar's secret police dominated the country's political life, while "censors were unleashed on Russian literature like a pack of bloodhounds," according to one contemporary. Paradoxically, in the thirty years of Nicholas's rule, writers and philosophers flourished. Herzen wrote, "We devoted ourselves to science, philosophy, love, military art, mysticism, in order to forget the monstrous shallowness about us."

Pyotr Chaadayev, the religious philosopher who was the first Russian dissident to be forcibly confined in a madhouse, claimed in 1837, "There is something in our [Russian] blood that repels all true progress," and he defined the opposing positions in Russian thought that have persisted until the present. Slavophiles determined to expel all foreign ideologies and Westernizers such as Chaadayev, seeking Russia's salvation in imported liberalism, clashed in an atmosphere of ferocious governmental repression in a land that was 90 percent illiterate. Vissarion Belinsky (1811-1848), poor and desperately ill, became Russia's first and most influential literary critic, still cited today in the Soviet Union as "a great teacher." Belinsky called literature "the vital spring from which all human sentiments percolate into society," and he insisted that "he who deprives art of its rights to serve social interests debases the reader instead of elevating him."

Belinsky's fellow believer in Western ideals, Herzen, looked to Russia's "naturalness of peasant life" and "our remarkable ability to assimilate foreign ideas" for his country's rebirth. From his exile in Europe, Herzen propagandized against the czarist government, while Belinsky defended the Russian natural school of literature, whose chief concern was social problems and whose leading representative was Nikolai Gogol. Herzen and Belinsky initiated Russian Socialism, while Mikhail Bakunin, later Karl Marx's opponent in the First International, promulgated revolutionary anarchism.

As Turgenev, Fyodor Dostoevski, and Leo Tolstoy were shaping their immense contributions to the world's great fiction, creating amazingly diverse panoramas characterized by acute political, social, and psychological analysis, Russian poetry developed along two distinct paths. One group espoused art for art's sake as an escape from everyday Russian reality, submerging themselves in stylistic simplicity, folk emotionalism, and Belinsky's dictum that poetry was "thinking in images."

NIKOLAI NEKRASOV

In contrast, civic realism in poetry found its voice in the works of Nikolai Nekrasov (1821-1878). Nekrasov's father had turned him out of the house because of his obsessive desire to become a man of letters. "Famished every day for three years," he managed to become the foremost publisher of Russia's new realistic school of fiction. A contemporary remarked that if the ceiling collapsed on a soirée given by Nekrasov's mistress, "Most of Russian literature would have perished."

Nekrasov chose to "sing of your suffering, O my people" in intensely emotional language and innovative metrical usage. His most important work was a satiric epic, *Komúna Rusí žit' chorošó?* (1870-1874, 1879; *Who Can Be Happy and Free in Russia?*, 1917), which traces the wanderings of seven peasants through "wretched and abundant, oppressed and powerful, weak and mighty Mother Russia." His "Reflections Before a Mansion Doorway" observes unequivocally, "Where the people are, the moan is."

Because of Nekrasov's message and his immense popularity, the government allowed only one edition of his works during his life. He felt the disparity between his peasant sympathies and his wealthy position keenly, and he was large enough in spirit to recognize and encourage his talented contemporary Fyodor Tyutchev, who pursued pure art. Though Tyutchev was overshadowed during his lifetime by Nekrasov, the Symbolists of the Silver Age claimed Tyutchev as their spiritual ancestor.

FYODOR TYUTCHEV

Fyodor Tyutchev (1803-1873) was Tolstoy's favorite poet, and like the great novelist, Tyutchev was a fervent Slavophile who, despite his noble rank, wrote, "I love poetry and my country above all else in this world." While a diplomat in Germany, he was profoundly affected by the pessimistic philosophy of Arthur Schopenhauer, and Tyutchev's poetry shows the influence of a dualistic universe in which a Manichaean chaos and the "all-engulfing, all-pacifying abyss of the cosmos" dominate human existence. For Tyutchev, a Schopenhauerean affinity between love and death was inherent in human nature, a confirmation for Dostoevski, too, of dark tendencies he recognized in his own writing. Tyutchev's four hundred short poems range from a perverse joy in destruction to a sublime desire to be "diffused in the slumbering Universe." His oratorical fervor continued the tradition established by Derzhavin of public poetic performance, and Tyutchev was the "last great master of the High Style," in which Old Church Slavonic rhetoric is supreme. Marc Slonim calls Tyutchev, after Pushkin, Lermontov, and Nekrasov, "the fourth great leader of Russian poetry . . . the profound interpreter of cosmic mysteries."

TOWARD THE SILVER AGE

Except for Count Aleksei Konstantinovich Tolstoy (1817-1875), a popular neo-Romantic poet in the German vein who opposed civic poetry bitterly and sought to reestablish the old norms of art, the 1860's and 1870's were dominated in Russia by fine poetic translations, not native Russian poetry. The costly Crimean War (1854-1856), a shocking waste of Russian lives brought about by the neglect and shortcomings of Russian leadership, had drained the nation's spirit. Russian prestige suffered a mortal blow through the ill-advised conduct of this war, and Alexander II and his government reluctantly faced the necessity of domestic reform. After taking the throne in 1855, Alexander freed the forty million Russian serfs in 1861, two years before Abraham Lincoln's Emancipation Proclamation, but taxes and land payments created tensions that resulted in many peasant uprisings throughout 1862. "The plague of Russian life" had ended, though, and the *zemstvos*, new self-governing bodies, relieved enough of the pressure on Russia's lower classes to maintain the status quo until 1905.

After 1865, Alexander's policies became more conservative. He was stalked and at last assassinated in 1881, ironically on the same day he had granted the *zemstvos* a larger voice in government, as the liberal intelligentsia had urged. Alexander III, his son, threw all reform proposals to the bitter winds from Siberia, increasing police powers, tightening the noose of censorship, and persecuting religious minorities, especially the Jews. His creation of a police state at home, coupled with his expensive and unsuccessful foreign ventures in Europe and Central Asia, made his reign a dismal time for literature. The last vestiges of the Golden Age had faded, and the Silver Age was waiting to be born.

In the 1880's, drought and poor agricultural practices resulted in massive famines and epidemics through out Russia. Capitalism was fortifying a formidable industrial expansion, but the lives of ordinary Russians became increasingly miserable. Political theorists envisioned a necessary alliance of the peasantry, the workers, and the intelligentsia, and a new form of Russian populism began to become part of the country's cultural atmosphere, tinged by more ideas from the West, the doctrines of Karl Marx.

The precise date of the beginning of modernism in Russian literature is uncertain. Some critics date the period from the publication in 1893 of Dmitri Merezhkovsky's lecture *O prichinakh upadka: o novykh techeniyakh sovremennoy russkoy lityeratury* (on the origins of the decline of Russian literature and on new currents in it), a theoretical work that announces the principles of Russian Symbolism. Others believe modernism began later, with the turn of the century or even with the 1905 Revolution, which Merezhkovsky and his wife, the poet Zinaida Gippius, supported. The Bolshevik Revolution of 1917, however, concluded the modernist period in Russia, just as it decisively ended the Russian monarchy forever.

In the 1890's, young Russian artists began to look inward, reassessing their values and redefining the function of the artist and his or her art. They became absorbed in the creative individualism evident in translations of the works of Friedrich Nietzsche,

Stefan George, the English Pre-Raphaelites, and the French Symbolists, especially Charles Baudelaire. Merezhkovsky and others protested against the radical intellectuals who had been dominating Russia's literary life and pronounced a new cultural dogma involving Western-style humanism, Russian tradition, mysticism, intuition, mystery, and myth—a spiritual obbligato to the strange goings-on of Grigory Rasputin at the Imperial Court.

At first, the new writers were dismissed as Decadents, but their successors became the spokespersons for a remarkable explosion of Russian art and literature, a conscious transmutation of Pushkin's Golden Age later known as the Silver Age of Russian letters. More Russian philosophical works appeared between 1890 and 1910 than during the part of the nineteenth century up to that point, and an abundance of small literary magazines provided an outlet for poetry and criticism.

Until 1903, the Russian literary scene was dominated by the Decadents' reaction against realism. They were led by Valery Bryusov (1873-1924), sometimes called the Peter the Great of Russian literature. After translating Maurice Maeterlinck and Paul Verlaine at the age of fourteen, Bryusov "sought a new body for the new art" in synaesthesia, "the subtle ties between the shape and the scent of a flower." The keynote of the landmark anthology *Russkiye simvolisty* (1894) is the slogan, "The personality of the artist is the essence of art." In 1903, Bryusov and his mesmerized followers founded *Vesy* (first published in January, 1904), which became the most important Russian Decadent literary periodical and preached such Baudelairean themes as erotic nihilism and Arthur Rimbaud's *dérèglement des sens* ("disorder of the senses").

Konstantin Balmont (1867-1943), the other great Decadent, a public performer as Bryusov was not, became "the Poet" of turn-of-the-twentieth-century Russia. Balmont drew a large and mostly youthful following at his public recitations. He was a spontaneous poet whose first poetic credo, "Words are chameleons," developed into Nietzschean vehemence by 1903: "I want daggerlike words and lethal moans of death. . . . Who equals my might in song? No one—no one!"

"Moans of death" erupted throughout Russia with the disastrous Russo-Japanese War (1904-1905), followed by the 1905 Revolution, which started on "Bloody Sunday," January 22. The following October, after months of turmoil, Nicholas II granted some civil liberties and the democratic election of a duma (legislative assembly). The czar's manifesto split the revolutionaries into three major camps: the Octobrists, satisfied with the czar's action; the Constitutional Democrats, liberals who wanted far more power invested in the Duma; and the Social Democrats, who had organized a soviet (workers' council) at St. Petersburg and attempted to force additional reform by strike. The czar put them down, trying to stamp out the revolutionaries and limiting the power of the Duma in late 1905. Counterrevolutionary forces in the Second and Third Dumas (1906-1912) prevented any advancement of liberalism prior to World War I.

After 1903, the Decadent movement in literature had an older faction and a younger one, the original Decadents being more occupied with social and political themes and the new Symbolists turning to the neo-Romantic inspiration of Lermontov and Tyutchev. Most critics agree, however, that no stated doctrinal differences distinguished the two groups in the prewar period, and that they lived harmoniously with each other in Moscow and St. Petersburg.

A startling manifestation of the Decadent movement appears in the work of the Satanist poet-novelist Solugub (the pen name of Fyodor Teternikov, 1863-1927). He regarded modern humanity as a horde of living dead, and he believed a poet inhabited a shadowy limbo, where, sorcerer-like, he had to make himself the only credible god in a universe as evil as its creator. His nihilism is somewhat restrained in his lyrics, which he compares in "Amphora" to a fine vase carried so carefully that no drop of the venom it contains is spilled. In his later years, he abandoned poetry for a perverse fictional vision of human debasement.

An antidote to Solugub's horrid view of humankind was offered by the metaphysical *Weltbild* drawn from the cult of Dostoevski at the end of the nineteenth century. The diverse works of Merezhkovsky and of Vladimir Solovyov (1853-1900) depart from Decadent nihilism and seek individual concepts of "Godmanhood," an absolute achieved through Sophia, the incarnation of Divine Wisdom, the archetypal Eternal Feminine. The German Neoplatonic idealism that had fostered the creativity of Lermontov and Tyutchev influenced many of the Symbolist disciples of Solovyov, who accepted the notion of the poet's intermediation between God and humans, conveying to ordinary mortals his experience of the ideals of Truth and Beauty reflected in the principle of Sophia. Solovyov himself accepted Christ's incarnation as proof of humanity's redemption. He believed that despite all of history's evils, humanity will at last attain divinity, and his concept of the Divine Sophia appeared frequently in his own verse, although he occasionally treated the symbol lightly, as in his long poem *Tri svidaniya* (1898; three encounters). Solovyov hoped for the reunion of all Christian denominations, and during his last years, he preached salvation through collective effort. Solovyov's teachings indelibly marked the entire religious movement connected with Russian Symbolism.

Each of the Symbolist triumvirate, Vyacheslav Ivanov, Andrey Bely, and Aleksandr Blok, owed a profound spiritual and artistic debt to Solovyov's definition of poetry as the "incantatory magic of rhythmic speech, mediating between man and the world of divine things."

Ivanov (1866-1949) considered all of human culture the path to God, and he believed that artistic intuition grasped symbols in the ordinary world that reflect the "real" reality of God. Hence the artist, having been given greater gifts, has the responsibility to lead men to the Divine Presence.

Bely (the pen name of Boris Bugayev, 1880-1934), whose strong enthusiasms bordered on the pathological, incorporated Solovyov's doctrine of Divine Wisdom in his lyrics *Zoloto v lazuri* (1904; god in azure), but within a few years, he had become the leading Russian disciple of Rudolf Steiner's Anthroposophy. An important novelist as well as a poet, Bely embodied the mixture of mysticism, diabolism, and obsession with the special fate of Russia that was so characteristic of his time.

ALEKSANDR BLOK

Despite the considerable achievements of Ivanov and Bely, Aleksandr Blok (1880-1921) was the culminating figure of the Silver Age. His lyrics place him with Pushkin and Lermontov, and his ideals remain a rare blend of ecstasy and despair. The young Blok experienced a supernatural vision of a "beautiful lady from Beyond," the Solovyovian Sophia, who inspired more than 240 of his lyrics. In "Gorod" ("The City"), however, set in St. Petersburg's "artificial paradises," disillusionment shattered Blok's Romantic dreams, and in "Nezna Komka" ("The Stranger"), one of his most powerful poems, his ideal woman appeared as an expensive prostitute. Such blasphemous irony caused Blok's break with the Moscow Symbolists. After 1906, Blok continued to suffer from his irreconcilable inner conflict; he wrote, "I see too many things clearly, soberly," and he hurled himself into intense experiences, trying to reconcile art and morality at the same time that he was frantically avoiding confrontation with himself. By 1909, he had become infatuated with his "beloved fatal country," and his lyric cycle "On the Battle of Kulikova Field" celebrates the fourteenth century victory of the Russians over the Tartars. Just prior to August, 1914, Blok predicted in poetry Russia's "road of the steppe and of shoreless grief," and following the 1917 Bolshevik Revolution, in a Rilkean "dictated" composition, Blok produced his masterpiece, *Dvenadtsat* (1918; *The Twelve*, 1920), a poetic vision of a revolution that would cleanse Russia and redeem its soul from its long agony. By 1921, however, representatives of every segment of Blok's postrevolutionary world, from Communist officials to his old intellectual friends, had ridiculed *The Twelve*, and Blok died convinced that "Vile, rotten Mother Russia has devoured me."

INNOKENTY ANNENSKY

Innokenty Annensky (1856-1909), the Russian poet who links the Decadents and the Symbolists, devoted fifteen years to translating the works of Euripides. Not surprisingly, his own themes were beauty, suffering, and death, the absolutes of a futile human existence that could be ennobled only through art and love. Annensky's finely honed meters and rhythmic effects influenced both the Symbolists and the Acmeists, the next major poetic group in Russia.

ACMEIST POETS

The Symbolists' nebulous Westernized ideals did not prevail for long against the literary realism being promoted by Maxim Gorky in the relatively stable bourgeois climate of Russia between 1910 and 1914. Acmeism was born in 1912, a movement primarily based in St. Petersburg and resembling the controlled, concrete Imagism of Ezra Pound and T. S. Eliot. The three major Acmeist poets, Nikolai Gumilyov, Anna Akhmatova, and Osip Mandelstam, despite significant differences in style and message, concurred that "we want to admire a rose because it is beautiful, and not because it is a symbol of mystical purity."

Nikolay Gumilyov (1886-1921), leader of the Acmeists, had a "bravura personality" that blossomed in physical danger and exotic landscapes. In his 1912 article "Acmeism and the Heritage of Symbolism," he stressed the Greek meaning of "acme" as "the point of highest achievement," as well as Théophile Gautier's rule, "The more dispassionate the material . . . the more beautiful will the work come out."

ANNA AKHMATOVA

Often likened to Rudyard Kipling's, Gumilyov's virile style could not have differed more strikingly from that of his wife for eight years, Anna Akhmatova (1889-1966). Akhmatova's earliest poetry, mostly small lyrics that sang of the woman's inevitably unhappy role in love, was extremely popular immediately upon publication, and her work has since completely overshadowed Gumilyov's. Even today Russian readers memorize Akhmatova's poetry, and she remains Russia's foremost woman poet, unforgettably uniting passion and asceticism. Periodically suppressed by the Soviets, Akhmatova's work has endured; among her greatest works is the cycle *Rekviem* (1963; *Requiem*, 1964), her lament for the victims of Joseph Stalin's purges.

INFLUENCE OF THE POLITICAL STATE

Russia's human losses in the twentieth century defy comprehension. The agony of World War I, closely followed by the February Democratic Revolution and the October Bolshevik Revolution, both in 1917, combined with the ravages of the civil war, cost millions of lives. Later, the famines, the collectivization of agriculture, and the purges of the 1930's established a dark backdrop for the staggering losses, estimated at twenty to twenty-five million lives, that the Soviet Union sustained during World War II.

The Bolshevik Revolution and the consequent establishment of the Soviet state enormously affected Russian literature, although seldom in Russia's history, if ever, has literature enjoyed the freedom of expression provided by Western democracies. In the Soviet era, works of prose and poetry have often been surreptitiously circulated in *samizdat* (editions) and clandestinely shipped abroad, to become *tamizdat* (literally, three-published) works in less restricted societies. The cost of the human devastation suffered by Russians during the century, however, is reflected in the estimates of those lost in Stalin's prison system, the "Gulag Archipelago," where hundreds of writers perished among countless numbers of their countrymen.

In response to the phenomenon of Soviet Communism, too, literature of the period after the 1917 Revolution evidenced two major tendencies. Those writers who remained within the Soviet Union and functioned within its intellectual and artistic borders often turned to apolitical themes or those acceptable to their government, in both cases revealing glimpses both accurate and distorted of life within their country; commentators such as Ronald Hingley observe that the distortions sometimes provide the truest insights. Writers who dissented from official Soviet positions eventually exported either their works or themselves, and from exile their writings occasionally found their way back to their native land, to circulate at considerable risk among readers of Russian *samizdat*.

Indeed, the tyranny of the Soviet state has produced three distinct "waves" of emigration. The first emigration, the largest of the three, took place during the decade following the 1917 Revolution. Among the many Russian poets who emigrated at this time, perhaps the foremost were Marina Tsvetayeva, who later returned to the Soviet Union, and Vladislav Khodasevich, who died in exile. The fate of Khodasevich (1886-1939) is particularly representative. Little read in the West, Khodasevich, like many émigrés, has suffered from what the critic and translator Simon Karlinsky calls the "Western self-censorship"—the conviction, inherited from the thirties, that a Russian writer who resides outside the Soviet Union cannot be of any interest to a Western reader. The second emigration, following World War II, brought to the West fewer writers of note, but the third wave, beginning in the 1970's and continuing to the present, has carried with it a host of brilliant writers, including Aleksandr Solzhenitsyn, Andrei Sinyavsky, and the poet Joseph Brodsky (1940-1996).

OSIP MANDELSTAM

Among the poets who have remained in the Soviet Union, the finest invariably have suffered persecution at the hands of the state. No loss to the world of poetry seems crueler than the death of Akhmatova's friend and fellow Acmeist Osip Mandelstam (1891-1938), who perished in a Far Eastern transit prison, bound for the mines of Kolyma beyond the Arctic Circle. Nadezhda Mandelstam retrospectively described her husband's spirit as endlessly *zhizneradostny*, which approximates the English phrase "rejoicing in life." Mandelstam never bowed to political pressures; he was an admirer of classicism in the oratorical style of Derzhavin and Tyutchev, a Jew more aware of Russian tradition than the Russians themselves were. "I am nobody's contemporary," he wrote, because as an inveterate Westernizer he yearned for world culture. His solemn and exquisitely crafted poems were his conscious effort to achieve "pure" poetry, often employing little-known historical detail and a "sprung" rhythm somewhat resembling Gerard Manley Hopkins's metrical experiments. Like Akhmatova, Mandelstam was forbidden to publish under Stalin, and his mental and physical health collapsed under torture. What sustained him so long as his frail constitution could endure was his concept of poetry as a moral obligation to his countrymen: "The people need poetry that will be their own secret/ to keep them safe forever. . . ."

FUTURIST POETS

The Acmeists' contemporaries, the Futurists, opposed literary and artistic tradition with a zeal that owed a considerable debt to Nietzsche. In 1912, their manifesto, "Poshchechina obshchestvennomu vkusu" ("A Slap in the Face of the Public Taste"), presented Russian readers with an extreme literary case of shocking the bourgeois. One of its authors, Vladimir Mayakovsky (1893-1930), described himself in his important poem *Oblako v shtanakh* (1915; *A Cloud in Pants*, 1965), as "the loudmouthed Zarathustra of our day," and his associate Velimir Khlebnikov (1895-1922), a linguistically experimental poet, rejected all emotional emphasis derived from previous ages from his powerful poems. Russia, he insisted, had "amplified the voice of the West as though transmitting the screams of a monster," and he explored new symbolic uses of language to rouse the world from its petrification.

Aleksei Kruchonykh (1886-1968) provided Futurism with its most famous poem, "Dyr bul shchyl" (1913), written in words that have "no definite meaning," that is, in *zaum* (transrational language), which he and Khlebnikov pioneered. *Zaum* is akin to abstractionism in art in that it is intended to have a direct evocative power without a specific, definable referent, and it was one of the most avant-garde innovations in Russian poetry. Kruchonykh wrote quite a number of usually short poems in *zaum* and published them in primitive-looking handmade manuscript booklets. The *zaum* "opera" *Pobeda nad solntsem* (pr. 1913; *Victory Over the Sun*, 1971), which in St. Petersburg rivaled the premiere of Igor Stravinsky's *Rite of Spring* in Paris of the same year, was one of the signal Russian avant-garde events of the age.

Although the Moscow group of Futurists was most prominent and inventive, the St. Petersburg group included Vasilisk (Vasily) Gnedov (1890-1978), who became famous as the author of "Poema kontsa" (1913, "Poem of the End"). This proto-minimalist poem consisted of a blank space on a page where a text was supposed to be. Gnedov performed it with a silent gesture to much acclaim. Just after the Bolshevik Revolution, the Futurists dominated Soviet cultural life briefly, mainly through the achievements of the dynamic Mayakovsky, who, like Nietzsche, called forcefully for the destruction of the old world and the invention of a new one to supercede it.

The Russian Formalist critic Viktor Shklovsky, Mayakovsky's contemporary, claims that Mayakovsky's chief accomplishment was the broadening of verse semantics, building an oratorical language that changed the very syntax of the Russian language. Mayakovsky's ego and his anarchic inclination feasted on the Bolshevik Revolution, but in "Homeward" (composed in 1925) he wrote, "From poetry's skies I plunge into Communism." In 1930, openly critical of Soviet bureaucracy, Mayakovsky committed suicide, which he described as "my final performance." The Soviet Union has enshrined Mayakovsky with their supreme poets, praising his declaration of the artist's obligation to the state. Mayakovsky's savage individuality is said to have stamped poets as diverse as Brodsky, Yevgeny Yevtushenko, and Andrei Voznesensky.

Diametrically opposed to Mayakovsky's idiosyncratic poetic style is that of Sergei Esenin (1896-1925), a "peasant poet" who harked back to Russia's rich folklore and its Orthodox religion. Esenin, a poet from the people, founded the Imaginist school of poetry between 1914 and 1919. His personal excesses led to a self-image he described in *Ispoved' khuligana* (1921; *Confessions of a Hooligan*, 1973), and his unhappy marriages, first to the American dancer Isadora Duncan and then to Tolstoy's granddaughter Sofya, contributed to his final breakdown. He attempted to write political poetry on contemporary topics, but near the end of his life his work was filled with nostalgia for the past and sadness at the fate of his home village, and his later poems made him the voice of many of his countrymen in their disenchantment with Soviet policies. After his suicide in 1925, Esenin's work was out of favor with the Soviet government, but he has since been fully rehabilitated.

MARINA TSVETAYEVA

Something of Mayakovsky's originality and force and something of Esenin's tender devotion to his Russian heritage meet in Russia's *inneres Mädchen*, as Rainer Maria Rilke called Marina Tsvetayeva (1892-1941), Akhmatova's friend and only rival as Russia's most famous woman poet. At eighteen, Tsvetayeva described her poetry as "torn from me like droplets from a fountain . . . their themes made up of youth and death." She emigrated to Paris in 1921, outraged at events in Russia, but she and her family returned in 1939 on the eve of war. After her husband, a Soviet secret agent, was shot by the government as a traitor and one of her children was sent to a labor camp, Tsvetayeva hanged herself in 1941.

As a daughter of the Russian intelligentsia, she wrote for this audience. Her intricate romanticism, like Rilke's, verged on the mystical, and she shared with him, as his long 1926 poem to her reveals, an awareness of "the other world" and the possibility of a new myth that would lead humankind to a better future. Akhmatova hailed Tsvetayeva's creative vitality in one of her last poems, a tender memory of "A fresh, dark elder branch/ Like a letter from Marina." Tsvetayeva, like Boris Pasternak, was one of the outstanding idealists in Russian poetry. Her impressionistic technique and elliptic imagery show evidence of Pasternak's influence, and she once remarked that he was the only poet among her contemporaries whom she considered her peer.

BORIS PASTERNAK

Boris Pasternak (1890-1960), child of a gifted musician and a famous painter, synthesized the classical tradition in Russian verse, the musical qualities of the Symbolists, and the near-telegraphic style of the mature Tsvetayeva. Pasternak wrote poetry early, at first attracted and soon repelled by the flamboyant Mayakovsky. Pasternak found his own voice in *Sestra moyazhizn* (1922; *My Sister, Life*, 1959), a collection that immediately established him as one of the leading poets of his generation.

In his autobiographical sketch *Okhrannaya gramota* (1931; *A Safe-Conduct*, 1949), Pasternak wrote, "Focused on a reality which feeling has displaced, art is a record of this displacement." A sense of the artist's isolation pervades Pasternak's life and work. As Max Hayward has suggested, Pasternak believed it essential "by responding submissively to high and lonely destiny . . . to contribute in some vital way to the life of the times." Already during World War I, Pasternak had pondered his "contribution," later to become his novel *Doktor Zhivago* (1957; *Doctor Zhivago*, 1958), the record of the Russian intelligentsia caught in the savagery of those revolutionary times. For writing the novel, Pasternak was expelled from the Soviet Writers' Union and forbidden to accept the 1958 Nobel Prize in Literature. The novel closes on "The Poems of Doctor Zhivago," in which Pasternak reaffirms the Christian sanctity of his poetic mission: "If Thou be willing, Abba, Father,/ Remove this cup from me."

ABSURDIST POETS

It was not until the 1980's that the Russian reading public became fully aware of the work of a small group of absurdist poets from the 1920's and 1930's who named themselves Oberiu (Association for Real Art), the existence of which was declared in a 1928 manifesto. The leading figures in the group were Daniil Kharms (Yuvachov; 1905-1942), Aleksandr Vveden sky (1904-1941), and Nikolai Zabolotsky (1903-1958), the primary drafter of the manifesto. Zabolotsky was able to publish one book of poems, *Stolbtsy* (1929, columns), but the other two were able to publish only a few individual poems and stories for children. Their work, which included plays and, in the case of Kharms, short prose sketches that have since become famous, involves totally unexpected, illogical, and sometimes tautological twists of action, imagery, and thought, such as "The sun shines in disarray,/ and the flowers fly in their beds" (Vvedensky) and "This is This./ That is That./ This is not That./ This is not not This./ The rest is either this or not this./ All is either that or not that" (Kharms). They reveal a philosophical depth beneath an absurd, often nightmarish surface. The group ran afoul of the Stalinist regime, and Kharms and Vvedensky both died in prison. Their work has come to be perceived as a major literary movement and the last gasp of the pre-revolutionary Russian literary avant-garde. It became extremely popular among young intellectuals.

POST-STALIN ERA

The cooperation between the Western Allies and the Soviet Union during World War II dissolved in Cold War tension during the 1950's, but after Stalin's death in 1953 a degree of artistic freedom was temporarily achieved by Russian writers. An amnesty decree a month after Stalin's death led to the release of prisoners who had survived the rigors of the gulag, and the Writers' Union restored the membership of Akhmatova in 1954. By 1955, the "thaw" had occasioned the posthumous rehabilitation of many writers who had died in the camps and prisons; this revisionist movement reached its peak with Nikita Khrushchev's famous speech at the Twentieth Party Congress in February, 1956, denouncing Stalin. Despite the suppression of *Doctor Zhivago*, the thaw lasted long enough to permit the publication of Solzhenitsyn's novel *Odin den Ivana Denisovicha* (1962; *One Day in the Life of Ivan Denisovich*, 1963), but soon thereafter Leonid Brezhnev ousted Khrushchev from power. After Brezhnev's accession in 1964, literature in the Soviet Union was subject to rigid Stalinist controls, and one after another, the most talented Russian writers emigrated to the West or were forcibly exiled.

Nevertheless, the Soviet Union continued to exhibit an immense thirst for poetry, attested by the immense popularity of such poets as Yevtushenko and Voznesen sky. Both rose to prominence in the early 1960's as spokespeople for liberal forces during that time of the thaw.

YEVGENY YEVTUSHENKO

Yevgeny Yevtushenko (born 1933), as the first poet to enunciate the shift in mood in his country, gained considerable acclaim at home and abroad for his revelation of Soviet anti-Semitism in "Babii Yar" (1961) and the effects of Stalinism as a social force in "Nasledniki Stalina" (1962; "The Heirs of Stalin"). Yevtushenko has used his travels abroad in several volumes of his works, such as the poetic drama *Pod kozhey statuey sbobody* (1972; under the skin of the Statue of Liberty). Certain of his more personal poems are reminiscent of Esenin's candor and nostalgia, but Yevtushenko's "novella in verse," *Golub' v Sant'iago* (1978; *A Dove in Santiago*, 1982), a tale of a tormented young art student in Chile at the time of the Augusto Pinochet coup, reflects the tragedy of a talented individual who is caught between his politics and his art.

ANDREI VOZNESENSKY

Like Yevtushenko, Andrei Voznesensky (1933-2010) survived the artistic restrictions imposed first by Khrushchev in 1963 and subsequently by Brezhnev and his successors. Voznesensky's histrionic style of poetic delivery, modeled on Mayakovsky's, made him popular with large and youthful audiences, while American critics have praised his imagery and originality. One of his translators, W. H. Auden, has cited the broad range of Voznesensky's subject matter as evidence of his imaginative power. Although Voznesensky was the object of articles in the Soviet press accusing him of intelligibility and "supermodernism," he was able to continue publishing. He published a number of works after the breakup of the Soviet Union and organized provincial poetry festivals before his death in 2010.

POEMS "TO REMEMBER"

The stream of *samizdat* and *tamizdat* poetry that emerged from the Soviet Union bears the self-imposed charge: "to remember"—to memorialize the victims of Stalin's gulag, and to speak out against the punishment of dissenters in labor camps and psychiatric hospitals. Poets who dissented against the Soviet government had to choose between writing "for the desk drawer," exile, or death, as the fate of Yuri Galanskov (1939-1972) demonstrates. In 1956, when the Hungarian revolt was suppressed by the Soviets, Galanskov gathered a *samizdat* collection of protest poems. After he set forth his "Human Manifesto," "calling to Truth and Rebellion . . . a serf no more," Galanskov was held in a Soviet special psychiatric hospital; he later died in a labor camp for his role in the human rights movement within the Soviet Union. The themes of *samizdat* and *tamizdat* poetry reflect the mediocrity of everyday Soviet life, the horrors of war, and the martyrdom of earlier poets such as Tsvetayeva, who perished under Stalin. Occasionally, too, this clandestinely exported poetry is quietly illuminated by the folk values of Old Russia, as in Gelb Garbovsky's "To the Neva": "I will come back, no matter what, even if, when I do return, I'm dying."

JOSEPH BRODSKY

The most famous poet-exile was Joseph Brodsky (1940-1996), who felt himself to be a poet by the grace of God and therefore for whom no other social role was necessary. A native of Leningrad, in the late 1950's, he became associated with the circle of young poets around Akhmatova and was recognized by her as a significant new talent. Though his poems were apolitical, his independence of mind caused him to be arrested in 1964 for "parasitism," that is, not having a legally approved job, and he was sentenced to five years of internal exile in the north. Released in a year, he was ultimately forced into exile in the United States, where he spent most of the rest of his life teaching, writing, and reciting his poetry, which he did with a unique intensity and melodiousness. In 1987, he won the Nobel Prize in Literature, and in 1991, he became the United States poet laureate, the first nonnative to be so honored. Although he did not complete high school, his poetry is characterized by the erudition of someone steeped in classical learning and world culture. It has a philosophical depth and complexity of imagery comparable to his favorite English Metaphysical poets and modernists such as T. S. Eliot and W. H. Auden. His verse forms are basically traditional, but within them he created an unusual degree of lyrical tension. His typical themes are loneliness and suffering, death and salvation, often ventriloquized through some famous historical or mythological figure in a moment of realization or crisis. Though he had the opportunity in the late twentieth century to visit and even return to Russia, he chose not to do so, but instead to die in exile and to be buried in Venice.

THE UNDERGROUND

Parallel to the public existence of poetry in the post-Stalin period represented on one hand by Yevtushenko and Voznesensky, and on the other by Galanskov and Brodsky, there was a more private, underground development that occurred in formal and informal poetry circles. Formal circles centered around officially sponsored clubs and seminars in which senior poets mentored younger aspiring poets. This was in part a subtle way for the authorities to keep an eye on the younger generation, but in the better groups, for example, those led by Mikhail Svetlov (1903-1964) and Kirill Kovaldzhi (born 1930), some talented poets did find useful mentoring and occasional outlets to publication. More important were the informal groups of the underground. One of the earliest of these, the Nebyvalisty (Unprecedentists, 1939-1940) headed by Nikolai Glazkov (1919-1979), who coined the term *samizdat*, actually began before the war at the Moscow Pedagogical Institute as a continuation of Futurism. Though the group soon dissolved, Glazkov, and for their part Kruchonykh and Pasternak, were able to serve as personal mentors to several generations of younger poets. SMOG (Youngest Society of Geniuses), also in Moscow but in the early 1960's, like the Nebyvalisty, was not noted for the innovativeness of its members' poetry, but rather for their unrestrained behavior. It did include one lyric genius in the mold of Yesenin, Leonid Gubanov (1946-1983). On the other hand, the Lianozovo school, which centered around the suburban Moscow barracks apartment of Evgeny Kropivnitsky (1893-1979), fostered poets of genuine originality and innovation. Among them were Vsevolod Nekrasov (Kholin; 1920-1999), Genrikh Sapgir (1928-1999), and even the scandalous Eduard Limonov (born 1943), all of whom emerged as major literary figures in the glasnost period. In Leningrad in the late 1950's, the Philological school, which included Vladimir Ufliand (1937-2007), Lev Losev (1937-2009), Aleksandr Kondratov (1937-1993), and Mikhail Yeryomin (born 1936), was one of the first such underground groups. A monumental contribution to an awareness of this period, especially in Leningrad, is Konstantin Kuzminsky's nine-volume *Blue Lagoon Anthology of Modern Russian Poetry* (1980-1986).

BARD POETRY

Along with the poetry underground there developed another trend that had its roots in popular and folk song, namely, the guitar poetry of the so-called bards. These poets chose to set their texts to melodies with simple guitar accompaniment and sing them in private gatherings and around campfires. The recognized founder of this trend was Bulat Okudzhava (1924-1997), who began to compose such songs immediately after World War II. With the advent of readily available tape recorders in the 1960's, Okudzhava's songs became well known and popular throughout the Soviet Union, despite the lack of official recordings. Other important figures in this genre were Aleksandr Galich (1918-1977), whose songs developed a social protest edge that resulted in his being exiled abroad, and Vladimir Vysotsky (1938-1980), whose broadranging themes and personae made him immensely popular with all levels of Russian society, a popularity that only increased after his untimely death from heart failure. What distinguishes the work of the bards from popular song is the high quality of the poetic text itself, which can usually stand on its own as fine poetry, regardless of its musical aspects.

POETRY OF FREEDOM

With Gorbachev's accession to power in 1985 and his introduction of a policy of glasnost, official censorship began to be reduced. By 1989, it was virtually eliminated, producing an ever-increasing wave of poetry publications. Initially, much of this was past work that finally emerged from the underground to reach the general reading public. Soon new voices and new work by older generations began to flood the public sphere, creating an impression of postmodern Babel. Where earlier there had been only a handful of published poets worth reading, there now were dozens, if not hundreds, with a range of orientations and styles. Parallel with this was a sharp decline in popular interest in poetry. What had been a narrow and exciting passageway to freer speech was made to face competition from a deluge of popular entertainment and the unfettered news media. At the same time, however, poetry has enjoyed a major flowering. Attempts to categorize the new poetry into trends such as metametaphorism and conceptualism are useful to some extent but do not do justice either to the richness and complexity of the situation or to such unique major figures as Gennady Aygi (1934-2006), Viktor Sosnora (born 1936), Aleksandr Kushner (born 1936), Ry Nikonova (born 1942), Lev Rubinstein (born 1947), Ivan Zhdanov (born 1948), Olga Sedakova (born 1949), Nina Iskrenko (1951-1995), Timur Kibirov (born 1955), and Vitaly Kalpidi (born 1957), to name just a few. Moreover, with the freedom to travel, publish, and distribute books, the separation among Russian poets living throughout Russia and those living abroad has been eliminated. The landscape of modern Russian poetry more and more resembles that in the West.

BIBLIOGRAPHY

Blok, Aleksandr. *Us Four Plus Four: Eight Russian Poets Conversing.* New Orleans, La.: UNO Press, 2008. An extensive collection of poetry from eight important Russian poets. The poems are arranged as a conversation.

Bristol, Evelyn. *A History of Russian Poetry.* New York: Oxford University Press, 1991. Covers Russian literature from the tenth century to the 1970's, placing writers and literary movements in a historical context. Biographical essay and commentary on each poet.

Bunimovitch, Evgeny, ed., and J. Kates, trans. and ed. *Contemporary Russian Poetry: An Anthology.* Champaign: Dalkey Archive Press, University of Illinois, 2008. A bilingual collection, consisting of works of forty-four living Russian poets, all born after 1945, who were selected for inclusion by Bunimovitch, a prominent Moscow poet.

Cornwell, Neil, ed. *A Reference Guide to Russian Literature.* Chicago: Fitzroy Dearborn, 1998. Detailed entries on some 273 writers, each consisting of a brief biographical sketch, a list of major works, and a selected bibliography. There are also thirteen essays on general topics. Russian-English title index.

_____. *The Routledge Companion to Russian Literature*. New York : Routledge, 2001. A reliable and accessible volume that spans a thousand years of Russian literature with essays on diverse subjects, each by an recognized authority in his or her area. Ideal both for students and for general readers. Bibliography and index.

Kates, J., ed. *In the Grip of Strange Thoughts: Russian Poetry in a New Era*. Brookline, Mass.: Zephyr Press, 2000. A collection of 118 poems by thirty-two writers, including fourteen women. A bilingual edition. Introduction and afterword on translation by the editor. Foreword by Mikhail Aizenberg. Annotated. Index of titles and first lines. Bibliography.

Nabokov, Vladimir Vladimirovich, comp. and trans. *Verses and Versions: Three Centuries of Russian Poetry*. Edited by Brian Boyd and Stanislav Shvabrin. Orlando, Fla.: Harcourt, 2008. Nabokov's English translations of Russian poems, preserving the rhyme schemes of the originals and presented side-by-side with them. Also includes Nabokov's translations from French to English and his comments about translation. Index of poets, index of titles and first lines. An invaluable volume.

Polukhina, Valentina, and Daniel Weissbort, eds. *An Anthology of Contemporary Russian Women Poets*. Iowa City: University of Iowa Press, 2005. English translations of works by more than eighty poets, some well established and others still unknown outside of Russia. Preface by Stephanie Sandler, concluding comments by Dmitry Kuzmin and Elena Fanailova. Biographical notes, bibliography, and index.

Scherr, Barry P. *Russian Poetry: Meter, Rhythm, and Rhyme*. Berkeley: University of California Press, 1986. One of the best treatments of the principles of Russian versification.

Smith, Gerald S. *Songs to Seven Strings: Russian Guitar Poetry and Soviet "Mass Song."* Bloomington: Indiana University Press, 1984. The main general source in English for information on the "bards."

Wachtel, Michael. *The Cambridge Introduction to Russian Poetry*. New York: Cambridge University Press, 2004. Discusses such matters as versification, poetic language, and traditional genres, drawing illustrations from poems by major Russian writers of the last three centuries.

_____. *The Development of Russian Verse; Meter and Its Meanings*. New York: Cambridge University Press, 1999. The first full-length study of Russian verse, demonstrating the influence of earlier uses of form on later poets, as well as the integral relationship between form and content. The author illustrates his ideas with close readings of more than fifty poets. A major scholarly achievement.

Yevtushenko, Yevgeny, et al., eds. *Twentieth Century Russian Poetry: Silver and Steel, an Anthology*. New York: Anchor Books, 1994. A large, sometimes quirky and inaccurate, but useful anthology of translations.

Mitzi M. Brunsdale
Updated by Gerald Janecek

ANNA AKHMATOVA
Anna Andreyevna Gorenko

Born: Bol'shoy Fontan, near Odessa, Ukraine, Russian Empire (now in Ukraine);
June 23, 1889
Died: Domodedovo, near Moscow, Soviet Union (now in Russia); March 5, 1966

PRINCIPAL POETRY

Vecher, 1912
Chetki, 1914
Belaya staya, 1917
Podorozhnik, 1921
Anno Domini MCMXXI, 1922
Iz shesti knig, 1940
Izbrannye stikhotvoreniia, 1943
Stikhotvoreniia, 1958
Poema bez geroya, 1960 (*A Poem Without a Hero*, 1973)
Rekviem, 1963 (*Requiem*, 1964)
Beg vremeni, 1965
Sochineniya, 1965-1983 (3 volumes)
Poems of A., 1973
Requiem, and Poem Without a Hero, 1976
Selected Poems, 1976
You Will Hear Thunder, 1976
Way of All the Earth, 1979
Anna Akhmatova: Poems, 1983
The Complete Poems of Anna Akhmatova, 1990 (2 volumes)

OTHER LITERARY FORMS

In addition to poetry, Anna Akhmatova (ak-MAH-tuh-vuh) wrote an unfinished play and many essays on Russian writers. Her spirited book *O Pushkine: Stat'i i zametki* (1977), published in its complete version posthumously, is one of the most discerning tributes to the greatest Russian poet, Alexander Pushkin, by a fellow poet. Akhmatova also translated poems from the Old Egyptian, Hindu, Armenian, Chinese, French, Italian, and many other languages, most of these in collaboration with native speakers.

ACHIEVEMENTS

Anna Akhmatova enriched Russian literature immeasurably, not only with the quality of her poetry but also with the freshness and originality of her strong talent. Through

Acmeism, a literary movement of which she was one of the founders and leading members, she effected a significant change of direction in Russian poetry in the second decade of the twentieth century. The Acmeists' insistence on clarity and precision of expression—much in the spirit of the Imagists, although the two movements developed independently of each other—represented a reaction against the intricate symbols and otherworldly preoccupations of the Symbolists. Akhmatova's youthful love poems brought her early fame, and her reputation was further enhanced during the long reign of terror in her country, through which she was able to preserve her dignity, both as a human being and as a poet. With Boris Pasternak, Osip Mandelstam, and Marina Tsvetayeva, Akhmatova is universally regarded as one of the four great poets of post-revolutionary Russia. Having been generously translated into English, Akhmatova's works are constantly gaining stature in world literature as well.

BIOGRAPHY

Anna Akhmatova—the pen name of Anna Andreyevna Gorenko—was born in a suburb of Odessa in 1889, into the family of a naval officer. Akhmatova began to write poetry when she was eleven, and her first poem was published in 1907. She achieved great popularity with her first books, *Vecher* and *Chetki*. After joining the literary movement called Acmeism, she played an important part in it together with Osip Mandelstam and with her husband, Nikolay Gumilyov, from whom she was later divorced. During World War I and the Russian Revolution, Akhmatova stood by her people, even though she did not agree with the ideas and methods of the revolutionaries. Never politically inclined, she saw in the war and the revolution an evil that might eventually destroy the private world in which she had been able to address herself exclusively to her own problems. When the end of that world came, she refused to accept it, believing that she would be able to continue her sequestered life. She also refused to emigrate, saying that it took greater courage to stay behind and accept what came.

The effect of the revolution on her life and creativity was not immediately evident, for she subsequently pub lished two more collections of poetry. When her former husband and fellow Acmeist Gumilyov was shot, however, Akhmatova realized that the new way of life was inimical to her own. Compelled to silence, she ceased to exist publicly, instead remaining an inner émigré for eighteen years and occupying herself mostly with writing essays and translating. This silence may have saved her life during the purges of the 1930's, although she was not spared agony while trying to ascertain the fate of her only son, a promising scholar of Asian history, who had been sent to a labor camp three times. Only World War II brought a change to Akhmatova's dreary and dangerous life. Like many Soviet writers and intellectuals, she once again sided with her people, suppressing her reservations and complaints. She spent the first several months of the war in besieged Leningrad and then was evacuated to Tashkent, where she stayed almost to the end of the war. In Tashkent, she was brought closer to the other part of her ancestry, for her grandmother, from whom she took her pen name, was a Tartar.

When the war was over and the authorities again resorted to repression, Akhmatova was among the first to be victimized. In a vitriolic speech by Andrei Zhdanov, the cultural dictator at that time, she and the satirist Mikhail Zoshchenko were singled out as examples of anti-Soviet attitudes among intellectuals and charged with harmful influence on the young. They were expelled from the Writers' Union, and their works ceased to be published. Thus, Akhmatova vanished from public view once again in 1946, this time involuntarily, and did not reappear until ten years later. In 1958, a slender collection of her poems was published as a sign of rehabilitation. A few more of her books were subsequently published, both at home and abroad, thus reinstating the poet as an active member of society.

During the last decade of her life, she wrote some of the best poetry of her career. Shortly before her death, she received two richly deserved accolades for her work. Ironically, the recognition came from abroad: She was awarded the prestigious Italian Etna Taormina Prize in 1964 and an honorary doctorate from Oxford University in 1965. Ravaged by long illness, she died in 1966, having preserved her dignity and independence by asking for and receiving a church funeral according to the Russian Orthodox rites. After her death, Akhmatova was almost unanimously eulogized as the finest woman poet in all Russian literature.

Analysis

Anna Akhmatova's poetry can conveniently be divided into three distinct periods: 1912 to 1923, 1940 to 1946, and 1956 to 1966 (with a few poems published in 1950). The interim periods were those of enforced silence. The first silence, from 1923 to 1940, came as a result of tacit admission on her part that the changed way of life in Russia was not fully acceptable to her. The second, from 1946 to 1956, was a direct result of the authorities' intervention. Needless to say, Akhmatova kept busy by further refining her poetry, by writing essays, and by translating.

Vecher and Chetki

Akhmatova's development as a poet can be traced from book to book. Her first books, *Vecher* and *Chetki*, impressed readers with the freshness of a young woman's concern about her feelings of love. In almost all the poems having love as a focal point, Akhmatova presents love from a woman's point of view, in a form resembling a diary. It is difficult to say whether the female voice in these poems belongs to the poet herself; probably it does, but in the last analysis it is immaterial. The beloved is almost always silent, never fully revealed or described, and at times he seems to be almost secondary— only a catalyst for the woman's feelings. She is so entranced by his mere presence that, in her anguish, she draws her "left-hand glove upon [her] right." The poet expresses the whole spectrum of love—from the playfulness of a young woman trying to dismay her partner (to prove that she, too, can wield some power over him) to moments of flaming passion.

To be sure, passion is presented implicitly, in the time-honored tradition of Russian literature, yet it is also vividly indicated in unique ways. As she says, "In human intimacy there is a secret boundary,/ Neither the experience of being in love nor passion can cross it/ Though the lips be joined together in awful silence/ And the heart break asunder with love." Her fervent passion is coupled with fidelity to her partner, but as her loyalty is professed time and again, a note of frustration and a fear of incompatibility and rejection become noticeable. The prospect of unrequited love is confirmed by betrayal and parting. The ensuing feeling of loneliness leads to despair and withdrawal. The woman's reaction shows a mixture of anger, defiance, even resignation: "Be accursed . . ./ But I swear by the garden of angels/ By the holy icon I swear,/ By the passionate frenzy of our nights,/ I will never go back to you!" (These lines, incidentally, prompted Zhdanov, in his merciless attack many years later, to call Akhmatova "a nun and a harlot.") Thus, celebration, parting, and suffering receive equal play in Akhmatova's approach to love, although the ultimate outcome is a markedly unhappy one. Her love poetry is a vivid testimony both to the glories and to the miseries of her gender.

The feminine "I" of the poems seeks refuge, release, and salvation in religion, nature, and poetry. The refuge in religion is especially evident in *Chetki*. The work has a peculiar religious tone, pervaded, like Akhmatova's sentiments of love, with a mood of melancholy and inexplicable sadness. The persona seems to have found consolation for unhappiness in love when she says: "The King of Heaven has healed my/ Soul with the icy calm of love's/ Absence." Her prayers are mostly in the form of confession or intercession. It is easy to see, however, that they are used primarily to compensate for her feeling of loneliness and weariness of life. Thus, privations and misfortunes are closely tied to her religious feelings; sin and atonement are inseparable, and her passions of the flesh are tempered by spiritual fervor. Akhmatova's poems with religious overtones have little in common with customary religious experience. They are also much more complex and psychologically laden than any of her other poetry.

BELAYA STAYA AND ANNO DOMINI MCMXXI

In Akhmatova's third collection, *Belaya staya*, a new theme joins those of love and religion: a presentiment of doom. Nourished by the horrors of war and revolution, this presentiment grows into a wake for a world on the verge of annihilation. As the revolution dragged on, Akhmatova's mood turned bleaker and more hopeless. She sought rapport with the events by writing poetry with political motifs, but to no avail.

The poems in *Anno Domini MCMXXI* clearly reveal Akhmatova's state of mind and emotions at this difficult time, as well as her awareness that an era had come to an end. "All is sold, all is lost, all is plundered,/ Death's wing has flashed black on our sight,/ All's gnawed bare with sore, want, and sick longing," she laments in one poem. She refused to emigrate, however, knowing instinctively, as did Boris Pasternak many years later when he was threatened with expulsion from the Soviet Union, that for a poet to leave his or her native land is tantamount to a death worse than physical death. She did not hesitate to criticize those who had left their country in its worst hour: "Poor exile, you are like a prisoner/ To me, or one upon the bed/ Of sickness. Dark your road, O wanderer,/ Of wormwood smacks your alien bread." These lines have been quoted often by Soviet critics for propaganda purposes, although Akhmatova wrote them sincerely, as a poet who could not tear herself away from her own land.

WAR AND LOVE OF COUNTRY

In the poems in which Akhmatova grappled with the problems of present-day reality, a gradual shift from intimate love poetry toward more worldly themes can be seen. This shift can be considered as an overture to another kind of Akhmatova's poetry. Tormented by the turbulent years of war and revolution, in which she made many personal sacrifices and witnessed many tragedies (the loss of friends, for example, including her former husband Nikolay Gumilyov), she was forced to face reality and to express her feelings and opinions about it. The silence imposed on her in 1923 only postponed further development in that direction.

When she was allowed to reappear shortly before World War II, Akhmatova wrote little in her old idiom. In many poems written during the war, she extols the beauty of her land and the magnitude of the martyrdom of her people under attack by a ruthless enemy. Leningrad, the city of her life and of her dreams, is especially the object of her affection. Tsarskoe Selo—a settlement near Leningrad, which was the residence of the czars; the town of young Alexander Pushkin; and the town of Akhmatova's favorite poetry teacher Innokenty Annensky as well as of her own youth—remained vividly and forever etched in her memory, even when she saw it almost totally destroyed in the war.

Leningrad and Tsarskoe Selo were not the only places to which Akhmatova paid homage; indeed, all Russia was her home. Her attitude toward her country is typical of many Russian intellectuals, who, despite a thick veneer of cosmopolitanism, still harbor a childlike, sentimental, and sometimes irrational love for their country. From her earliest poems to her last, Akhmatova expressed the same feeling for Russia, a strange mixture of abstract love for her country, on one hand, and down-to-earth concern for its people, on the other. In the poem "Prayer," for example, she prays to the Lord to take even her child and to destroy "the sweet power of song" that she possesses if it would help to change "the storm cloud over Russia . . . into a nimbus ablaze."

This willingness to sacrifice what is dearest to her if it would benefit her country is no mere affectation—it is expressed with utmost sincerity and conviction. In a poem written almost thirty years later, "From an Airplane," she again expresses her love for her country in no less sincere terms: "It is all mine—and nothing can divide us,/ It is my soul, it is my body, too." Perhaps the most profound and meaningful testimony to her patriotism can be found in the poem "Native Land," written in the last years of her life. For her, her country was "the mud on our gumboots, the grit in our teeth . . ./ And we mill, and we mix, and we crumble/ This innocent earth at our feet,/ But we rest in this earth at the roots of the flowers,/ Which is why we so readily say: It is ours!"

Akhmatova did not limit her gaze to European Russia, where she was reared and where she spent most of her life. Through her experiences in Tashkent, the city in which her ancestors had resided, she acquired a great admiration for, and understanding of, the Asian mind and soul. A mystical bond with Asia inspired her to write some of her most beautiful descriptive poems, such as "From the Oriental Notebook."

REQUIEM

Nevertheless, Akhmatova could not close her eyes to the Soviet reality, in which she was personally caught in a most tragic way. In a unified cycle of poems, *Requiem*, a masterpiece unpublished in the Soviet Union until 1987, she expresses her deep sorrow about not only her personal loss but also the suffering to which the Russian people were being subjected. *Requiem* was her closest approach to public castigation of the regime in her country. The tone for the entire work is set by the motto, which sadly admits that the circumstances are not those of a foreign country but, more personally, those of the poet's own country and people. In a short foreword in prose, Akhmatova tells how during the horrible years of the purges she spent seventeen months waiting in line in front of a prison to discover the fate of her son. Another woman recognized her and whispered, "Can you describe this?" "Yes, I can," Akhmatova replied.

She kept her promise by writing *Requiem*. Although much of it reflects the universal sorrow and despair of a mother on the verge of losing her son, it is the *injustice* of her suffering that most pains the poet. Using her personal sorrow to speak for all human beings who suffer unjustly, the poet created in *Requiem* a work of lasting value. Moreover, there is much encouragement to be gained from *Requiem*. The persona does not lose hope and courage. She perseveres, knowing that the victims are unjustly persecuted and that she is not alone in suffering. In the epilogue, she recalls the trying hours and the faces she has seen in those seventeen months; in her final words, she begs that her monument be erected in front of the prison where she has stood for "three hundred hours," so that the thawing snow from the face of her monument will glide like tears. Even if overt references to the political terror are overlooked, *Requiem* is still one of the twentieth century's most eloquent poetic testimonies to human tragedy.

FINAL POEMS

Akhmatova's poetry from the last decade of her life shows the greater maturity and wisdom of old age. Her approach to poetic themes is more epic and historical, with a deeper perspective. This mature poetry is also more philosophical and psychological. The best example is the autobiographical *A Poem Without a Hero*, a panoramic view of the previous century as it pertains to the present. It is a subtle and at times complex poem, difficult to fathom without a proper key.

In her last poems, Akhmatova speaks as if she has realized that her active role is over and that nothing else can hurt her. Her work at this time shows a mixture of sadness, resignation, relief, and even slight bewilderment as to what life really is after more than seven decades of coping with it: "The grim epoch diverted me/ As if I were a river./ I have been given a different life. In a new bed/ The river now flows, past the old one,/ And I cannot find my shores. . . ." She finds solace in her increasing loneliness, contemplating the past, trying to reevaluate it and to find the correct perspective on it. In one of her last poems, written slightly more than a year before her death, she speaks of the "Supreme Mystery." It has been on her mind from the beginning, changing its face from period to period. In her early poetry, it was the mystery of the man-woman relationship. Later, it became the mystery of the man-to-man relationship, with the emphasis on the cruelty of man to man. In her last years, it became the mystery of the relationship of man to eternity, indeed, the mystery of the meaning of existence. Through such organic development, Akhmatova reached the pinnacle of her poetic power, the power found in Pasternak's late poetry and in the work of other great poets of the century.

FORM AND STYLE

The stylistic aspect of Akhmatova's poetry is just as important as the thematic one, if not more so. She shows several peculiarly Akhmatovian features. Above all, there is the narrative tone that points to a definite affinity with prose. Formalist critic Viktor Zhirmunsky calls her entire oeuvre "a novel in verse." It is this affinity that enables her to switch easily from emotion to description. Connected with this skill is a dramatic quality, expressed either through inner monologue or dialogue. The second striking feature is the brief lyric form, usually consisting of three to four stanzas, rarely five to seven, and never more than seven. (Later in her career, Akhmatova wrote many poems in free verse.) Parallel to the brevity of form is a pronounced laconism: A few carefully selected details suffice to convey an entire picture. Akhmatova's economy of words, spare almost to the point of frugality, led her to the epigrammatic form and to fragmentation, understatement, and improvisation. As a result, her sentences are sometimes without a verb and even without a subject (that being quite possible in Russian). Another peculiarity is the concreteness of her images, especially with reference to space and time. She tells the reader exactly where and when, almost to the minute, the events in her poem take place. The colors are vividly and exactly given. She avoids metaphors, instead using pointed, explanatory epithets. Finally, her intonation, never scrupulously measured or regulated, is that of a syncopated rhythm, approaching the rhythm of some forms of folk poetry. Many of these stylistic features result from her adherence to the tenets of Acmeism, but many others are uniquely her own and are easily recognizable as such.

Of the poets who influenced her, Akhmatova herself admits indebtedness to Gavrila Derzhavin, Pushkin, and Annensky. The latter two can be said to have exerted the greatest influence on her, although traces of other poets' influences—Nikolai Nekrasov, Aleksandr Blok, Mikhail Kuzmin—can be found. Even Fyodor Dostoevski, who never wrote poetry, is sometimes mentioned as a possible source of influence. As for her impact on other poets, Akhmatova's influence, like that of her great contemporaries, Mandelstam, Pasternak, and Marina Tsvetayeva, is pervasive, elusive, impossible to measure. In her old age, she recognized the talent of Joseph Brodsky—then only twenty-two years old—and passed on her mantle, as Nadezhda Mandelstam has said, in a kind of poetic succession. Akhmatova, "Tragic Queen Anna," as literary historian Alexander Werth calls her, is a poet without whom modern Russian literature is unthinkable and by whom world literature has been significantly enriched.

OTHER MAJOR WORK

NONFICTION: *O Pushkine: Stat'i i zametki*, 1977.

BIBLIOGRAPHY

Driver, Sam N. *Anna Akhmatova*. New York: Twayne, 1972. This is the first English biography, written six years after Akhmatova's death. The first third of the book deals with biographical facts, and the remainder with a thematic explanation of the poetry. It is a concise yet scholarly work, still serving as the best primary introduction to Akhmatova's life.

Feinstein, Elaine. *Anna of All the Russias: The Life of Anna Akhmatova*. New York: Knopf, 2007. The extensive details of this biography bring to life Akhmatova's complex personality and grant readers insight to her poetry.

Gerstein, Emma. *Moscow Memoirs: Memories of Anna Akhmatova, Osip Mandelstam, and Literary Russia Under Stalin*. Translated and edited by John Crowfoot. Woodstock, N.Y.: Overlook Press, 2004. Literary scholar Gerstein describes her experiences with Mandelstam and Akhmatova, including the poet's reactions to her son's imprisonment.

Ketchian, Sonia. *The Poetry of Anna Akhmatova: A Conquest of Time and Space*. Munich: Otto Sagner, 1986. A brilliant scholarly study of themes and method in Akhmatova's poetry. Contains a recapitulation of Akhmatova scholarship, both Soviet and Western.

Leiter, Sharon. *Akhmatova's Petersburg*. Philadelphia: University of Pennsylvania Press, 1983. A review of Akhmatova's life in her beloved St. Petersburg and of political circumstances providing the material for, and leading to, her poetry inspired by St. Petersburg. The book also discusses Akhmatova's vision of this city.

Reeder, Roberta. *Anna Akhmatova: Poet and Prophet*. Rev. ed. Los Angeles: Figueroa Press, 2006. Reeder discusses in scholarly fashion all facets of Akhmatova's life and work. Stressing the artistic aspects of her poems, the author also examines the political circumstances in which she had to live. A forty-six-page bibliography is particularly useful.

Rosslyn, Wendy. *The Prince, the Fool, and the Nunnery: The Religious Theme in the Early Poetry of Anna Akhmatova.* Amersham, England: Avebury, 1984. An examination of the interplay of religion and love in Akhmatova's early collections, this book also contains considerable biographical detail. Poems are included in both Russian and English translation.

Wells, David N. *Anna Akhmatova: Her Poetry.* Oxford, England: Berg, 1996. Wells offers a succinct overview of Akhmatova's life and poetry from the beginnings to her later works. His is a penetrating study, with many citations from her poetry in both Russian and English, stressing her main achievements.

Vasa D. Mihailovich
Updated by Mihailovich

INNOKENTY ANNENSKY

Born: Omsk, Siberia, Russia; September 1, 1855
Died: St. Petersburg, Russia; December 13, 1909

PRINCIPAL POETRY
Tikhie pesni, 1904
Kiparisovy larets, 1910 (*The Cypress Chest*, 1982)

OTHER LITERARY FORMS

In addition to his two collections of poetry, for which he is best remembered today, Innokenty Annensky (uhn-YEHN-skee) wrote four tragedies and was a critic and pedagogue of note. His tragedies include *Melanippa-Filosof* (pb. 1901), *Tsar Iksion* (pb. 1902), *Laodamiia* (pb. 1906), and *Famira Kifared* (pb. 1913). Annensky's major critical effort consists of the essays constituting the two collections entitled *Kniga otrazhenii* (1906) and *Vtoraia kniga otrazhenii* (1909). They were reissued in a single volume in 1969. The remainder of Annensky's critical and pedagogical essays have never been collected in book form; they remain scattered throughout the Russian journals in which they first appeared.

ACHIEVEMENTS

Innokenty Annensky has always been considered a "poet's poet" because of the subtlety of his poetic imagery and the intricacy of his thought. In contrast to such contemporary poets as Aleksandr Blok and Konstantin Balmont, who were enormously popular in their own time, Annensky's main impact was rather on the aesthetic theory of Acmeism, one of the great Russian poetic schools of the twentieth century. Two gifted and famous Acmeists, Anna Akhmatova and Osip Mandelstam, were especially drawn to Annensky both as a poet and as a formulator of poetic doctrine.

Although he has often been regarded as a member of the older, "first generation" of Russian Symbolists (in contrast to the younger or "second generation"), Annensky does not truly fit into a particular category. His style can be designated as Symbolist insofar as his use of literary allusions is concerned, yet his worldview and aesthetic ideals, as well as his treatment of non-Symbolist stylistic elements, set him apart from this movement. Annensky differs from his contemporaries in his aesthetic independence. He is considered unique among twentieth century Russian poets in that he combined aspects of Symbolism with experimental stylistic devices to produce verse that cannot easily be labeled. He is regarded today as one of the more interesting and significant modern Russian poets, and he has a reputation far exceeding that which he enjoyed during his own lifetime.

BIOGRAPHY

Innokenty Fyodorovich Annensky was born in Omsk, Siberia, on August 20, 1856, but the family returned to St. Petersburg in 1858. Both parents having died when Annensky was quite young, he was reared by his brother, Nikolay Fyodorovich Annensky, publisher of the important journal *Russkoe bogatstvo*. Nikolay and his wife, Alexandra Nikitichna Annenskaya, held liberal political and social views typical of the positivistic thinkers of their generation.

Educated at home, possibly because his health was poor, Annensky mastered several foreign languages, including Latin and Greek. He completed a degree in philology at the University of St. Petersburg in 1879; in the same year, he married a widow named Dina Khmara-Barshchevskaya. The marriage was apparently a happy one; he was close to his two stepsons, and his own son Valentin was born in 1880.

Annensky embarked on his pedagogical career following graduation. After teaching Greek and Russian in several private institutions in St. Petersburg, he went to Kiev between 1890 and 1893, where he became director of the Pavel Galagan College. He returned to St. Petersburg in 1893, assuming the directorship of a high school there, and in 1896, he was appointed head of the famous lyceum at Tsarskoe Selo. It was during his tenure at Tsarskoe Selo that he issued his first volume of original verse and translations, *Tikhie pesni*; the book was virtually unnoticed by the critics.

Annensky's last post was as inspector of the St. Petersburg School District; he also lectured on classical literature at a private university for women. During this period, his friendship with the Acmeist poet and theoretician Nikolay Gumilyov gave him entrée into the literary world of St. Petersburg and brought him belated fame. Annensky died of a heart attack on November 30, 1909, the very day his retirement had been granted.

ANALYSIS

Innokenty Annensky's lyrics reflect an intimate knowledge of French poetry, particularly the verse of the Parnassians and the French Symbolists. Like many of these French poets, Annensky heeded Stéphane Mallarmé's dictum that to name was to destroy, while to suggest was to create. Like the French, Annensky concentrated a lyrical theme in one symbolically treated subject or in a complex of interconnected subjects. Although he made use of symbol and suggestion, the fact that the lyrical theme was related to a single subject or a complex of related subjects lent greater impact to his poems.

Annensky's link with the French Symbolists was paralleled by his close ties with the Parnassians. The latter, particularly their principal poet, Théophile Gautier, advocated art for art's sake and the composition of a carefully constructed poetry equally removed from subjective emotions and contemporary events. The Parnassians also expressed a renewed interest in the classical world; indeed, the Parnassians had a greater impact on Annensky than did the Symbolists, for he shared with the former a cult of poetic form and a love of the word as such, as well as subscribing to their notion that there was no affinity between aesthetics and ethics.

Annensky's relationship with the Russian Symbolists is somewhat ambiguous for there was an absence of any kind of organizational tie or even any close relationship between him and representatives of the "new poetry." Unlike his contemporaries, he considered Symbolism to be an aesthetic system rather than a literary school. He neither rebelled against civic poetry, for example, as the Symbolists generally did, nor rejected his poetic heritage. Unlike the later Symbolists, he did not regard art as a means of mystical escape, maintaining that Symbolism was intended to be literature rather than a new form of universal religion.

The approximately five hundred lyrics that Annensky wrote are the center of his creative work and can be divided into six major themes: death, life, dream, nature, artistic creation, and time. The themes of death, life, dream, and nature are actually subordinate to that of time, which binds all of them together. In this very emphasis on temporality, Annensky transcended Symbolism and anticipated later poetic movements. His exemption of artistic creation from the strictures of time illustrates the enormous emphasis he placed on aesthetics.

Death played an important role in Annensky's verse, for he considered it as an ever-intruding end to a life without hope. He devoted a number of lyrics to this theme, one of the most important of which was "Siren' na kamne" ("Lilac on the Gravestone"). Here Annensky touches on the transitory nature of human life, on the contrast between life and death, and on the awareness that the seemingly infinite possibilities of the intellect are thwarted by the intrusion of an awareness of physical death. Annensky's realization that death is a physical, inescapable end demonstrates his acceptance of the limitations of the material world and stresses thereby one of the most significant differences between him and the Symbolists.

"DEPRESSION" AND "THE DOUBLE"

One of Annensky's major themes is life. This category is dominated by lyrics about *toska* (depression, melancholy, or yearning personified), as exemplified by the poem "Toska" ("Depression"). The persona in "Depression" is an invalid, suspended, as it were, between life and death. The setting for the poem is a sickroom decorated with flowered wallpaper, around which flies hover. The unnaturalness of the surroundings, coupled with Annensky's frequent use of participles rather than finite verbs, separates both persona and reader from the normal, lively world of action and imprisons them in a static, banal realm. Like his poems on death, Annensky's lyrics about life are characterized by pessimism derived from his constant awareness of the limitations and frustrations of life.

In *The Influence of French Symbolism on Russian Poetry*, Georgette Donchin suggests that because the dream symbolizes an escape from reality, it was a common poetic theme for Russian Symbolists. The dream also occupies a special place in Annensky's poetry. Simon Karlinsky, in his 1966 essay "The Materiality of Annensky," argues that the dream represents a world divorced from the strictures of time, an alternative existence for the poet. Annensky's dream verses can be subdivided into three categories according to theme: disorientation, oblivion, and nightmare. In "Dvoinik" ("The Double"), the persona experiences a loss of orientation, with the primary differentiation of identity, that between the I and the non-I, blurred. Annensky's deliberate grammatical confusion of the first, second, and third persons destroys the normal distinctions between conversation and narration, even of existence. When the distinct separateness of the individual consciousness is eradicated, nothing is certain. Annensky has, in fact, placed the rest of the poem outside reality by erasing the conceptions of definite time and space, with all existence transformed into a dream.

EPHEMERALITY AND DEATH

In "Kogda b ne smert', a zabyt'e" ("If There Were Not Death, but Oblivion"), oblivion represents the cessation of time. It is a state divorced from temporality, which is seen in the poem as the creator and destroyer of beauty. The poet's awareness of the ephemerality of artistic as well as natural beauty is a source of torment for him; he is trapped by time and is doomed to solitude.

Unlike disorientation and oblivion, the nightmare threatens the sufferer with annihilation. In "Utro" ("Morning"), Annesky has erased the distinction between dream and reality, making the nightmare vividly real. When day comes at the end of the poem, it is not merely a unit of time but a symbol of the force of light against the power of darkness, good against evil, life against death.

NATURE

Nature is the backdrop against which thoughts and emotions can be projected, the external mirror of human existence. As such, it constitutes a significant theme in Annensky's verse. The winter poem "Sneg" ("Snow") is characterized by a sharpness of line and by the specificity resulting from the repeated use of the definite demonstrative adjective *eto* ("this"). In addition to crispness of outline and color contrast, Annensky's employment of oxymoron makes his images clearer still. The clarity of nature has become a foil for the clarity of the thought of the persona.

"TO A POET"

In contrast to the later Symbolists, Annensky considered the poet a creator of clear, linear art. His divergence from the Symbolists is especially marked in the lyric "Poetu" ("To a Poet"), a lesson in how to write poetry. Annensky focuses on the importance of clarity and concreteness, opposing them to abstraction and indefiniteness. He asserts that poetry is a "science" governed by certain laws and is, within limits, exact, as the measuring triad of dimensions in the poem suggests. The figure with the triad is the

Muse, who in turn symbolizes the art of classical Greece with its emphasis on clarity and beauty of form. The link with Greece is reinforced by the reference to Orpheus and the significance of form. The Muse is juxtaposed to veiled Isis, emblematic of the mystery and distortion of the later Symbolists. She perhaps stands for the figure of Eternal Wisdom that informed much of the philosophy of the Symbolist philosopher-poet Vladimir Soloviev. The poet is not an intermediary between Earth and a higher realm; he is not a seer or transmitter, but a writer.

"POETRY"

Like "To a Poet," "Poeziia" ("Poetry") is a metapoem, in which art transcends the everyday world and allows the poet limited access to a realm of absolute beauty. The poem is set in the Sinai Desert, a region of intense light and heat; the word "flaming" in the first line not only describes the concentrated heat of the desert but also carries the religious connotation of the fire that can purge sin and memory (as in Alexander Pushkin's famous poem "Prorok," "The Prophet"). Annensky personifies poetry in the last stanza, where he speaks of the "traces of Her sandals." The narrator never sees Poetry directly; he entreats Her, although not "knowing Her."

The desert can be seen here as a haven from society and from the decay of the established religion (in this case, Symbolism) from which the poet seeks to escape. Poetry is contrasted to the vision of Sophia (Eternal Wisdom) that Soloviev saw in Egypt, and the poem as a whole may well represent Annensky's escape from a burdensome, "official" school of poetry in his quest for pure art.

"THE STEEL CICADA"

Time is centrally important in Annensky's verse, for it is the regulator of the days and seasons, the ruler of life. Time connects and dominates all of Annensky's other themes, providing a focal point for understanding his conception of the material world and his emphasis on art. "Stalnaia cikada" ("The Steel Cicada") portrays time as an invention of the mind. In this lyric, Annensky has equated the timepiece with a cicada and has thus transformed it into something alive, thereby implying process and change. When the lid of the watch has been slammed shut in the last stanza, time has stopped. The intrusion of *toska*, having cut the poet off from external events (by shutting the watch lid), has stopped time.

Time, the medium of change, causes the alteration of moods and conditions that is the antithesis of depression. Annensky speeds up time through his poetic lexicon, employing short phrases without enjambment to achieve a staccato effect. Near the end of the poem, the persona has become reconciled to the return of depression; his companionship with the cicada is called a "miracle" that will last only for a minute. With the removal of the cicada comes the realization that the passing moment is beyond recall. The poet's attempt to escape from constancy into a realm of change that he has invented himself (symbolized throughout the poem by the watch, a mechanical object) has failed. In the end, he is the victim of his own immutability.

SYMBOLISM OF TIME

For Annensky, time symbolizes process and the final disintegration that characterizes life, nature, and death, while life represents the temporary immersion in process. It is the poet's realization of the relentless flow of time that produces the psychological state of depression, an awareness that the extreme limitations of existence are nevertheless the highest human achievement. Annensky's cognizance of depression amounts to a rejection of mysticism, separating him irrevocably from the later Symbolists. Time represents reality and is inescapable except through the momentary conquest by the mind and spirit of the artist.

USE OF PERSONIFICATION

Although he did not experiment in metrics and rhyme, Annensky was more adventurous stylistically in his employment of personification. He frequently capitalizes the first letter of a word denoting an object or abstract term to identify it with a human being, utilizing the simile and metaphor for the same purpose. Annensky's reliance on personification causes the reader to view nature, at least within the scope of these poems, as an extension of the conscious mind. His poetic universe centers on the mind, extends to artifacts, includes surrounding nature (especially the garden), and is limited only by the clouds. Beyond the clouds lies infinity, which cannot be understood and hence cannot be encompassed within the realm dominated by the mind. Because his universe can be considered as having a rational basis, Annensky should be regarded as a precursor of the rationalism of the Acmeists.

ROLE IN THE SYMBOLIST MOVEMENT

Although classified as a Symbolist by a number of critics, Annensky should rather be regarded as a transitional figure between Symbolism and later poetic developments in Russia. Annensky differs from the Symbolists in his use of conversational elements and in his preference for concrete, distinct objects as poetic images. Like his thematic emphasis on time, his predilection for the concrete and real as opposed to the abstract and mystical denotes an acceptance of the actual world. His literary orientation was toward new poets rather than toward those who were already established. His later poetry contains stylistic elements more compatible with Acmeism, even with Futurism, than with Symbolism.

Annensky's ambiguous position in relation to the Symbolists is underscored by his avoidance of the polemics characterizing the Symbolist school. This may have been partially a result of the fact that he was not a professional poet but instead was an educator who lacked sufficient time or opportunity to develop extensive personal contacts with the Symbolists. His abstention from the literary quarrels that were to climax in 1910, the year after his death, indicates an unwillingness to involve himself in the intricacies of literary battles. In addition, Annensky's avoidance of Symbolist polemics parallels his emphasis on poetry as an artistic phenomenon rather than a literary school. He believed that the intrinsic aesthetic value of poetry precluded its use as a vehicle. His abstention from mysticism and literary polemics resulted from a desire to preserve the integrity of the art and thus to prevent its prostitution to other ends.

INFLUENCE ON ACMEISTS

Annensky stood out from the poets of his time in devising a poetic world that was concrete rather than abstract, worldly rather than mystical. He employed personification and focused on images and objects that made his language concrete. Although he was interested in the musical elements of poetry, he emphasized its pictorial and visual aspects. He thus created a definitive background for the philosophical or aesthetic argument of a particular lyric. These factors, coupled with a respect for the intrinsic worth of art, relate him more closely to writers following him, particularly to such poets as the Acmeists, than to his contemporaries. In tracing the development of Russian poetry and, indeed, of Russian literature as a whole in the twentieth century, the pivotal position of Annensky and the great scope of his contribution must be taken into account.

OTHER MAJOR WORKS

PLAYS: *Melanippa-Filosof*, pb. 1901; *Tsar Iksion*, pb. 1902; *Laodamiia*, pb. 1906; *Famira Kifared*, pb. 1913.

NONFICTION: *Kniga otrazhenii*, 1906; *Vtoraia kniga otrazhenii*, 1909.

BIBLIOGRAPHY

Fedorov, Andrei V. *Innokentij Annenskij: Lichnost' i tvorchestvo*. Leningrad: Khudozhestvennaia Literatura, 1984. A succinct biography by a leading Russian scholar on Annensky. It details the poet's life and discusses the essential aspects of his lyrics, prose, and plays, with the emphasis on poetry. In Russian.

Ljunggren, Anna. *At the Crossroads of Russian Modernism: Studies in Innokentij Annenskij's Poetics*. Stockholm: Almqvist & Wiksell International, 1997. A thorough discussion of Annensky's poetry, addressing both the Russian and international links of his work, with the emphasis on how the French Symbolists were received and transformed by Annensky within the Russian Symbolist poetry. His poetics are discussed at length. His similarities with Boris Pasternak, Ivan Bunin, Vladislav Khodasevich, and Vladimir Nabokov are also discussed.

Setchkarev, Vsevolod. *Studies in the Life and Work of Innokenty Annensky*. The Hague, the Netherlands: Mouton, 1963. This seminal work includes a biography and a discussion of Annensky's works and is one of the best on the subject. Setchkarev discusses in detail Annensky's rise to prominence and his contribution to the Russian literature of the first decade of the twentieth century. The author analyzes Annensky's significance in the second wave of Russian Symbolists. A must for students of Annensky by a Russian scholar transplanted in the West.

Tucker, Janet G. *Innokentij Annenskij and the Acmeist Doctrine.* Columbus, Ohio: Slavica, 1986. In this studious examination of Annensky's poetry, the author analyzes the poet's contribution to Symbolist poetry, the themes and devices of his poetry, his role as a literary critic, and, above all, his views of, and relationship to, the doctrine of Acmeism and his links with that movement. A valuable contribution to the critical evaluation of Annensky by a Western scholar.

Janet G. Tucker
Updated by Vasa D. Mihailovich

ALEKSANDR BLOK

Born: St. Petersburg, Russian Empire (now in Russia); November 28, 1880
Died: Petrograd, Russian Soviet Federation of Socialist Republics (now St. Petersburg, Russia); August 7, 1921

PRINCIPAL POETRY

Stikhi o prekrasnoy dame, 1904
Nechayannaya radost, 1907
Snezhnaya maska, 1907
Zemlya v snegu, 1908
Nochyne chasy, 1911
Skazki, 1912
Krugly god, 1913
Stikhi o Rossii, 1915
Sobraniye stikhotvoreniy i teatr v 4 kigakh, 1916 (4 volumes; includes the poetic cycles *Puzyri zemli*, *Gorod*, *Faina*, etc.)
Dvenadtsat, 1918 (*The Twelve*, 1920)
Skify, 1918 (*The Scythians*, 1982)
Solovinyy sad, 1918
Iamby: Sovremennye stikhi, 1907-1914, 1919
Sedoe utro, 1920
Za granyu proshlykh dnei, 1920
Vozmezdie, 1922 (wr. 1910-1921)
Poems of A. B., 1968
Selected Poems, 1972

OTHER LITERARY FORMS

Aleksandr Blok wrote three lyrical plays, the first of which, *Balaganchik* (pr., pb. 1906; *The Puppet Show*, 1963), was staged immediately and widely. The second, *Korol' na ploshchadi* (pb. 1907; *The King in the Square*, 1934) was never staged, although its material was absorbed into other works. *Roza i krest* (pb. 1913; *The Rose and the Cross*, 1936) was popular in print and had more than two hundred rehearsals at the Moscow Art Theater, but was never publicly staged. Several additional dramatic monologues failed before presentation. Blok also wrote critical essays on poetry and drama as well as a series of articles dealing with the role of the intelligentsia in Russian cultural development, translated several plays from French and German for stage production, and edited his mother's translation of the letters of Gustave Flaubert. Much of his work was reissued in various collections during his lifetime, and posthumous editions, in-

Aleksandr Blok
(Library of Congress)

cluding diaries, letters, and notebooks, have appeared regularly. A scholarly collected works in nine volumes has been completed in the Soviet Union.

ACHIEVEMENTS

Aleksandr Blok was the leading Russian Symbolist and is universally regarded as one of the most important Russian poets of the twentieth century. The Symbolists were interested in poetic reform to reshape the partly sentimental, partly social-oriented poetic idiom of the second half of the nineteenth century. They favored a return to mysticism, albeit with modern overtones, free from the rational tenor of the scientific age. The movement's early exponents, notably Konstantin Balmont and Valery Bryusov, incorporated French Symbolist ideas into their work, but when Blok began to write at the turn of the century, Symbolism was no longer a single unit. It had disintegrated into literary factions that reflected the movement's precepts in their own way. Though Blok paid homage to the search for spiritual values, his mysticism owes as much to the writings of his uncle, the religious philosopher Vladimir Solovyov, as to Stéphane Mallarmé, with whom he shared the striving to give shape to the "music of the spheres," the elusive entities beyond reality.

In contrast to his eccentric fellow Symbolists and the equally whimsical linguistic experimenters of other movements, Blok stood out as a contemplative, sincere individual whose philosophical concerns were as important as the language used to express them. He attached an almost metaphysical significance to the creative power of the poet, and this belief in the transcendental quality of art led him to reach beyond the partisan interests of his contemporaries to create a solid, coherent poetical system reminiscent of the "golden age" of Alexander Pushkin, Mikhail Lermontov, and Fyodor Tyutchev almost a century earlier. Blok's considerable talent and natural sense of rhythm facilitated the realization of these aspirations, resulting in an amazing output during twenty years of literary activity. Thematically, Blok brought the cult of the Eternal Feminine to Russia, using the concept as focal point in his search for spiritual unity. The immense range of this vision, incorporating, among others, the Virgin Mary, Holy Sophia, Mother Russia, Blok's wife, and St. Petersburg prostitutes, permitted the poet to extend early mystical longings to the concrete realities of his own life and to revolutionary changes. His verse cycles dedicated to his native land, his perceptive essays on the role of the intelligentsia, and his refusal to emigrate during the famines of the civil war brought him deference from all segments of the Russian public. Stylistically, he honored the conventions of the past by building on existing rhyme schemes in much of his work, even as he changed from the traditional counting of syllables in a metric foot to modern tonic verse patterns.

Blok's poetry appealed to fellow poets, critics, and the public at large alike. He managed to avoid censorial confrontations with both prerevolutionary and postrevolutionary regimes to emerge as the most esteemed writer of the Silver Age, at once a preserver of tradition and a precursor of modern poetry. His work is widely translated and discussed abroad, and he remains a respected literary figure in Russia.

BIOGRAPHY

The artistically, academically, and socially illustrious family into which Aleksandr Aleksandrovich Blok was born on November 28, 1880, contributed significantly to his poetic development and success. His maternal grandfather was Andrey Beketov, the prominent botanist and rector of St. Petersburg University, and his grandmother was an editor and translator—from English, French, and German—of artistic and scientific works. Blok's mother, one of the prime influences on his life, wrote poetry herself and established a reputation as a translator of French literature. Several other female members of the family were also engaged in literary activity, especially the interpretation of French writers to the Russian public, thus exposing Blok early to the ideas of European literature. The Blok side of the family consisted of outstanding professional people, though tainted with a strain of insanity that affected Blok's father, a law professor at Warsaw University. Blok believed that his father's mental instability contributed to his own frequent despondency. Blok's parents, highly individualistic and incompatible in personality, did not remain together for long. The poet was born in his mother's ancestral home and reared by a household of solicitous women, who nourished both his physical and artistic development until age eleven, when he was finally enrolled in a boys' school. By that time, he had already written poems, coedited an informal family journal, and taken part in domestic theatricals. Blok's lifelong attachment to the feminine principle in his poetry and his first book of verse specifically devoted to that concept may well reflect the influence of the women in the Beketov household.

In 1898, Blok entered the law school of St. Petersburg, but changed three years later to the philology department, from which he graduated in 1906. In 1903, he published his first verses and married the daughter of the scientist Dmitry Mendelyev, a family friend. He had also become interested in mystic philosophy, contributing essays to the Religious-Philosophical Society, of which he was a member. By the time his first verses were printed, he had amassed more than six hundred poems, most of which found ready acceptance after his debut. From this point on, a steady stream of poems, dramas, and essays issued from Blok's pen with seeming effortlessness. In 1904, the collection *Stikhi o prekrasnoy dame* (verses about the Beautiful Lady) appeared, to be followed in 1907 by his second book, *Nechayannaya radost* (unexpected joy), and several plays. Under the influence of his mystical beliefs, Blok had transferred the cult of a divine feminine vision to his wife, Lyubov, an aspiring actress, to whom many of the Beautiful Lady poems were dedicated. Blok's close friend and fellow mystic, the poet Andrey Bely, carried this adoration to extremes, causing family disharmony. Blok's wife rejected all mysticism, lived a life of her own, and bore a short-lived son conceived in an extramarital liaison. Nevertheless, the couple remained together as trusted friends. Blok to the end admired, needed, and relied on Lyubov's strong, earthy personality, as he had earlier relied on his mother and grandmother.

The shattered idealism of Blok's marriage and the miscarried 1905 uprising drew the poet away from the otherworldly themes of his early work. As he developed a more skeptical, practical outlook, he immersed himself in the street life of St. Petersburg, giving himself up to several passions. His infatuation with Natalia Volokhova, an actress in his play *The Puppet Show*, inspired the verse cycles *Snezhnaya maska* (the snow mask) and "Faina," which are among his finest works. A happier love affair with the opera singer Lyubov Delmas in 1914 engendered the cycle "Karmen."

Blok made five journeys abroad. As a young man, he accompanied his mother twice to Germany. Later, in 1909, he traveled with his wife to Italy and transformed his impressions of that country into the group of "Italyanskie stikhi." In 1911, the Bloks toured Europe, which provided inspiration for the verse tale *Solovinyy sad* and the play *The Rose and the Cross*, reflecting experiences on the Basque coast and in Brittany respectively. A nagging feeling of guilt about having neglected his father is reflected in the unfinished epic "Vozmezdie" (retribution).

Blok's political involvements were minor, though controversial. His ideas on the state of the country were published in *Rossia i intelligentsia* (1918), a series of essays spanning a decade. Blok accuses his own upper class of having created a cultural schism by looking to Europe while slighting its own people and heritage. This negative attitude toward the existing ruling circles encouraged him not to condemn the revolution, though he did not welcome it enthusiastically. A stint at the front contributed to his unhappiness, as he saw the philosophical unity sought in his work disappear in the ravages of war and revolution. He served briefly on a provisional government commission investigating suspect czarist officials, then composed his best-known and most controversial poem, *The Twelve*, which depicts a murderous Red Army detachment as disciples to an ineffectual, effeminate Christ. The equally provocative *The Scythians* followed a few days later. Between 1918 and his death on August 7, 1921, Blok wrote little, though he continued work on "Vozmezdie." The Bolshevik government, grateful for his conciliatory stance, printed and reissued many of his works and appointed him to several literature boards and artistic commissions. Through these activities, his material circumstances became less desperate than those of his fellow citizens, but his health declined quickly just the same. Depression and doubts about the future of his country hastened his end. Russia's artistic, literary, and governing elite and more than a thousand people followed his coffin in recognition of his cultural contributions.

ANALYSIS

Aleksandr Blok sought to give a metaphysical dimension to his poetry by creating a persona that pays homage to a supernatural ideal, in his own words "an essence possessed of an independent existence." This ideal is usually represented by the concept of the Eternal Feminine, which takes on a range of embodiments in the various stages of Blok's development. Initially, he depicted an ephemeral, distant spirit, the Beautiful Lady, whose presence the poet perceives in almost every poem, but who is never made manifest. As Blok matured, his mental discipline, inquiring mind, and sensuous disposition prompted him to alter the image, until it became more of a literary device and less of a religious inspiration. While the vision retained some of its ethereal, purifying characteristics in later works, it also assumed demoniac, physically alluring aspects. In many other poems, desperate city women, whose misfortunes Blok ascertained from newspapers, represent the feminine ideal, as do the poet's female friends and relatives. The persona's attitude to the changing image is ambiguous. He is inexplicably and fatally drawn to some embodiments, observing others wistfully and indifferently. Eventually, social pressures, war, and revolution drew Blok further from the transcendental sphere, causing him to blend his vision with the concept of Mother Russia. Blok then saw the Beautiful Lady in the lined faces of praying peasant women and urban prostitutes, and even in the Russian landscape. A final attempt to revive the religious dimension of the image occurs in the revolutionary poem *The Twelve*, in which an effeminate,

Christ-like ghost silently and gently accompanies marauding Bolshevik revolutionaries.

Blok was the forerunner of modern Russian poetry. He replaced the realistic, low-quality verse of the second half of the nineteenth century with a new lyricism, to which he gave a mystical dimension. Technically, he freed Russian verse from rigid meter and led the way to modern tonic patterns. The social upheavals of his era are reflected in his work but are always subordinate to artistic requirements. Blok appealed to all segments of the public and continues to be popular at home and abroad.

"Gorod" and "Arfy i skripki"

Although the Eternal Feminine is a constant in Blok's work, it does not exhaust his poetic themes. After witnessing the bloodbath of the unsuccessful 1905 uprising in St. Petersburg, he devoted an entire cycle, "Gorod," to his hometown. Only a few of these poems express political observations; most of them deal with the darker aspects of street life. Feelings of impending catastrophe, both personal and societal, pervade the poetic atmosphere. The later cycle "Strashny mir" (a terrible world) extends this theme of urban degradation and misery. In one of the sections of the cycle, "Plyaski smerti" (dances of death), which echoes Charles Baudelaire's "Danse Macabre," Blok evokes the disintegration of his society, which the persona views in the shape of a corpse, no longer believing in transcendence, while soulless St. Petersburg citizens dance their own deaths through empty lives. In the seventy-two-poem cycle "Arfy i skripki" (harps and violins), Blok endeavors to link poetry to music, and several of his verses were later set to music. He manages to reproduce the rhythm of ballads, romances, and factory and folk songs in these and many other poems. Finally, the unfinished epic "Vozmezdie" is a lyrical chronicle of his family's and nation's destiny. Blok's general poetic mood ranges from mystical belief and idealistic expectation to false rapture, skeptical, even cynical visions of life, and eventually sadness, despair, and critical aloofness.

Poetic style

Stylistically, Blok stands between the traditional syllabic meter and modern tonic patterns. In his earlier work, metric regularity and exact rhyme dominate, to be followed by syllabotonic verse and experiments with *vers libre*. His rhymes become approximate, until he evolves a very modern, conversational style. Typically, his line has three stresses, interrupted by one or two unstressed syllables, but his rather extensive output shows great stress and syllable diversity within the line. He favors lexical repetition and occasionally repeats the first stanza as the last, with slight lexical change, to achieve a musical effect. Not the least of his skills is to transform vague, mystical notions into concise, elegant verse. Blok's poetry is more accessible than the linguistic experiments of the Futurists and other innovators, and theme or thought are not as completely subordinated to technique. This accessibility, achieved with no loss of artistic quality, and the generally held belief that he re-created the great poetic traditions of the nineteenth century, give him a fame and exposure not matched by other modern Russian poets.

CELEBRATION OF THE ETERNAL FEMININE

Blok's celebration of a feminine ideal is a twentieth century version of earlier cults, encompassing the Gnostic image of Holy Sophia, the adoration of the Virgin Mary in its various guises, Dante's devotion to Beatrice, and Johann Wolfgang von Goethe's evocation of the Eternal Feminine in *Faust: Eine Tragödie* (pb. 1808, 1833; *The Tragedy of Faust*, 1823, 1838). Blok was not directly influenced by Western manifestations of the concept, though he employed all of them. His interest in the symbol came from the writings of the mystic philosopher Vladimir Solovyov, who incorporated Holy Sophia into his ideological system. Blok called his ideal more generally the Beautiful Lady, devoting not only his first collection, *Stikhi o prekrasnoy dame*, to her, but also extending the vision in diverse guises in all major subsequent work. His choice of an ancient symbol was influenced by the belief that familiar, even proverbial, concepts call forth deeper emotions than newly created metaphors. The more than three hundred poems of his first collection portray the Beautiful Lady as a godlike essence which can never assume concrete, earthly shape, but is accessible in spirit to the perceptive poetic persona. The image thus appears in fleeting poses, in the flickering of a candle, the rustle of a curtain, a breeze, or simply as a felt presence. Particularly prominent is Blok's evocation of a distant shadow: "I waited for You. But Your shadow hovered/ In the distance, in the fields . . ." or "You are leaving into crimson sunset/ Into endless circles."

In this semblance, the Beautiful Lady is sometimes an elemental, an almost pagan spirit, enveloped in mists and twilight, floating by in a snowflake or glistening in a star. She appears as a figure in a song and is herself a song, perceived in snatches of distant melodies. In line with traditional symbolism, she is frequently represented by a radiant light: "I wait. Unexpectedly a door will open,/ And vanishing light will fall on me." The association with light extends naturally to religious settings, in which the Beautiful Lady is an incarnation of the Virgin. She is anticipated by the persona at the temple entrance: "The church steps are illuminated/ Their stones alive—and waiting for Your steps," and immediately perceived within: "Holy Lady, how caressing the candles,/ How comforting Your features." The poems tend to follow a rigid scheme: a physical setting empty of other people, the persona's anticipation, his ritualistic incantations, and the resultant perception of the vision.

Blok often used dark/light contrasts to separate image from persona and the rest of the world. In a well-known poem of this type, "I Go into Darkened Temples," the worshiper waits in the dim edifice, contemplating the flickering candle before the icon of the Virgin. The intense longing produces a state of excitement, in which real or imaginary creaks, rustles, and movements translate into a perception of her presence. The icon seems to come alive as the worshiper falls into a trance, engulfed by dreams and fairy-tale images. The final impression is an instant of joy and relief. These verses are not so much a lyrical diary, though Blok designated them as such, as they are a glimpse of his spiritual search. The intensity of his emotions carries a hint of immaturity, even sentimentality, which is redeemed, however, by the careful transmutation of the ecstasy into a restrained poetic idiom, and by the gossamer quality of the dreamlike reflections.

Several factors led the poet to change the image and thus extend the range of his spiritual odyssey. The idea of constant longing and expectation, interrupted only by vague, insubstantial moments of revelation, failed to satisfy the poet on a permanent basis. Doubt in the validity of his adoration, even in the existence of the Beautiful Lady and impatience with her remoteness already appear in the first collection. Blok sees himself as her "Obscure slave, filled with inspiration/ Praising You. But You don't know him." He also reproaches her: "You are different, mute, faceless,/ Hidden away. You bewitch in silence." In the end, he challenges the symbol more directly: "You are holy, but I don't believe You." In one of Blok's most quoted poems, "I Have a Premonition of You," he fearfully anticipates other embodiments: "The entire heaven is on fire, and Your appearance near,/ But I am terrified that You will change your visage." The changes were inevitable in the light of the poet's determination to transfer some of the mystique to his fiancé Lyubov, who became his wife in 1904. This attempt at earthly incarnation miscarried, for while he implored Lyubov to serve as his inspiration, addressing her with the same capitalized "You" often lavished on the Beautiful Lady, she refused all mysticism and insisted on an ordinary flesh-and-blood relationship.

NECHAYANNAYA RADOST

Blok's second book, *Nechayannaya radost*, features an altered image of the Beautiful Lady. The thirteen-poem lead cycle "Puzyry zemli" identifies the symbol with the Macbethian witches, described by William Shakespeare: "The earth has bubbles, as the water hath/ And these are of them." Religious adoration is here replaced by riotous cavorting amid the demons of the St. Petersburg marshes. The second cycle of the book, "Nochnaya fialka," a fantastic tale composed in 1905-1906, expands this underground involvement. A new version of the Eternal Feminine appears in the form of a graceful but lethally poisonous flower princess. The dreamer-poet leaves his city and friends to venture far into a swampy netherworld, where he encounters a faceless, ageless vegetable female. This sweet-smelling woman flower eternally spins, casting her devastating marsh breath over others, while she herself blooms in the poisonous atmosphere. The sleepy hero perceives distant echoes of a happier land, now forever lost to him. The style of "Nochnaya fialka" demonstrates Blok's increasing technical mastery. Though he preserves traditional regular rhythm, he uses free verse and uneven rhyme and syllable schemes . This poem is considered one of Blok's best.

In Blok's subsequent collections, the Eternal Feminine assumes whatever aspect suits the poetic theme. When casting his unrequited love for Natalia Volokhova into verse in the cycle *Snezhnaya maska*, the vision becomes a glacial force, indifferently condemning the persona to a frozen wasteland. In "Faina," she is a cruelly teasing gypsy. Blok's most famous poems feature other embodiments of the ideal. In "The Stranger," she is a prostitute, uncannily reflecting the purity and mystery of the Beautiful Lady, and in "A Girl Sang in a Church Choir," she is a young singer transformed into a ray of light, promising salvation, while the piercing cries of a child reveal her deception. When the poet does make contact with his vision, the encounter is usually unsatisfactory or violent, as in "Humiliation," where the persona wrestles with a prostitute and shouts in despair: "I am neither your husband, nor bridegroom, nor friend!/ So go ahead, my erstwhile angel and plunge/ Your sharp French heel into my heart."

THE TWELVE

Blok's most controversial manifestation of a divine vision occurs in the final stanza of his revolutionary poem *The Twelve*. Technically, *The Twelve* is a masterpiece. It pits the icy, howling snowstorm of the revolution against the vulnerable population, seen as unsure of its footing and slipping on the ice. All segments of society confront and attempt to hurdle the Bolshevik snowdrift. A fur-clad upper-class lady fails and lies prostrate; a fat-bellied priest attempts to squeeze by furtively; a bourgeois stands undecided at the crossroad; an intellectual shouts his dissent; and a peasant woman, not understanding the political event, succeeds in clambering across the snowdrift. Prostitutes using incongruous political jargon establish union fees for their services. These scenes are background for the main drama dealing with twelve Red Army men who think they safeguard the revolution, but really loot and kill. One of them murders his lover in a jealous rage, only to be overcome by religious scruples and feelings of guilt. At poem's end, the revolutionaries continue on their violent path, boldly asserting their freedom from religion, but—unknown to them—they are led by the shadowy, gentle, garlanded figure of an effeminate Christ, whose unexpected appearance transmutes the marauders into the twelve disciples. Blok was vilified by both the Left and the Right for this inexplicable ending, but insisted that his poetic instinct dictated it. The controversy over this image for a long time obscured appreciation of the poem's exquisite artistic craftsmanship. Blok wrote very little after *The Twelve*.

OTHER MAJOR WORKS

PLAYS: *Balaganchik*, pr., pb. 1906 (*The Puppet Show*, 1963); *Korol' na ploshchadi*, pb. 1907 (wr. 1906; *The King in the Square*, 1934); *Neznakomka*, pb. 1907 (*The Unknown Woman*, 1927); *Pesnya sudby*, pb. 1909, 1919 (*The Song of Fate*, 1938); *Roza i krest*, pb. 1913 (*The Rose and the Cross*, 1936); *Ramzes*, pb. 1921; *Aleksandr Blok's Trilogy of Lyric Dramas*, 2003 (Timothy C. Westphan, translator and editor).

NONFICTION: *Rossia i intelligentsia*, 1918; *Katilina*, 1919; *O simvolizme*, 1921 (*On Symbolism*, 1975); *Pis'ma Aleksandra Bloka*, 1925; *Pis'ma Aleksandra Bloka k rod-*

nym, 1927; *Dnevnik Al. Bloka, 1911-1913,* 1928; *Dnevnik Al. Bloka, 1917-1921,* 1928; *Zapisnye knizhki Al. Bloka,* 1930; *Pis'ma Al. Bloka k E. P. Ivanovu,* 1936; *Aleksandr Blok i Andrey Bely: Perepiska,* 1940.

Bibliography

Berberova, Nina. *Aleksandr Blok: A Life.* Translated by Robyn Marsack. New York: George Braziller, 1996. A biography originally published in 1996 by Carcanet Press Limited, Britain, and by Alyscamps Press, France.

Briggs, A. D. P. *A Comparative Study of Pushkin's "The Bronze Horseman," Nekrasov's "Red-Nosed Frost," and Blok's "The Twelve": The Wild World.* Lewiston N.Y.: Edwin Mellen Press, 1990. Blok's "The Twelve" is compared to works by Nikolai Nekrasov and Alexander Pushkin.

Chukovsky, Kornei. *Alexander Blok as Man and Poet.* Translated and edited by Diana Burgin and Katherine O'Connor. Ann Arbor, Mich.: Ardis, 1982. A very good Soviet monograph, equally divided between biography and critical analysis of Blok's work. Best known as a scholar of children's literature, Chukovsky was a friend of Blok, and his account is enriched by personal reminiscence.

Hellman, Ben. *Poets of Hope and Despair: The Russian Symbolists in War and Revolution, 1914-1918.* Helsinki: Institute for Russian and East European Studies, 1995. Surveys and compares the work of half a dozen Russian Symbolists of the World War I period, including Blok. Includes bibliographical references.

Pyman, Avril. *The Life of Aleksandr Blok.* 2 vols. New York: Oxford University Press, 1979-1980. One of the most exhaustive treatments of Blok as a man and a writer by a leading scholar of Russian literature. The emphasis is on biography, but there are also discussions of Blok's poems. Excellent illustrations.

Rylkova, Galina. *The Archaeology of Anxiety: The Russian Silver Age and its Legacy.* Pittsburgh, Pa.: University of Pittsburgh Press, 2007. This discussion of the Silver Age (c. 1890-1917) in Russia contains a chapter on Blok and his work.

Sloane, David A. *Aleksandr Blok and the Dynamics of the Lyric Cycles.* Columbus, Ohio: Slavica, 1987. A penetrating study of Blok's lyrics, especially of his tendency to write in cycles throughout his career.

Soboleva, Olga Yu. *The Silver Mask: Harlequinade in the Symbolist Poetry of Blok and Belyi.* Oxford, England: Peter Lang, 2007. The author compares and contrasts how Blok and Andrey Bely use the harlequin in their Symbolist poetry.

Vickery, Walter, ed. *Aleksandr Blok Centennial Conference.* Columbus, Ohio: Slavica, 1984. A collection of twenty-one essays on various aspects of Blok's life and work, prepared for a seminar in Chapel Hill, North Carolina, in 1981, the centennial of Blok's birth. The topics tend to concentrate on the stylistic elements of his poetry and other aspects of Blok's portrait.

Vogel, Lucy, ed. *Blok: An Anthology of Essays and Memoirs.* Ann Arbor, Mich.: Ardis,

1982. A collection of informative memoirs by people who knew Blok, including Lyubov Mendeleeva (his wife), Maxim Gorky, Osip Mandelstam, and Boris Pasternak. Includes a twenty-six-page bibliography.

Margot K. Frank

JOSEPH BRODSKY

Born: Leningrad, Soviet Union (now St. Petersburg, Russia); May 24, 1940
Died: Brooklyn, New York; January 28, 1996

PRINCIPAL POETRY

Stikhotvoreniya i poemy, 1965
Elegy to John Donne, and Other Poems, 1967
Ostanovka v pustyne: Stikhotvoreniya i poemy, 1970
Debut, 1973
Selected Poems, 1973
Chast' rechi: Stikhotvoreniya, 1972-1976, 1977
Konets prekrasnoi epokhi: Stikhotvoreniya, 1964-1971, 1977
V Anglii, 1977
A Part of Speech, 1980
Verses on the Winter Campaign 1980, 1980
Rimskie elegii, 1982
Novye stansy k Avguste: Stichi k M.B., 1962-1982, 1983
Uraniia: Novaya kniga stikhov, 1987
To Urania: Selected Poems, 1965-1985, 1988
Chast' rechi: Izbrannye stikhi, 1962-1989, 1990
Bog sokhraniaet vse, 1991
Forma vremeni, 1992 (2 volumes; volume 2 includes essays and plays)
Rozhdestvenskie stikhi, 1992 (*Nativity Poems*, 2001)
Izbrannye stikhotvoreniya, 1957-1992, 1994
So Forth, 1996
Collected Poems in English, 2000
Nativity Poems, 2001

OTHER LITERARY FORMS

The essays and reviews of Joseph Brodsky (BROD-skee), some of which have been collected in *Less than One: Selected Essays* (1986), are valuable in their own right; brilliant, arrogant, and idiosyncratic, they establish Brodsky as one of the finest poet-essayists of the twentieth century. Among Brodsky's subjects are Osip and Nadezhda Mandelstam, Marina Tsvetayeva (unlike most of his prose, his two essays on Tsvetayeva, one brief and one extended, were written in Russian, the language Brodsky normally reserves for his poetry), W. H. Auden, Constantine P. Cavafy, and Eugenio Montale. The essay "Less than One" is an extraordinary meditation on the city of Leningrad, part memoir and part cultural history.

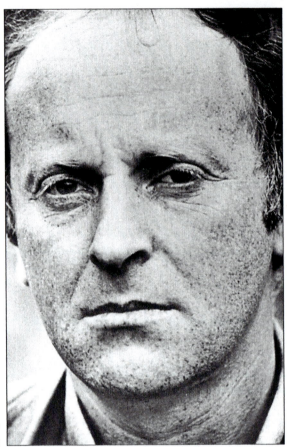

Joseph Brodsky
(Library of Congress)

ACHIEVEMENTS

Joseph Brodsky is generally recognized as one of the most gifted poets writing in Russian in the twentieth century; for many, there is little question of his having any rivals. Perhaps Brodsky's most remarkable achievement was his ability to continue writing poems in Russian despite the hardships of political persecution within the Soviet Union and, later, the alienation from the everyday rhythms of the Russian language imposed by his exile to the United States. Brodsky matured as a poet in a Leningrad devoid of poetic movements; indeed, the sense of being alone as a poet pervades his work to an unusual degree. It is difficult to assess Brodsky's generation of poets. The work of contemporaries whom he has praised, poets such as Evgeni Rein and Anatol' Naiman, is available only sporadically in the West, and then in the limited distribution of the émigré presses.

Brodsky's poems have been translated into many languages, including French, German, Italian, Swedish, Czech, and Hebrew, but it is the English translations that won him high regard and a rather wide audience in the West. Brodsky's participation in the translation process, given his own fine skills as a translator, ensured high-quality versions that sound like anything but adaptations from another language. Brodsky was accorded many honors, including Guggenheim and MacArthur Fellowships, an honorary doctorate from Yale University, membership in the American Academy of Arts and Letters, and the Nobel Prize in Literature in 1987. He served as the United States poet laureate consultant in poetry in 1991-1992.

BIOGRAPHY

Joseph Aleksandrovich Brodsky was born in Leningrad on May 24, 1940. Brodsky's mother worked as a translator, an occupation her son was to take up as well; his father worked as a news photographer. During the German blockade of the city, Brodsky spent some time with his grandparents. He has recalled a somewhat later time of fear during the government-orchestrated anti-Semitic hysteria of 1953, when it seemed that his family might be "resettled" far from Leningrad. During these last years of Stalinism, Brodsky was an unenthusiastic student; he left school in 1955 to pursue independent studies in various languages and literatures. In 1956, he began learning Polish, a language that gave him access to Western literature not available in Russian; he recalled that he first read the works of Franz Kafka and William Faulkner in Polish translation, and he encountered the poetry of Czesław Miłosz, whom he called "one of the greatest poets of our time, perhaps the greatest."

The year 1956, when Brodsky was only sixteen, was crucial in establishing his sense of himself and of Russia. When Brodsky referred to himself as a member of the "generation of 1956," he had in mind the shock of recognition forced by the invasion of Hungary, a recognition of his status as a poet in a totalitarian state. If Brodsky saw Stalinism less as a political era than as a "state of mind," then the events of 1956, three years after the death of Stalin, proved the ugly endurance of a repressive regime that soon began to harass Brodsky personally.

Brodsky made several trips away from Leningrad on geological expeditions, traveling throughout the Soviet Union to the Amur River near China, Central Asia, the Caspian Sea region in the south, and the White Sea area in the north, where he was to spend nearly two years in exile a few years later. These travels exposed Brodsky to a variety of landscapes and may in part account for the powerful, if unattractive, natural descriptions in his mature verse. His travels permitted him a great deal of freedom, but his vaguely unorthodox movements and affiliations eventually drew the attention of KGB officials. Brodsky was first arrested in 1959 and twice confined to mental hospitals. These visits provided the setting for his most ambitious long poem, a dialogue between "Gorbunov i Gorchakov" ("Gorbunov and Gorchakov"). Brodsky had begun writing poems as early as 1958, though he later dated his first serious work from about 1963 (the year of his elegy to John Donne).

Arrested again and tried in 1964, Brodsky was sentenced in March to five years exile and hard labor; the charge was "parasitism." In effect, Brodsky was put on trial for identifying himself as a poet without "proof" in the form of a university degree or membership in the Writers' Union. The notes from his trial, smuggled out of Leningrad and excerpted often in articles about Brodsky, make for perverse evidence for his belief that the spiritual activity of writing poetry cannot be tolerated by a state that defines writing as a political act. Many Soviet cultural figures of international renown, including Dmitri Shostakovich and Kornei Chukovskii, testified on Brodsky's behalf and agitated for his early release, often at great professional and personal risk. As a result, Brodsky served only twenty months of his term, doing agricultural work in a small "village"—actually just a few huts in the wilderness—near Arkhangel'sk. He continued reading and writing; his first acquaintance with the works of Auden came in 1965, in translation. (He had known Robert Frost's poems as early as 1962 and was astonished by Frost's "hidden, controlled terror.")

Auden's influence is apparent in Brodsky's poem written on the occasion of T. S. Eliot's death in 1965; the lament looks ahead to the mature verse that Brodsky was writing on his return to Leningrad that year. It was at this time that his friends succeeded in shortening the length of his prison term. Anna Akhmatova, whom Brodsky had first met in 1960, was chief among this group of friends. Though he did not recall initially feeling an affinity with Akhmatova, Brodsky and she became close friends. His work owes more to the style and preoccupations of Mandelstam than to Akhmatova, but Brodsky found in Akhmatova a living link to Russia's great poetic tradition, a poet who had known Mandelstam well, a poet who incarnated Russia's great upheavals in her life and in her verse.

Brodsky matured a great deal as a poet between 1965 and 1972. He gave readings to small groups of students and even managed to have four of his poems published in 1966 and 1967 in official publications of Soviet cultural organs. A first volume of his poems had appeared without his authorization in the United States in 1965; a revised version, which included new poems, came out in 1970. Brodsky supported himself in Leningrad as a translator during these years, producing Russian versions of writers ranging from Andrew Marvell and Donne to Tom Stoppard. Brodsky did nothing, however, to become more acceptable to the Soviet regime during these seven years in Leningrad. In 1972, he was exiled from the Soviet Union; he was not even told where the airplane he was boarding would take him—to Siberian exile, or to freedom in the West. The plane landed in Vienna, where Brodsky was met by an American Slavicist, Carl Proffer, with an invitation to teach in Ann Arbor, Michigan. In Vienna, Brodsky sought out Auden, who arranged for him to participate in the Poetry International in London and generally smoothed his way for his introduction to the West.

Settling in the United States, Brodsky slowly began a life of teaching, writing, giving readings, and meeting fellow poets. He taught at the University of Michigan, Queens

College, the Five Colleges (Amherst, Hampshire, Mount Holyoke, Smith, and the University of Massachusetts), New York University, and Columbia University. In 1981, he became the Five College Distinguished Professor of Literature, with tenure at Mount Holyoke College; he also spent time teaching at Columbia. Brodsky became a U.S. citizen in 1977. He won the Nobel Prize in Literature in 1987. He died in Brooklyn, New York, on January 28, 1996.

ANALYSIS

In describing his poetry, Joseph Brodsky had said that his "main interest is the nature of time," a theme that also recurs with obsessive frequency in his essays. Beginning even before his exile to Arkhangel'sk in 1964 and persisting in his later works, there is a preoccupation with endings, with concluding moments that illuminate with sudden new depth the meaning of all that has come before. Brodsky, whose stance as a poet is that of a watcher and listener rather than that of a participant and speaker, records his sense of a period of time in a manner that is more transcendental than teleological. In a 1962 poem, "Ogon', ty slyshish' . . ." ("The Fire Is Dying Down"), Brodsky observes how the room and objects around him absorb the shifts in time marked by the changing fire. A sense of lateness advances on the poet "from the corners"; he finds himself "suddenly at the center." Time has paused so palpably that the "clock hands have completely disappeared." The fire dies by the end of this twenty-line poem, but its brightness does not abandon the attentive watcher, who remains behind in the room's darkness. Just as it is important that the clock hands are not only invisible but also silent, silence being the analogue of time's halt, so it is crucial in the last line that the fire glows not in the poet's eyes but in the room itself. The encroaching darkness of the dying fire becomes an external event that marks the inner fact of the poet's eyes growing cold, "motionless."

"SONNET"

In another short lyric of 1962, a poem of fourteen lines with only a few near-rhymes and simply titled "Sonet" ("Sonnet"), Brodsky explores a moment defined by a different kind of ending. Speaking to a loved woman, the poet envisions a new eruption of Vesuvius that will someday cover their dusty city with ash. He hopes that when the eruption begins, he will be able to set off for her house, so that future excavators will find them still embraced. The poem stops time in that final embrace, preserved by a layer of ash. The embrace and the ash are equally sustaining for the poet, who notes the passing clouds, a frequent emblem for the passing of time in Brodsky's poems. It is typical of Brodsky's poems that the very moment that destroys a city and all life in it also contains the possibility of preservation against decay.

The poem mirrors this contrast between the threat of change and the saving power of volcanic ash in its formal arrangement. As in many early Brodsky poems, the unit of division in the poem is the line. Without enjambments and virtually without rhyme (there is some sound interlocking in the first four lines), the poem's ordering principle is the sequence of its thoughts, expressed at the even pace of one clause per line. The exception is line 12, "then I would like for them to find me," a single thought in two clauses (in Russian), the crucial turning point of the poem. The meter of the poem is iambic, mostly feminine pentameter, five-footed iambs being the commonest line length in Brodsky's repertoire in the 1960's, and the most successful. The sonnet feels experimental, though, because there are two lines of two and four metric feet, respectively, and virtually no rhyme, as if it were testing the boundaries of its own timing. Like Brodsky's many unrhymed sonnets, the poem shows how time can be controlled, slowed or hurried, within the conventions of meter and rhyme; the final picture of an unending embrace literally suspends time, so that the poem challenges, visually as well as verbally, the unspoken condition of all Brodsky's work, the effect of time on humans.

The tender lyrics of early, as well as later, Brodsky, are balanced by verses of ironic distance and glittering wit. In some poems, such as the famous "Pamiatnik" ("Monument"), the serious if slightly mocking tones of the first lines ("Let's build a monument/ at the end of a long city street") turns toward a sarcastic finale—in this case prepared for by the poem's accumulation of petty details from Leningrad life: "Let's build a monument to lies." That final sentence indicts monument building as yet another hypocritical activity in a society whose public life proves inevitably false. In a longer poem, "Dva chasa v rezervuare" ("Two Hours in a Reservoir"), Brodsky mixes German and Yiddish phrases into a running monologue. The speaker pronounces his thoughts as they furiously charge past him in whatever language comes to his lips: "Enter and *exeunt* devils, thoughts./ Enter and *exeunt* guests, years." Narrative fragments about Faust and Johann Wolfgang von Goethe, Dr. Faustus and Thomas Mann, interrupt speculations about God and poetry and the fact that humans are hurtling toward their deaths. The poem extends Brodsky's preoccupation with time, quoting Faust's famous desire to seize and hold one beautiful moment, a line Brodsky might be expected to appreciate—indeed, one he uses more than once. The poem's pace, though, is breakneck, the puns (particularly between languages) rampant, and the humor of the piece as pungent as it is inventive. Brodsky's search for ways to understand the passing of time, often defined by its endpoints, emerges in poems as varied as the witty "Odnoi poetesse" ("To a Certain Poetess"), where a relationship has outlived love, or the delicate "Aeneas i Dido" ("Aeneas and Dido"), in which the moment of parting is captured poignantly by details—passing clouds, the hem of a tunic, a fish chasing after a ship at sail.

"AENEAS AND DIDO"

"Aeneas and Dido" deals with the end of a myth, and the poem concludes with a memorable picture. Dido watches Aeneas looking through a window, both of them realizing that the new gusts of wind will make it possible for Aeneas to set sail and leave Dido behind. Windows appear frequently in Brodsky's poems, often framing a landscape seen from within a room. Indeed, space becomes almost the conceptual framework through which time is explored in Brodsky's poems: His remark that literature shows what time does to a person was made in a talk titled "Language as Otherland," and the titles of his poems often locate lyrics spatially as well as temporally. Examples of this can be found in each stage of his career, including "Zimnim vecherom v Ialte" ("A Winter Evening in Yalta"), "Dekabr' vo Florentsii" ("December in Florence"), and "Osen' v Norenskoi" ("Autumn in Norenskaia").

SETTINGS

Brodsky's settings are occasionally interiors; small rooms become intimate settings for discovering the world outside and, always, oneself. In "Sumev otgorodit'sia . . ." ("Now that I've walled myself off from the world"), glimpses of puddles and fir trees merge with the domestic drama of a poet studying his face in a mirror. Brodsky has moments of self-description, framed by mirrors and windows, reminiscent of the later works of Akhmatova, though Brodsky always seems in search of some truth deeper than the self-image a piece of glass presents him. Self and other, interiors and landscapes interpenetrate one another in Brodsky's poems; as furiously as he seeks boundaries, walling himself off spatially, or describing endpoints in time, spaces and periods of time run into one another, and the confusions press the poet all the more in his attempt at self-definition.

Brodsky's landscapes are inseparable from the homesickness that pervades his verse. There is no place called "home" that is exempt. While he was in internal exile in Arkhangl'sk, Brodsky compared himself to Ovid; in the West, he has described scenes as diverse as Cape Cod and Cuernavaca, hills and lagoons and sluggish rivers, stopovers in St. Mark's Piazza or along Roman roads. Brodsky loves Venice, a city that glows through his poems like Leningrad, but there is not any landscape, any visual image of indoor or outdoor space with which the poet is not somehow at odds.

New places provide fresh scenes for seeing, new ways to show what one must see. If the goal of his poetry is, as Brodsky said in 1972, "to show man the true scale of what is happening," then landscape and cityscape finally offer a figurative vocabulary for philosophical apperceptions. The "scale" for Brodsky is never political but always personal, a fact that made him politically suspect in the Soviet Union.

PHILOSOPHY

Brodsky's philosophical preoccupations (the nature of "reality," and what it means for time to pass) and figures of expression (mythological plots, interior and exterior landscapes) are constants in his poetry, of which he continued to find new variations. There is, however, a more distinct sense of development in the prosodic features of Brodsky's poems, and these changes provide the clearest indications of his battle with Russian poetic tradition. Certain Brodskian themes resemble those of poets whom he is known to admire: the parting and exile of Mandelstam, the meditations on death of Evgeni Baratynskii, the monuments of Alexander Pushkin if not of Gavrila Derzhavin, the epistolary acts of self-definition of Dmitry Kantemir. In the case of Brodsky's verse forms, however, there are only a few poems with rather self-conscious and specific models, the most notable being his poem on the death of Eliot, written in the form and spirit of Auden's "In Memory of W. B. Yeats."

POETIC FORMS

Brodsky's early poems strive to carve their own prosodic molds, using simple, assertive sentences, and a structuring free-verse line the firm closure of which allows few enjambments. The rhymes are experimental, often only hints at sound repetitions. In the early 1960's, Brodsky experimented with the placement of the line in such poems as "Ryby zimoi" ("Fish in Winter") and "Stikhi pod èpigrafom" ("Verses with an Epigraph"). Poems such as these make the most startling break with Russian prosodic tradition, spread over a page in complex patterns of indentation like those of E. E. Cummings (whom Brodsky admired in his youth). More deeply radical, though, and more difficult to sustain, are poems with very long verse lines, such as "Proplyvaiut oblaka" ("Clouds Swim By"). Here Brodsky repeats and interweaves similar phrases to break up long lines, while subtly binding them more tightly one to another. In later poems, Brodsky has used refrains to the same effect: The word "stifling" recurs as a one-word sentence in "Kolybel'naia Treskovogo Mysa" ("Lullaby of Cape Cod"). The long line led Brodsky to explore ternary meters (several poems use anapest pentameter); in some cases, various kinds of ternary meters appear fleetingly with rhymes or near- rhymes structuring the poem. The impression in "Clouds Swim By" is one of fluidity that is being formidably if flexibly shaped, perhaps the most appropriate form for a poem that describes the changing shapes of clouds overhead.

Longer verse lines came into Brodsky's work with complex sentences, as well as enjambments more abrupt than those previously found in Russian poetry. Regular meters are usually used, though they are the less common meters of iambic pentameter (not the common meter in Russian as it is in English; Russian depends far more on iambic tetrameter) and anapest pentameter. There are striking ventures in stanzaic form, the most remarkable in "Gorbunov and Gorchakov." In this long poem, Brodsky limits himself to an *abababab* sequence in each ten-line stanza; the poem contains fourteen sections of ten such stanzas and is actually a conversation, sustaining the rhythms and dictions of colloquial speech within its very demanding form.

With these additional formal complexities, Brodsky entered a grammatical universe adequate to the expression of his metaphysical questions. As has been noted by Richard Sylvester, Brodsky's complex sentences convey an ever-changing nexus of logical relationships, where words such as "because," "despite," "when," "where," and "if" become the all-important links in sentences dependent on several semantic fields. In such later poems as the cycle "Chast' rechi" ("A Part of Speech"), subject matter, diction, even stylistic level may change in such quick succession as to seem arbitrary: One poem in the cycle begins "A list of some observations." However, Brodsky's poetry is anything but inscrutable; his complex forms provide myriad vehicles perfectly suited for exploring themes of fragmentation, decay, solitary observation, and intense recollection.

A PART OF SPEECH

In Brodsky's well-received *A Part of Speech*, images and underlying questions extend the issues raised in his earlier poems. The desire to focus on particular points in time finds him often retreating into memory. This orientation toward the past was felt keenly in poems from the 1960's; one of Brodsky's best-known poems is "Ostanovka v pustyne" ("A Halt in the Wilderness"), where the razing of an Orthodox church is witnessed as a gesture of senseless modernization. Time as a category has tragic dimensions for Brodsky, as he himself has said. Near the end of "A Halt in the Wilderness," he speaks acerbically of "the relay race of human history." That poem looks ahead to ask what sacrifices the new era might demand, but there is no redeeming belief in progress for Brodsky. In his essays, Brodsky dwelt on the evils of the twentieth century; he offers his readers little consolation and certainly no respite from personal responsibility in the dogmas of ideology or religion. In "Lullaby of Cape Cod," Brodsky defines his sense of human knowledge and its limitations in lines that resonate beyond his experience of emigration: "Having sampled two/ oceans as well as continents, I feel that I know/ what the globe itself must feel: there's nowhere to go."

Akhmatova found that in Brodsky's first poems the speaking voice was extremely solitary. The sense of bearing a unique vision is undiminished in Brodsky's later poems, ranging from the varieties of quantification in "Lullaby of Cape Cod" to the equation that acts as a fluctuating refrain in "Èkloga IV-ia (Zimniaia)" ("Winter Eclogue: IV"): "Time equals cold." The more nearly oxymoronic Brodsky's declarations, the more finely he has sharpened his sense of the metaphysical conceit into an instrument for measuring a vision that is always just evading the poet's means of expression.

There is no expectation of finding the "right" metaphor, as frequent images of echoless space imply. "A glance," wrote Brodsky in "A Part of Speech," "is accustomed to no glance back." Brodsky's poems are less a relief from solitude than a journey forth, a journey deeper and farther into the "otherland" of language. To say that the journey is "merely long" is to say nothing, and to say everything. Brodsky writes in "Lullaby of Cape Cod":

> Far longer is the sea.
> At times, like a wrinkled forehead, it displays
> a rolling wave. And longer still than these
> is the strand of matching beads of countless days;
> and nights.

To observe that the break between "days" and "nights" is radical in terms of syntax and prosody is to describe Brodsky's poetics; to add that the break is unbearably long, that it expresses a discontinuity central to his metaphysical premises, is to initiate an examination of Brodsky's underlying themes at the level on which he deserves to be understood.

TO URANIA

Two collections of Brodsky's poetry contain translations of his Russian poems, by him and by others, as well as poems written in English. For this reason, there is a noticeable incongruence of themes and styles. *To Urania* contains poems from his earlier collections *A Part of Speech* and *Uraniia*. They express the poet's nostalgia for his homeland and are elegies for parents and friends, mixed with his musings about historical events and European cities, in which intellectually he felt at home as much as in his homeland. Moreover, fourteen cantos in his peculiar bardic style are actually a dialogue between two patients in a Soviet psychiatric ward. Brodsky indulges in his familiar attempts to fathom the mysteries of memory of the things past and to reconcile the limits of time and space, as he did throughout his poetic career. References to political matters, especially their seamy side, are also vintage Brodsky. Elements of a realistic and a spiritual, almost metaphysical approach to poetry are masterfully proportioned, as in many of his collections. Subdued sorrow of an exile unable or unwilling to forget the old and fully accept the new breaks through the veneer of bombastic intonations. Finally, his difficulties in mastering fully the idiom of a foreign language are manifested in sporadic rough renditions of English idioms.

SO FORTH

So Forth offers poems written during the last decade of Brodsky's life. As in *To Urania*, they are both translations and poems written originally in English. Considered by some critics as a collection of perhaps his best poetry (while others point out his awkwardness in juggling the two languages), *So Forth* displays Brodsky's ability to conform his remarkable erudition and never fully satisfied curiosity to his unique style. Even though, as in *To Urania*, he tries his best to be a poet-citizen of the world, the deep sorrow that he was forced out of his homeland is beautifully expressed in the poem "In Memory of My Father: Australia," in which the poet sees in a dream his father sailing as a ghost to Australia, that is, being free to travel. Not all poems are somber and heavy. Some are surprisingly light, as is the poem "A Song"—dancing, as it were, like a child in play. However, most of Brodsky's later poems are elegiac, somber, ironic, always reminding his readers of sorrow and death.

OTHER MAJOR WORKS

PLAY: *Mramor*, pb. 1984 (*Marbles*, 1985).

NONFICTION: *Less than One: Selected Essays*, 1986; *Vspominaia Akhmatova*, 1992;

Watermark, 1992; *On Grief and Reason: Essays*, 1995; *Homage to Robert Frost*, 1996 (with Seamus Heaney and Derek Walcott).

BIBLIOGRAPHY

Bethea, David M. *Joseph Brodsky and the Creation of Exile*. Princeton, N.J.: Princeton University Press, 1994. A critical analysis that compares and contrasts Brodsky to the poet's favorite models—John Donne, W. H. Auden, Osip Mandelstam, and Marina Tsvetayeva—and analyzes his fundamental differences with Vladimir Nabokov. Various critical paradigms are used throughout the study as foils to Brodsky's thinking. Includes a bibliography and index.

Brodsky, Joseph. Interviews. *Joseph Brodsky: Conversations*. Edited by Cynthia L. Haven. Jackson: University Press of Mississippi, 2002. Contains numerous interviews with Brodsky in which he talks about life in exile and his poetry.

Grudzinska-Gross, Irena. *Czesław Miłosz and Joseph Brodsky: Fellowship of Poets*. New Haven, Conn.: Yale University Press, 2010. Examines the relationship between the two poets and how their work was influenced.

Jason, Philip K., ed. *Masterplots II: Poetry Series*. Rev. ed. Pasadena, Calif.: Salem Press, 2002. Contains analysis of two of Brodsky's poems, "A Part of Speech" and "Elegy for John Donne."

Loseff, Lev, and Valentina Polukhina, eds. *Joseph Brodsky: The Art of a Poem*. New York: St. Martin's Press, 1999. These essays concentrate on individual poems and on purely aesthetic aspects of Brodsky's poetry. The essays, written in both Russian and English, analyze the most significant of Brodsky's poems, using citations in Russian and English.

MacFadyen, David. *Joseph Brodsky and the Baroque*. Montreal: McGill-Queen's University Press, 1998. A thorough analysis of the baroque elements in Brodsky's poetry and of the affinities with, and influence of, philosophers Søren Kirkegaard and Lev Shestov and the poet John Donne. The comparison of Brodsky's poetry before and after exile is especially poignant.

_____. *Joseph Brodsky and the Soviet Muse*. Montreal: McGill-Queen's University Press, 2000. An assessment of Brodsky's significance as a shaper and remaker of Soviet poetry in his early years. The contact with, and influence of, the writings of James Joyce, John Dos Passos, Ernest Hemingway, Robert Frost, Boris Pasternak, and Marina Tsvetayeva are chronicled, with suitable citations, in Russian and English, from Brodsky's poetry. Very useful for the understanding of Brodsky's development as a poet.

Polukhina, Valentina. *Brodsky Through the Eyes of His Contemporaries*. Rev. ed. 2 vols. Boston: Academic Studies Press, 2008. A leading Russian expert examines the poet as his fellow poets saw him.

Rigsbee, David. *Styles of Ruin: Joseph Brodsky and the Postmodernist Elegy*. Westport,

Conn.: Greenwood Press, 1999. Rigsbee examines Brodsky's contribution to post-modernist poetry, particularly through his pronounced trend toward elegy. A poet himself and a translator of Brodsky, the author adds to his analyses a personal touch as well as that of an expert of the craft.

Turoma, Sanna. *Brodsky Abroad: Empire, Tourism, Nostalgia*. Madison: University of Wisconsin Press, 2010. This biography of Brodsky focuses on his life as an exile.

Stephanie Sandler
Updated by Vasa D. Mihailovich

SERGEI ESENIN

Born: Konstantinovo (now Esenino), Ryazan province, Russia; October 3, 1895
Died: Leningrad, Soviet Union (now St. Petersburg, Russia); December 28, 1925

PRINCIPAL POETRY

Radunitsa, 1915 (*All Soul's Day*, 1991)
Goluben', 1918 (*Azure*, 1991; includes "Preobrazhenie," "Transfiguration";
"Prishestvie," "The Coming"; and "Inonia")
Ispoved' khuligana, 1921 (*Confessions of a Hooligan*, 1973)
Pugachov, 1922
Stikhi skandalista, 1923
Moskva kabatskaia, 1924
Anna Snegina, 1925
"Cherni chelovek," 1925
Persidskie motivi, 1925
Rus' sovetskaia, 1925
Strana sovetskaia, 1925
Sobranie sochinenii, 1961-1962 (5 volumes)
Selected Poetry, 1982
Complete Poetical Works in English, 2008

OTHER LITERARY FORMS

Sergei Esenin (yihs-YAYN-yihn) wrote little besides poetry. Some autobiographical introductions and a few revealing letters are helpful in analyzing his poetry. The short story "Bobyl i druzhok" and the tale "Yar" are rarely mentioned in critical discussion of Esenin's work, but his theoretical treatise "Kliuchi Marii" (1918; the keys of Mary) helps to explain his early revolutionary lyrics. This economically written, perceptive study traces the religious origins of various aspects of ancient Russian culture and art.

ACHIEVEMENTS

Perhaps the most controversial of all Soviet poets, Sergei Esenin is certainly also one of the most popular, among both Russian émigrés and citizens. The popularity of his poetry never diminished in Russia, despite a period of twenty-five years during which his work was suppressed and his character defamed. Officially, Esenin was labeled the Father of Hooliganism, and his works were removed from public libraries and reading rooms. In the early 1950's, however, his reputation was fully rehabilitated, and his poems have become widely available in Russia. In the twenty-first century, Esenin rivals

Aleksandr Blok, Vladimir Mayakovsky, and even Alexander Pushkin as the most popular of all Russian poets.

Although Esenin welcomed and supported the 1917 October Revolution, he soon began to have second thoughts. He did not like the transformation that was taking place in the rural areas, and he longed for the traditional simple peasant life and the old "wooden Russia." His flamboyant lifestyle, his alcoholism, and his dramatic suicide eventually brought him the scorn of the Soviet authorities.

The most important representative of the Imaginist movement in Russian poetry, Esenin at his best achieved a distinctive blend of deep lyricism, sincerity, melancholy, and nostalgia. Calling himself "the last poet of the village," Esenin used folk and religious motifs, images of nature, and colorful scenes from everyday village life, which he painted with a natural freshness and beauty. His disappointment with his own life, his unhappy marriages, and his apprehensions concerning the changes he saw at every hand—all are reflected in the mood of unfulfilled hope and sadness that pervades his poetry.

BIOGRAPHY

Sergei Aleksandrovich Esenin was born in the small village of Konstantinovo, since renamed Esenino in the poet's honor, in the fertile Ryazan province. His parents were poor farmers, and because his mother had married against the will of her parents, the Titovs, the couple received no support from their families. Esenin's father had to go to Moscow, where he worked in a butcher shop, in order to send home some money. When he stopped sending the money, his wife had no other choice but to find work as a live-in servant. Her parents at last decided to help and took the young boy to live with them.

Esenin's grandfather, Feodor Andreevich Titov, belonged to a religious sect known as the Old Believers; he frequently recited religious poems and folk songs, and he approached life with an optimistic vigor. Esenin's grandmother sang folk songs and told her grandson many folktales. Both grandparents adored the young Esenin, who lived a happy and relatively carefree life. They made a great impression on the young boy.

From 1904 to 1909, Esenin attended the village school, where, with little effort, he graduated with excellent marks. His grandfather Titov decided that Esenin should become a teacher and sent him to the church-run Spas-Klepiki pedagogical school from 1909 to 1912. At first, Esenin was extremely unhappy in the new surroundings; he even ran away once and walked forty miles back to his grandparents' home. Eventually, however, he became reconciled to his fate, and he was noticed by his teachers and peers for the unusual ease with which he wrote poetry. The boy with the blond, curly hair became self-confident and even boastful, which made him unpopular with some of his fellow students.

At the age of sixteen, after his graduation in 1912, Esenin decided not to continue his studies at a teacher's institute in Moscow. Instead, he returned to his grandparents' home and devoted his life to poetry. He was happy to be free to roam aimlessly through the fields and the forests, and his early poems reflect his love for animals and for the rural landscape. Although he also used religious themes in his early poems, Esenin was probably not very religious, certainly not as devoted as his grandfather. He was, however, very familiar with the religious traditions of the Old Believers and with the patriarchal way of life.

Esenin realized that to become known as a poet, he had to move to a big city. In 1912, he moved to Moscow, taking a job in the butcher's shop where his father worked. He disliked the job but soon found work as a bookstore clerk, where he was happier. Esenin also joined the Surikov circle, a large group of proletarian and peasant writers.

Esenin lost his job in the bookstore, but in May of 1913, he became a proofreader in a printing shop. The work strengthened his interest in the labor movement, and though he never completely accepted the ideology of the Social Revolutionary Party, he distributed illegal literature and supported other revolutionary activities. To learn more about history and world literature, Esenin took evening courses at the Shaniavski People's University in Moscow. With his goal of becoming a great poet, he recognized the need to broaden his education.

The foremost Russian writers of the time, however, lived in St. Petersburg rather than in Moscow, and in March of 1915, Esenin moved to Petrograd (as St. Petersburg was known between 1914, when Russia went to war against Germany, and 1924, when it became Leningrad). Upon his arrival, Esenin went to see Blok, who helped the young "peasant" and introduced him to well-known poets such as Zinaida Gippius, Feodor Sologub, and Vyacheslav Ivanov and to novelists such as Ivan Bunin, Aleksandr Kuprin, and Dmitry Merezhkovsky. The young poet Anatoly Mariengof became Esenin's intimate friend. Esenin was appointed as an editor of the political and literary journal *Severnie Zapiski*, an appointment that brought him in contact with other writers and intellectuals. Through the help of a fellow peasant poet, Nikolai Klyuyev, Esenin met the publisher M. V. Averyanov, who published Esenin's first volume of poems, *All Soul's Day*, in 1915.

In the autumn of 1915, Esenin was drafted into the army, which for him was a tragedy. He agonized in the dirty barracks and under the commands of the drill sergeant. Eventually, he succeeded in being transferred to the Commission of Trophies, a special unit for artists, but he neglected his duties so flagrantly that he was ordered to a medical unit stationed near the czar's residence in Tsarskoe Selo. The czarina discovered that the young poet was stationed nearby and invited him to the court to read his poetry. Esenin was flattered, but he also carried in his heart a deep hatred for the monarchy. Under some still unclear circumstances, Esenin left Tsarskoe Selo before February of 1917, and in 1918 he published his second volume of poetry, *Azure*.

In August of 1917, Esenin married Zinaida Raikh, who was then working as a typist for a newspaper published by the Socialist Revolutionary Party. The marriage ended in divorce in October, 1921, following the birth of two children. Raikh, who subsequently became a famous actress, married the great theatrical director Vsevolod Meyerhold. Esenin maintained ties with Raikh until the end of his life, and the dissolution of his first marriage established the pattern that was to mark his last years.

In 1918, however, Esenin was hopeful and ambitious, on the verge of fame. In March of 1918, he again moved to Moscow and continued to write optimistic, mythical poetry about the future of Russia. He tried to understand the revolution, although he abhorred the suffering it brought. In late 1918, during a visit to his native Konstantinovo, Esenin observed the passivity of the peasants. With the poem "Inonia," he tried to incite them to positive action.

During this period, Esenin, with several minor poets such as Mariengof, formed a literary movement known as Imaginism. The Imaginists (*imazhinisty*) had been inspired by an article about the Imagist movement in English and American poetry, founded by Ezra Pound. Except for the name, however, and—more important—the doctrine that the image is the crucial component of poetry, there was little connection between Pound's Imagism and the Russian Imaginism. For Esenin, the movement encouraged liberation from the peasant themes and mythical religiosity of his early verse. In addition, as is evident in the Imaginist manifesto of 1919, the movement was useful in attracting publicity, of which Esenin was very conscious.

In the fall of 1921, at a studio party, Esenin met the well-known American dancer Isadora Duncan, who was giving a series of dance recitals in Russia. Although Esenin spoke no English and Duncan knew only a few phrases in Russian, they found enough attraction in each other for Esenin to move immediately into Duncan's apartment. The turbulence of the relationship became notorious. In 1922, Duncan needed to raise money for her new dancing school in Moscow. She wanted to give a series of dance recitals in Western Europe and in the United States, but she also realized the difficulties she and Esenin would face in the United States if they were not legally married. On May 2, 1922, they were married, and Esenin became the first (and the only legal) husband of Duncan.

The United States disappointed Esenin. He could not communicate, and even Prohibition did not slow down his acute alcoholism. In the United States, he was seen merely as the husband of Duncan, not as a famous Russian poet. The skyscrapers could not replace the gray sky over the Russian landscape. After a nervous breakdown, Esenin returned alone to Russia, and when Duncan returned some time later, he refused to live with her again.

After his return to the Soviet Union, Esenin became increasingly critical of the new order. He was never able to accept the atmosphere of cruelty and destruction during the civil war, and the ruthless law of vengeance carried out by many fanatics, even after the war, was criminal in his eyes. It was difficult for Esenin both as an individual and as a poet to conform to Lenin's new economic policy period. To some extent, he regarded this difficulty as a personal failure and reacted to it with spells of depression alternating with outbursts of wild revelry. He styled himself a "hooligan," and he excused his heavy drinking, drug taking, barroom brawls, blasphemous verse, and all-night orgies as fundamentally revolutionary acts.

At the same time, Esenin saw himself as a prodigal son. He yearned for motherly love, the healing touch of nature, and the peaceful countryside. In 1924, he returned to his native village, but he could not find the "wooden Russia" that he had once glorified in his poems. *Rus' sovetskaia* (Soviet Russia), his famous poem of 1925, expresses his isolation in his own country. The revolution had not fulfilled Esenin's dreams of a rural utopia, and he, "the last poet of the village," was among its victims.

From September, 1924, until February, 1925, Esenin visited Baku and the Crimea, a trip that resulted in the publication of the collection *Persidskie motivi* (Persian motifs). In 1925, he married Sofya Tolstaya, one of Leo Tolstoy's granddaughters. The marriage was predictably unhappy; Esenin's deteriorating health caused him to be admitted repeatedly to hospitals. He managed to write the somewhat autobiographical long poem *Anna Snegina*, which describes the fate of the prerevolutionary people in the new Soviet society. The poor reception of the poem and the harsh criticism it provoked devastated Esenin.

The poet began to mention suicide more frequently. Even though his physical health improved, Esenin remained very depressed. In December of 1925, he left his wife in Moscow and went to Leningrad, where he stayed at the Hotel Angleterre. He was there for several days and was frequently visited by friends. On December 27, Esenin cut his arm and in his own blood wrote his last poem, "Do svidan'ia, drug moi, do svidan'ia..." ("Good-bye, My Friend, Good-bye"); later that day, Esenin gave the poem to friends (who neglected to read it) and showed the cut to them, complaining that there was no ink in his room. In the early hours of December 28, the poet hanged himself on a radiator pipe.

Esenin's widow arrived the next day and took her husband's body in a decorated railroad car to Moscow. In Moscow, thousands of people waited for the arrival of the train. Fellow writers and artists carried the coffin from the train station to its temporary resting place in a public building, where thousands more paid their last respects. Esenin was buried on the last day of 1925.

ANALYSIS

Sergei Esenin's poetry can be divided into two parts: first the poetry of the countryside, the village, and the animals and, second, the primarily postrevolutionary poetry of *Moskva kabatskaia* (Moscow the tavern city) and of *Rus' sovetskaia*. Generally, the village poetry is natural and simple, while many of the later poems are more pretentious and affected. The mood of country landscapes, the joys of village life, and the love for animals is created with powerful melodiousness. The poet's sincere nostalgia for "wooden Russia" is portrayed so strongly that it becomes infectious. Esenin creates idylls of the simple Russian village and of country life with the freshness of a skilled painter, yet the musicality of his verse is the most characteristic quality of his poetry. His simple, sweet, and touching early lyrics are easy to understand and are still loved by millions of readers in Russia.

As a "peasant poet," Esenin differed from some other Russian peasant poets of the time, such as Nikolai Klyuyev and Pyotr Oreshin. Esenin stressed primarily the inner life of the peasant, while the others paid more attention to the peasants' environment. His peasants are free of material things, even though they are part of their environment, while in the work of other peasant poets, things are preeminent.

Esenin's early poems chiefly employ the vocabulary of the village; they reveal the influence of the *chastushki*, the popular folk songs widely heard in any Russian village. When he arrived in Petrograd, Esenin presented himself as "the poet of the people"; dressed in a peasant blouse adorned with a brightly colored silk cord, he chanted his poems about harvests, rivers, and meadows.

When Esenin moved to Petrograd, he began to learn the sophisticated techniques of the Symbolists, particularly from the poet Blok. Esenin was able to create a complete picture of a landscape or a village with a single image. He continued, however, to maintain the melancholy mood and the sadness that would always be typical of his poetry.

At the time of his suicide, Esenin was still quite popular, both in the Soviet Union and among Russian émigrés. Beginning in 1926, the State Publishing House published Esenin's collected works in four volumes, but many poems were missing from this edition. By that time, the "morally weak Eseninism" had been officially denounced. In 1948, a one-volume selection of Esenin's poetry was published, and it sold out immediately. By the early 1950's, Esenin was fully rehabilitated, and in 1961, a five-volume edition appeared, which has since been reprinted several times. According to Russian critics, Esenin's tremendous popularity can be explained by the fact that his poetry was consonant with the feelings of the Russian people during the most difficult days in their history.

ALL SOUL'S DAY

Esenin's first collection, *All Soul's Day*, radiates happiness, although it is not free of the melancholy typical of his works. These early poems express the joy of village life, the poet's love for his homeland, and the pleasures of youth; even the colors are light and gay: blue, white, green, red. Esenin employs religious themes and Christian terminology, but the poems are more pantheistic, even pagan, than Christian. *All Soul's Day* was well received by the critical Petrograd audience, and this response immeasurably boosted Esenin's confidence. The poet was only twenty years old when he proved his mastery of the Russian language.

AZURE

Esenin's second collection, *Azure*, appeared after the revolution, in 1918, but the majority of the poems were written during World War I. These poems reflect Esenin's uncertainty concerning the future, although he did accept and praise the October Revolution. He visualized the revolution as a glorious cosmic upheaval leading to a resurrection of Russia and its rural roots. The style, mood, and vocabulary of *Azure* reveal the influence of Blok and Klyuyev.

Although Esenin undoubtedly was initially on the side of the Bolsheviks, his vision of the revolution was a highly individual one. He saw a return to peasant communities and to a primitive democratic simplicity. The threatening industrialization and the technological development of the mysterious electricity, the hidden source of power, which he witnessed later, horrified him. Three long poems with religiously symbolic titles, which were part of the *Azure* cycle, reflect this attitude: "Preobrazhenie" ("Transfiguration") "Prishestvie" ("The Coming"), and "Inonia."

The well-known poem "Inonia" reflects with particular clarity Esenin's wish for a peasant utopia, an anticapitalist, agricultural republic that could resist the industrial giants. Esenin saw himself as the prophet of a new religion that had to overcome the peasants' traditional Christianity to bring about a happy, rural, socialist paradise. By 1920, however, Esenin realized that the results of the revolution were slowly destroying his "rural Russia," and he saw himself as "the last poet of the village."

PUGACHOV

During this period of growing disillusionment, Esenin began to forsake the simplicity and the rural spirit of his early verse, although folk elements never disappeared from his work. Among the most significant of his more experimental Imaginist poems was the long dramatic poem *Pugachov*, published in 1922. This unfinished verse drama exhibits the unusual metaphors and verbal eccentricities that were characteristic of the Imaginists. The hero of Esenin's poem, the Cossack leader of a peasant rebellion in the 1770's, is highly idealized and bears little resemblance to the historical Pugachev. In contrast to Pushkin, who treated the same subject in his novella *Kapitanskaya dochka* (1836; *The Captain's Daughter*, 1846), Esenin passionately sympathized with Pugachev and his peasants. He also drew parallels between Pugachev's revolt and the October Revolution: In his view, both had failed because of human egotism and people's unwillingness to sacrifice for the common good.

"STRANA NEGODIAEV"

In 1922 and 1923, partially during his trip to the United States and Western Europe and partially after his return, Esenin wrote another dramatic poem. "Strana negodiaev" (the country of scoundrels), influenced by Western cinema, marked a departure from the Imaginist style of *Pugachov*. In it, Esenin abandoned striking imagery in favor of a rather crude realistic style. He never completed the poem, however, realizing that it was a failure. In the poem, Esenin refers to America as a greedy trap in which deceit is the key to survival; at the same time, he acknowledges the industrial achievement of the West. In sympathizing with the anti-Soviet hero of this dramatic poem, Esenin confirmed that he had lost much of his enthusiasm for the revolution.

MOSKVA KABATSKAIA

Indeed, by 1923, Esenin saw himself as lost in his own country. He did not reject the revolution itself but the results of the revolution. He was already notorious for his alcoholism, his orgiastic lifestyle, and his escapades around Moscow. His most decadent poems were included in the collection *Moskva kabatskaia*. In these poems, he confessed that he would have become a thief if he had not been a poet, and he exposed all his vices. These poems reflect Esenin's disappointment with himself, with love, and with religion. The critics accused him of wallowing in filth.

The poet of the village and the countryside became overshadowed in the 1920's by the alcoholic of *Moskva kabatskaia*. Esenin's manner became harsher, reflecting the worsening crisis of his life. Gentle laments for the passing of the idealized countryside were replaced by nostalgia for lost youth and the search for a home. Esenin largely abandoned the devices cultivated by the Imaginists, returning to the materials of his early verse yet handling them in a new manner—stark, assured, despairing.

With the poems of *Moskva kabatskaia*, Esenin sought to reconcile himself with the new Russia. In the celebrated poem "Rus' sovetskaia," he admits that he is too old to change, and he fears that he will be left behind by younger generations. In a mixture of resignation and defiance, he accepts the new order and resolves to continue writing poetry not by society's standards but by his own.

PERSIDSKIE MOTIVI

Although Esenin never visited Persia, during his visit to Baku and the Caucasus in 1925, he wrote a cycle of short poems entitled *Persidskie motivi*. Technically, the poems are well written, but Esenin's love lyrics addressed to different girls, in which genuine nostalgia mingles with superficiality and a lack of conviction, suggest that the poet was nearing a dead end.

ANNA SNEGINA

In 1925, Esenin also published the long autobiographical poem *Anna Snegina*, written during his stay in Batum. The poem describes a love affair set in a Russian village during the civil war. Soviet critics, however, were not interested in decadent love affairs; they expected poetry promoting the revolutionary spirit. Esenin was not able to produce this; he remained the anachronistic dreamer of a rural utopia. In his eyes, Soviet society had no need of him nor of his poetry.

OTHER MAJOR WORK

NONFICTION: "Kliuchi Marii," 1918.

BIBLIOGRAPHY

Brengauz, Gregory. *Yesenin: Lyrics and Life—Introduction to Russian Poetry*. 2d ed. Tallahassee: Floridian Publisher, 2006. This biography, in Russian and English, looks at Esenin's life and works.

Davis, J. *Esenin: A Biography in Memoirs, Letters, and Documents*. Ann Arbor, Mich.: Ardis, 1982. Davis culls the autobiographical material from the poet's work and complements it with biographical commentaries, shedding light on various aspects of Esenin's life. These materials, in turn, shed light on his poetry.

De Graaff, Frances. *Sergei Esenin: A Biographical Sketch*. The Hague, the Netherlands: Mouton, 1966. In his valuable study of Esenin's life and poetry, De Graaff combines biography with the poet's works, bolstering his observations with citations from many poems, in Russian and English. Includes an extensive bibliography.

Esenin, Sergei. *Complete Poetical Works in English*. Translated by Victoria Bul. Tallahassee: Floridian Publisher, 2008. Contains an introduction and biography by the translator, poems by poets who influenced or were influenced by Esenin, and a section of Isadora Duncan's autobiography.

McVay, Gordon. *Esenin: A Life*. Ann Arbor, Mich.: Ardis, 1976. In this definitive biography of Esenin in English, the author encompasses the poet's entire life, including his tragic death by suicide. The book offers brief analyses of Esenin's works along with copious illustrations.

Mariengof, Anatoli. *A Novel Without Lies*. Translated by Jose Alaniz. Chicago: Ivan R. Dee, 2000. A detailed memoir of Mariengof's association with Esenin and the literary avant-garde of the 1920's.

Prokushev, Yuri. *Sergei Esenin: The Man, the Verse, the Age*. Moscow: Progress, 1979. In this biography of Esenin by a Russian scholar, Prokushev offers the Russian point of view of the poet and his poetry. The emphasis is on the biographical details. It is somewhat tinted ideologically, stressing Esenin's often failed efforts to adapt to the Soviet reality, his love for Russia, and the realistic aspects of his poetry.

Thurley, Geoffrey. Introduction to *Confessions of a Hooligan*, by Sergei Esenin. Cheadle, England: Hulme, 1973. A book of translations of Esenin's poems about his struggle against alcoholism. In the introduction, Thurley examines circumstances that led to the writing of these poems.

Visson, Lynn. *Sergei Esenin: Poet of the Crossroads*. Würzburg, Germany: Jal, 1980. Visson undertakes a thorough, expert analysis of the stylistic features of Esenin's poetry, with extensive quotations from the poems, in Russian and in English, offering penetrating insights into the artistic merits of Esenin's poetry.

Rado Pribic

VLADISLAV KHODASEVICH

Born: Moscow, Russia; May 28, 1886
Died: Paris, France; June 14, 1939

PRINCIPAL POETRY
Molodost', 1908
Shchastlivy domik, 1914
Putem zerna, 1920
Tyazhelaya lira, 1922
Evropeiskaya noch', 1927

OTHER LITERARY FORMS

In addition to his poetry, Vladislav Khodasevich (kuh-DAY-zah-vihch) published many critical essays and memoirs. The most important of these are collected in *Nekropol'* (1939), *Literaturnye stat'i i vospominaniia* (1954), and *Belyi koridor: Isbrannaia proza v dvukh tomakh* (1982). His biography of the eighteenth century poet Gavrila Derzhavin (*Derzhavin*, 1931) is also notable. As is the case with Khodasevich's poetry, very little of his prose is available in English translation.

ACHIEVEMENTS

Vladislav Khodasevich was one of the most highly regarded Russian poets of his time and is one of the least known poets in modern times. Twelve years of poetic silence before his death contributed to that obscurity, and a virtual ban on publishing his work in the then Soviet Union as well as difficult relations within the Russian émigré community in Western Europe negatively affected his reputation for years. Interest in him revived in the 1980's, when a growing interest in him emerged in both the Soviet Union and the West.

BIOGRAPHY

Vladislav Felitsianovich Khodasevich was born in Moscow on May 28 (May 16, Old Style), 1886. Neither his father nor his mother was a native Russian (Felitsian Khodasevich was Polish, Sophie Brafman a Jewish convert to Catholicism and a fervent Polish nationalist), but perhaps as much because of his background as despite it, young Khodasevich considered himself thoroughly Russian in both allegiance and sensibility. The youngest of six children, he was educated at Moscow's Third Classical Gimnazium. Even before he left school, his ambitions turned to writing, and it was through a schoolmate that he made his first shy forays into the febrile world of fin de siècle Moscow literary life—the world of Valery Bryusov, Andrey Bely, and Aleksandr Blok. After graduation, Khodasevich began writing and publishing, and except for an almost comic bureaucratic interlude immediately after the revolution, he practiced no other profession.

Chronic ill health aggravated by hardship and privation kept Khodasevich out of military service during World War I and the Russian Revolution. In April of 1921, Khodasevich moved with his second wife, Anna Chulkova, and her son Garik to St. Petersburg, the abandoned capital, to work and live in the subsidized House of the Arts. It was there that Khodasevich, in a concentrated burst of energy, wrote many of his finest poems. Roughly one year later, however, spurred by private difficulties and by doubts about the future for writers in the new Soviet state, he and young poet Nina Berberova left for Western Europe. Khodasevich, like many other artists and intellectuals who left at the same time, did not expect his sojourn there to be a permanent one, and he maintained literary and personal ties with his homeland. However, Khodasevich soon found himself on the list of those who were to be barred from returning, and his skepticism about the Soviet Union began to harden into conviction.

Khodasevich was not of like mind with much of the émigré community, and although he settled permanently in Paris in 1927, he—like Marina Tsvetayeva—found that their aesthetic isolation in Russian letters and their lack of a convenient niche was to become an oppressive physical and spiritual isolation as well. Khodasevich, unlike Tsvetayeva, was never ostracized by fellow émigrés and was able to earn a meager living writing criticism for Russian periodicals, but there were few kindred spirits to be found among his own countrymen, let alone among the left-leaning French intellectual community of 1930's Paris. Khodasevich believed that he was witnessing the final eclipse of Russian letters and, ironically, continued to insist on the primacy of tradition even as his own poetics were discarding their much-vaunted classical proportions.

Khodasevich's last years were difficult ones: He wrote practically no poetry after 1927, and a final break with Berberova in 1932, financial straits, and failing health all contributed to depression. He did remarry and continue to write remarkable prose, and he was at work on an Alexander Pushkin study when he was fatally stricken with cancer in 1939. He died in the spring of that year.

ANALYSIS

A pupil of the Symbolists who soon freed himself from their poetics if not their perceptions, a contemporary of Boris Pasternak, Anna Akhmatova, Tsvetayeva, and Osip Mandelstam but resembling none of them, Vladislav Khodasevich is a poet not easily classified. He is often described as a classicist because of his loyalty to Pushkin and Russian verse tradition, yet his always ironic and sometimes bleak vision of the world is no less a product of the twentieth century. His poetic output was small and his demands on himself severe, but his mature verse, with its paradoxical combination of domesticity and exile, banality and beauty, harmony and grotesquerie, places him among the finest Russian poets of the twentieth century.

Khodasevich made his poetic debut in the heyday of Russian Symbolism. For the Symbolists, passion was the quickest way to reach the limits of experience necessary for artistic creation, and so all the motifs that accompany the Symbolist/Decadent notion of love— pain, intoxication, hopelessness—are explored by Khodasevich, diligent student of Decadence, in his first collection.

MOLODOST'

In *Molodost'* (youth), Khodasevich treats the transcendent themes of death, love, art, and eternity (so dear to the Symbolist canon) to both facile versifying and facile dramatization. His lyric voice is that of the seer, the magus, the seeker—a pale youth with burning eyes, a self-conscious poet risking all for revelation and encounters with mystic dread. *Molodost'* is the work of a talented beginner, but no more.

The poems are infused with vague mystery and vague premonitions, full of hints of midnight trysts at crypts, of confounding of realities, of fashionable madness and jaded melancholy. Khodasevich's problem is the problem of Symbolism in general: Its claim to universality of experience was undercut by the lack of any universal, or even coherent, symbolic system. In seeking to create a language of those "Chosen by Art," they plumbed for the emblematic, "creative" meaning of words, but the choosing and the chosen—hence the meaning—might vary from salon to salon. No word or deed was safe from symbolic interpretation, but the poet's own self-absorbed consciousness was the sole arbiter of meaning. Indeed, at times it seemed that literature itself was secondary to the attempt to divine hidden meaning in everyday events, thereby creating a life that itself was art enough.

Khodasevich's poetics would begin to change with the advent of his next book, but his apprenticeship among the Symbolists would affect him for the rest of his life. From them, he learned to perceive human existence as the tragic incompatibility of two separate realities, and all his poetic life would be an attempt to reconcile them.

SHCHASTLIVY DOMIK

His second volume of verse, *Shchastlivy domik* (the happy little house), shows Khodasevich replacing his early mentors — Bely, Blok, Bryusov, Innokenty Annensky —with eighteenth and nineteenth century classics such as Pushkin, Evgeny Baratynsky, and Derzhavin. His new persona is both more accessible and more distant than the pale pre-Raphaelite youth of the first book: He is more personal and biographical, surrounded by more concrete visual imagery and fewer abstractions, although the stylization, the deliberate archaisms, and the traditional meter in which those details are given serve to keep the poet's mask a generalized one—one poet among many, the latest heir to an elegiac tradition. *Shchastlivy domik* is still a diary of the emotions, kept by a self-absorbed "I," but here the spheres of emotion and art begin to separate. This poet belongs to a guild of craftsmen, not a hieratic brotherhood intent on perceiving life as a work in progress. A sense of history and linear time replaces the boundless "I" of the Symbolist/Decadent, defining both past and present and imposing different sorts of limits on the power of language to conjure, transform, or even affect reality. In this context, death becomes an even rather than a sensuous state of mind, and art becomes a means of overcoming death by very virtue of its formality and conventionality. These characteristics, not sibylline utterances, will carry the work beyond its creator's physical end.

Gone, then, are sadness and frustration at the utter futility of words, replaced by a less literal quietism—elegiac contemplation, meditation, and pride not in one's own oracular powers but in a tradition. Dignified humility replaces bombast, domesticity replaces exotica, and Pushkin is the chief guide. Although Khodasevich never lost his sense of the split between the world of appearance and the higher reality, in this collection he discovered inspiration in everydayness, in ordinary, prosaic, humble moments. In his next collection, his first book of truly mature work, he worked out the poetics appropriate to that discovery.

PUTEM ZERNA

Most of the major poems in *Putem zerna* (the way of grain) were finished by 1918, but the book itself did not see print until 1920. In lexicon, choice of themes, and lyric voice, it is a testament to a sober but still joyful everyday life; the poet is an ordinary human, subject to the laws of time and space, vulnerable to cold, hunger, illness, and death, no more and no less significant than any other man on the street. Like his fellow Muscovites in times of war and revolution, he observes history, participates in it "like a salamander in flame," but possesses no Symbolist second sight and no power to guess, let alone prophesy, the future. Although the poet, unlike his fellows, does have occasion to transcend his human limits, his small epiphanies, too, depend on the physical world. Their source is earthly. They derive from moments in which the poet experiences an acute awareness of things heard, felt, seen, smelled, and tasted.

Straightforward syntax, simplicity of lexicon, an intimate, slightly ironic, conversational tone, and the unrhymed iambic pentameter of the longer poems all make *Putem zerna* a deliberately prosaic book of poetry. Its persona is both public and private—public in his identification with the lives and deaths of his fellow creatures, private in facing his own mortality. The two are linked by the central metaphors of the book; the biblical seed that dies to be born again and the life-giving bread baked from buried grain—the eternal cycle of being.

Many of the book's poems have an identifiable setting in both space and time, coordinates usually lacking in Khodasevich's earlier works. The homely images of Moscow neighborhoods lead to meditations on the passing of time, nations, generations, and the poet himself as he feels the onset of physical weakness, illness, and old age. The poems chronicle what Khodasevich called "holy banality": common, collective experiences such as hauling wood, selling herring rations to buy lamp oil, and watching the local coffin maker finish his latest order. Moments of transcendence come unrequested and unexpected, with the thump of a seamstress's treadle or the sight of an all-too-ordinary suicide in a local park. The thump of the poet's own rocking chair, for example, marking time, sparks this moment in "Epizod" ("Episode"). In this poem, the observer of others leaves his own body and instead observes himself—thin, pale, dying, cigarette in hand. He also observes all the objects surrounding him—a bookcase; the ubiquitous yellow wallpaper of modest; older apartments; Pushkin's death mask; the children and their sleds. As the soul returns to its body, it journeys over water—a crossing of Lethe described in painstakingly physical terms.

The balance achieved in *Putem zerna* is both an acrobatic and a poetic feat, as Khodasevich points out in one of his short poems. It requires both muscle and brain. In his incarnation as ordinary man, Khodasevich has to balance life against death; in his role as poet, he has to balance creativity and the everyday world. For the moment, poetry makes that reconciliation possible by imposing order on the chaos and disarray of everyday life. However, just as the poet cannot exist without the man, the poetry cannot exist without the chaos.

TYAZHELAYA LIRA

If earthly and divine principles complement each other in *Putem zerna*, they come into conflict in Khodasevich's 1922 collection, *Tyazhelaya lira* (the heavy lyre). Here the divine side of the poet's nature turns dominant and becomes a condition for the existence of all else. Poetic order is no longer simply one possible means of reconciliation but the only order possible if the "I" is to survive in any way. Equilibrium shifted, the prosy external world lends itself less and less to ordering. Unlike the poet in the previous collection (an ordinary man save for his flashes of kinship with "child, flower, beast"), the poet of *Tyazhelaya lira* is unmistakably a creature different from his fellows, one for whom the creative moment has expanded to fill his entire consciousness. His state is one of constant awareness of human limitations and his own duality, of constant service to his craft. This awareness reveals not affinities but differences, not community but isolation.

Exalted, yes, but smug—never. Khodasevich's version of the conventional antagonism between the two worlds of the poet is not at all simple and clear-cut. The two realities are mutually exclusive yet do, paradoxically, overlap. Each seeks to free itself of the other, but only in their uncomfortable union does the lyric "I" of this collection exist. This voice may be much more ironic and self-deprecating than that of the high priests of Symbolism, but the poet's gifts—vision and "secret hearing"—allow him to see and hear, not over, but through physical existence. They allow him to escape, however briefly, from his captivity in an aging, unattractive, bodily prison. Indeed, the collection is dominated by a set of images that provide that escape to the soul's true homeland: Eyes, windows, mirrors, and reflections all open onto another reality, an escape route for the spirit. Wings, wounds (sometimes mortal, death being the ultimate flight), verbs with transitional prefixes, and negative definitions also belong to a poetics whereby the word, the soul, and the spirit break out of the enclosed cell of body or world. Angels, Psyche, Lucifer, an automobile winged by headlights, and acid consuming a photographic negative move across and through the tissue of existence.

One of the most striking poems of the collection, "Ballada" ("Ballad"), describes another journey out of the body. Here, as in "Episode," the poet is transformed into a creature with knowledge of the realms of both life and death. In both cases, the journey to the underworld begins with the speaker of the poem alone in his room, surrounded by familiar objects; the room has a window, and time passes strangely. While "Episode" ends with a return to the mortal body and an understanding of life and death as kindred states, "Ballad" ends with the man transfigured, changed into Orpheus, and that transformation takes place because of poetry. Cut by the sharp blade of music, the man grows up and out of himself, setting dead matter into motion with him, re-creating both himself and the world around him. His instrument, his blade, is the heavy lyre handed him through the wind.

EVROPEISKAYA NOCH'

Khodasevich's last book, *Evropeiskaya noch'* (European night), did not appear separately but came out as part of his *Sobranie stikhov* (collected verse) of 1927. Like his two earlier books, *Evropeiskaya noch'* treats of both spiritual and material worlds. The epiphanies of *Putem zerna*, however, are long gone, as are the neat oxymorons and epigrammatic resolutions of *Tyazhelaya lira*. There are no escape routes here. Instead, there is the Gnostic's anti-Paradise, a grotesque Gogolian world of inferior time and space, demoniac in its unrelenting banality and tawdry stupidity. The poet is doubly exiled, for even language seems to have lost its ability to transform either the self or what surrounds it. Now the physical world shapes both the language and the voice, distorting them and depriving them of their fragile unity and identity. The possibility—or rather impossibility—of creativity involves three things: the victory of matter over spirit and the distortion of both; the confusion of masks, or the poet's inability to recognize even himself; and the dismemberment of the once coherent lyric "I," as in a poem that ends with the poet exploding, flying apart "Like mud, sprayed out by a tire/ To alien spheres of being."

Savagely funny, *Evropeiskaya noch'* covers a world densely populated by humans, animals, and objects as well as the trappings, gadgetry, and attitudes of the modern century. Animate and inanimate objects obey the same laws, are objects of the same verbs, undergo the same processes. The natural world is at best askew, at worst hostile. The luminous, sanctified domesticity of *Putem zerna* has turned paltry and pitiful, the entire universe reduced to a collection of "poor utensils." The lyric hero, a petty Cain, is exiled from his age and from himself: "Like a fly on sticky paper/ He trembles in our time." Too inarticulate to give voice, he merely groans in mute despair.

The breakup of coherent vision and the loss of sense of self and genuine creativity take poetic form in the breakup of a once smooth line, disjointed stanzaic structure, abrupt changes of rhythm, and incongruous rhyme. Imagery, too, disintegrates: The poet looks in mirrors and cannot recognize his past selves in the aging face confronting him, gazes at a shiny tabletop and sees his own severed head reflected in the window of a passing streetcar, looks at the "asphalt mirror" of a Berlin street at night and sees himself and his friends as monsters, mutants, and human bodies topped by dogs' heads. The creation of art, so closely tied to the re-creation of self, seems impossible in a world of dusty galleries and cheap cinemas. Appropriately enough, *Evropeiskaya noch'* ends with a counterfeit act of creation, a parody of Jehovah's Fourth Day and of the poet's ability to bring dead matter to life. In this last poem, called "Zvezdi" ("Stars"), the cosmos emerges at the wave of a seedy conductor's baton. The show begins, and light comes forth from darkness in the form of prostitutes: the chorus line as the Big Dipper and the soloists as the North Star and "l'Étoile d'Amour." In Khodasevich's earlier works, the poet had been able to create or re-create an earlier, truer existence, a cosmos of his own. He came to doubt his ability to perform such a task. In Khodasevich's later poems, it appears that corrupt and perverted forms—vaudeville comedians and down-and-out dancing girls—may be the only artistic order left to the modern world.

OTHER MAJOR WORKS

NONFICTION: *Derzhavin*, 1931; *Nekropol'*, 1939; *Literaturnye stat'i i vospominaniia*, 1954; *Belyi koridor: Isbrannaia proza v dvukh tomakh*, 1982.

MISCELLANEOUS: *Sobranie stikhov*, 1927.

BIBLIOGRAPHY

Bethea, David M. *Khodasevich: His Life and Art*. 1983. Reprint. Princeton, N.J.: Princeton University Press, 1986. A thorough study by a leading Western expert on Khodasevich. The monograph examines Khodasevich's life and works, underscoring his main achievements in poetic artistry and his contribution to the Russian literature at home and in exile.

Brintlinger, Angela. *Writing a Usable Past: Russian Literary Culture, 1917-1937*. Evanston, Ill.: Northwestern University Press, 2000. Contains two chapters on Khodasevich, one concerning *Derzhavin* and the other on the writer's view of Alexander Pushkin. Notes Khodasevich's devotion to the past.

Hughes, Robert P. "Khodasevich: Irony and Dislocation—A Poet in Exile." In *The Bitter Air of Exile: Russian Writers in the West, 1922-1972*, edited by Simon Karlinsky and Alfred Appel, Jr. Berkeley: University of California Press, 1977. Main stations in Khodasevich's life are marked, followed by brief but pertinent comments on his poetry and his place in Russian literature.

Khodasevich, Valentina, and Olga Margolina-Khodase vich. *Unpublished Letters to*

Nina Berberova. Edited by R. D. Sylvester. Berkeley, Calif.: Berkeley Slavic Specialties, 1979. Previously unpublished letters casting light on Khodasevich. Bibliographical references, illustrated.

Kirilcuk, A. "The Estranging Mirror: The Poetics of Reflection in the Late Poetry of Vladislav Khodasevich." *Russian Review* 61, no. 3 (2002): 377-390. Provides an analysis of the later poetry, which treats of spiritual and material worlds.

Miller, Jane A. "Kodasevi's Gnostic Exile." *South and East European Journal* 28, no. 2 (1984): 223-233. Miller concentrates on Khodasevich's exile poetry, notably on *Tyazhelaya lira* and *Evropeiskaya noch '*. She points out the success of the former and the relative failures of the latter. She also broaches the question of creativity and the artist, especially his mirror of himself and his relation to the material world around him.

Nabokov, Vladimir. "On Khodasevich." In *The Bitter Air of Exile: Russian Writers in the West, 1922-1972,* edited by Simon Karlinsky and Alfred Appel, Jr. Berkeley: University of California Press, 1977. A terse but significant article on Khodasevich, written in 1939 in Russian on his death. The article has added weight because it was written by another famous writer in exile.

Rubins, Maria. *Twentieth-Century Russian Émigré Writers.* Vol. 317 in *Dictionary of Literary Biography.* Detroit: Gale, 2005. Brief essay on Khodasevich discusses his life and works.

Jane Ann Miller

MIKHAIL LERMONTOV

Born: Moscow, Russia; October 15, 1814
Died: Pyatigorsk, Russia; July 27, 1841

PRINCIPAL POETRY

Pesnya pro tsarya Ivana Vasilyevicha, molodogo oprichnika i udalogo kuptsa Kalashnikova, 1837 (*A Song About Tsar Ivan Vasilyevitch, His Young Body-Guard, and the Valiant Merchant Kalashnikov*, 1911)
Stikhotvoreniya M. Lermontova, 1840
Demon, 1855 (*The Demon*, 1875)
The Demon, and Other Poems, 1965
Mikhail Lermontov: Major Poetical Works, 1983

OTHER LITERARY FORMS

In addition to his position as one of the foremost Russian poets of the nineteenth century, Mikhail Lermontov (LYAYR-muhn-tuhf) holds the distinction of producing what many consider to be the first major novel in Russia, *Geroy nashego vremeni* (1840; *A Hero of Our Time*, 1854). The state of Russian prose during the 1820's and 1830's was far from satisfactory. Although several writers had tried their hands at historical novels in the 1820's, writers in the 1830's were still wrestling with such basic matters as narrative structure and a suitable literary language for the larger forms of prose fiction. Lermontov himself had begun two novels in the 1830's—a historical novel, *Vadim* (1935-1937; English translation, 1984), and a novel of St. Petersburg life, *Knyaginya Ligovskaya* (1935-1937; *Princess Ligovskaya*, 1965)—but he never completed them. In *A Hero of Our Time*, he solved the problems of structure and point of view by turning to the current fashion for combining a series of discrete short stories in a single cycle and taking it a step further. *A Hero of Our Time* consists of five tales linked by the figure of the central protagonist, Grigory Pechorin. Lermontov uses the device of multiple narrators and points of view to bring his readers ever closer to this hero, first providing secondhand accounts of the man and then concluding with an intimate psychological portrait arising from Pechorin's own diary records, all the while maintaining his own authorial objectivity. The figure of Pechorin himself, a willful yet jaded egoist, made a strong impact on the reading public, and the Pechorin type had many successors in Russian literature.

Lermontov also wrote several plays, beginning with *Ispantsy* (pb. 1935; the Spaniards) and *Menschen und Leidenschaften* (pb. 1935; people and passions), which were inspired by the Storm and Stress period of Friedrich Schiller's career, and concluding with *Maskarad* (pb. 1842; *Masquerade*, 1973), a drama exposing the vanity of St. Petersburg society. Lermontov is most remembered, however, for his prose and poetry.

Mikhail Lermontov
(Library of Congress)

ACHIEVEMENTS

In poetry, Mikhail Lermontov stands out as a Romantic writer *par excellence.* Influenced in his youth by such writers as Schiller and Lord Byron, he transformed Russian verse into a medium of frank lyric confession. The reserved and often abstract figure of the poet found in earlier Russian poetry gave way to a pronounced and assertive lyric ego in Lermontov's work, and Lermontov's readers were struck by the emotional intensity of his verse. Striving to express his personal feelings as forcefully as possible, Lermontov developed a charged verse style unmistakably his own. Although he seldom invented startling new poetic images, he often combined familiar images in sequences that dazzled his readers, and he used repetition, antithesis, and parallelism to create pithy and impressive verse formulations. Lermontov's poetic vision and his unabashed approach to the expression of his emotions had a considerable effect on subsequent Russian writers, from Nikolay Nekrasov in the next generation to Aleksandr Blok and Boris Pasternak in the twentieth century.

Iconoclastic in his approach to genre as well, Lermontov completed a trend already apparent in Russian poetry of the 1820's—the dismantling of the strict system of genre distinctions created during the era of classicism in Russian literature. Lermontov drew on disparate elements from various genres—the elegy, ode, ballad, and romance—and forged from them new verse forms suitable for his own expressive needs. The poet also showed a willingness to experiment with diverse meters and rhythms, and he employed ternary meters, primarily dactyls and amphibrachs, to an extent not seen previously in Russian poetry. Lermontov's exploration of such meters would later be continued by writers such as Nekrasov.

Although Lermontov's career was exceptionally brief, his accomplishments were extensive. He is justly considered to be, along with Alexander Pushkin, one of the two most important Russian poets of the nineteenth century. He left a rich legacy for future generations of Russian poets. Having moved past the poetic practices of Pushkin and his contemporaries, Lermontov forged a new style for the expression of the poet's emotions, a style both rugged and pliant, charged and evocative. His bold assertiveness as a poet and his skilled handling of rhythm and meter found an echo in the work of several generations of later writers. These achievements have earned Lermontov the right to one of the foremost places in the pantheon of Russian poets.

Biography

Mikhail Yurievich Lermontov was born in Moscow on October 15, 1814. According to family tradition, the Lermontovs were descended from a Scottish mercenary named George Learmont, who entered the service of the Muscovite state in the seventeenth century. Mikhail's mother, Mariya Arsenieva, belonged to an old and aristocratic family, the Stolypins, and her relatives did not approve of her match with Lermontov's father. Mariya died in 1817, and the child was reared by his maternal grandmother, Elizaveta Arsenieva, on her estate, Tarkhany. Because Lermontov's father Yury did not get along with Elizaveta Arsenieva, he left his son at Tarkhany and seldom met with him again before dying in 1831.

Lermontov had a comfortable upbringing. His grandmother provided him with a series of private tutors, and he occupied himself with painting and music as well as his studies. He moved with his grandmother to Moscow in 1827, and in the following year, he entered a private preparatory school connected with the University of Moscow. There, he became interested in poetry and began to write voluminous amounts of verse, inspired by such authors as Schiller, Byron, Pushkin, Vasily Zhukovsky, and others. The influence of Byron and Pushkin is evident in Lermontov's first attempts at narrative poetry, "Cherkesy" ("The Circassians") and "Kavkazsky plennik" ("A Prisoner of the Caucasus"). It was also during this period that Lermontov began work on his most famous narrative poem, *The Demon*.

In the fall of 1830, Lermontov entered the University of Moscow, where he remained immersed in his own personal world, reading and writing poetry and drama, including *Stranny chelovek* (pb. 1935; *A Strange One*, 1965). At the same time, he began to make a name for himself in social circles and experienced his first serious infatuations. His romance with one woman, Varvara Lopukhina, left a lasting imprint on the young man. Lermontov's romantic experiences and his encounter with society as a whole were filtered through his absorption with the figure of Byron. Constantly comparing his life with Byron's, he would become excited by any perceived similarities.

In 1832, Lermontov withdrew from the University of Moscow and sought admission to the University of St. Petersburg. Because the university would not give him credit for work done in Moscow, Lermontov instead entered the School of Guard Ensigns and Cavalry Cadets. There, he took up the lifestyle of an average cadet and wrote little in the way of serious poetry. Most of his creative energies went into the composition of salacious verse for his comrades' amusement, although he did begin work on his first novel, *Vadim*, a historical piece depicting the activities of a demoniac hero during the time of the Pugachev rebellion in the 1700's. After receiving his commission in the Life Guard Hussar Regiment stationed outside St. Petersburg in Tsarskoe Selo, Lermontov continued to sustain an active social life and rather calculatingly tried to generate a reputation as a Don Juan. Lermontov's cynicism about the values and mores of St. Petersburg society found expression in his verse play *Masquerade*, which, because of censorship problems, was approved for publication only after his death. In addition to this dramatic piece, Lermontov began work on the novel *Princess Ligovskaya*, which depicts an encounter between a young aristocrat and a St. Petersburg clerk, but the book was never finished.

Lermontov's literary reputation received a dramatic assist in 1837, when he wrote a bold poem about Pushkin's untimely death as a result of a duel in January of that year. The duel—the culmination of Pushkin's long frustration with life in St. Petersburg and with the attentions paid to his wife by Baron Georges d'Anthès, a French exile and the adopted son of a Dutch diplomat—had taken place on January 27. Pushkin was mortally wounded and died on January 29. Lermontov immediately penned a sharp poem expressing his dismay at Pushkin's death and the sufferings he had endured that led him to the duel. When some of d'Anthès's supporters began to cast aspersions on Pushkin, Lermontov added sixteen more lines that gave vent to his indignation with the court aristocracy itself. The poem received wide circulation in manuscript form and created a sensation in St. Petersburg. When it came to the czar's attention, Lermontov was arrested and sent to serve in the Caucasus.

This exile did not last long, however, and after several months in the south, Lermontov was transferred to Novgorod and then back to St. Petersburg. There, the poet circulated in society as a figure of note, and he reacted to the situation with ironic amusement. He also entered into close relationships with other important literary figures of the day—Zhukovsky, Pyotr Vyazemsky, and Andrey Kraevsky, the editor of the new journal *Otechestvennye zapiski*, in which several of Lermontov's poems appeared. Although his production of lyric poetry declined at this time, he completed several noteworthy works, including the narrative poems "Tambovskaya kaznacheysha" ("The

Tambov Treasurer's Wife") and "Mtsyri" ("The Novice"), which contains the confessions of a young monk who had briefly fled the monastery to find out "if the earth is beautiful" and "if we are born into this world/ For freedom or for prison." The first portions of his great novel *A Hero of Our Time* also began to appear in 1839.

Early in 1840, however, Lermontov again found himself in trouble with the authorities. Within the span of a few weeks, he succeeded in insulting the czar's daughters at a masquerade ball and took part in a duel with Erneste de Barante, the son of the French ambassador. Again Lermontov was arrested, and again he was sent to the Caucasus for military service. Once there, Lermontov managed to obtain an assignment with a regiment actively engaged in fierce battles with rebel Caucasian tribes, and he soon distinguished himself in hand-to-hand combat with the rebels. Suitably impressed, Lermontov's commanders recommended that he be given a gold saber in recognition of his valor, but he never received this commendation, perhaps because he continued to incur the disfavor of the authorities back in St. Petersburg.

Having been given permission to take a two-month leave in the capital early in 1841, Lermontov overstayed his leave and was ordered to depart for the Caucasus within forty-eight hours. He was in no hurry to rejoin his regiment, however, and his return journey became a leisurely affair, during which he wrote several of his finest lyrics. Reaching the town of Pyatigorsk in May, he spent several weeks taking the waters and indulging in pleasant diversions with a company of friends and other young people. Unfortunately, Lermontov chose to mock a certain Nikolay Martynov, an officer and former schoolmate at the Guards' School who had adopted the habit of wearing native dress in an attempt to impress the women in town. Martynov took umbrage at Lermontov's repeated needling, and he finally challenged him to a duel. The duel took place on July 27, 1841. Deadly serious, Martynov advanced to the barrier with determination and shot Lermontov, killing him instantly. Lermontov was subsequently buried at Tarkhany.

ANALYSIS

The hallmark of Mikhail Lermontov's mature verse—a fine balance between the intensity of the poet's emotion and the controlled language he uses to express it—took several years to achieve. In his early work, Lermontov did not check his desire to convey his feelings directly, and his verse seems raw and effusive, often hyberbolic and unformed. He wrote hundreds of poems as an adolescent, and he later recognized their immaturity, for he refused to publish them with his subsequent work. They would appear only after his death.

EARLY POETRY

A study of the early poetry reveals Lermontov's aggressive absorption of the work of other writers. Imagery, phrases, and individual lines are taken whole from the poetry of such authors as Zhukovsky, Pushkin, Alexander Polezhaev, and Ivan Kozlov among the Russians, and of Byron, Thomas Moore, Alphonse de Lamartine, and Victor Hugo among foreign writers. Lermontov's tendency to lift excerpts from one work and to insert them into another was a lifelong characteristic of his artistic method. He not only appropriated elements from other writers' works but also cannibalized his own poetry. The narrative poem "The Novice," for example, contains elements drawn from an earlier work, "Boyarin Orsha" (the Boyar Orsha), which in turn contains elements from an even earlier work, "Ispoved" (a confession). As the Russian Formalist critic Boris Eikhenbaum put it in his noted study of 1924, *Lermontov* (English translation, 1981): "His attitude was not directed toward the creation of new material, but to the fusion of ready-made elements." In his greatest works, however, Lermontov's art of fusion resulted in some very distinguished pieces.

LORD BYRON'S INFLUENCE

Perhaps the most influential figure in Lermontov's formative years as a poet was Byron. Lermontov's early lyrics repeatedly feature heroes who possess a special sensitivity or gifted nature but who have been crushed by fate. Such characters may carry a dark secret or wound in their souls, but they bear their suffering proudly and without complaint. Typical are these lines from a poem of 1831, "Iz Andreya Shenie" ("From André Chénier"): "My terrible lot is worthy of your tears,/ I have done much evil, but I have borne more." Lermontov himself recognized his affinity with Byron, while seeking at the same time to assert his individuality; a poem of 1832 begins, "No, I am not Byron, I am another/ As yet unknown chosen one." This sense of his own uniqueness is characteristic of the young Lermontov, and his fascination with the traits of the Byronic hero is further evident as he compares himself to Byron: "Like him, I am a wanderer persecuted by the world/ But with a Russian soul." Other Romantic features in the poem include a comparison between the unfathomable depths of his soul and the depths of the ocean (recalling Byron's celebrated verses on the same theme), a statement about the separation of the poet from "the crowd," and a complaint about the difficulty of expressing one's inner feelings. Lermontov airs this last concept in a demonstrative final line. Asking "Who will tell the crowd my thoughts?" the poet exclaims: "I—or God—or no one!" Many of Lermontov's poems conclude with such dramatic flair. Also characteristic here is Lermontov's penchant for concise lines structured by parallelism and antithesis. Comparing himself with Byron, he writes: "I began earlier, I will end earlier." This line seemed particularly prophetic to the Russian reading public when the poem first appeared in 1845, after Lermontov's early death. Curiously, Lermontov's apprehension of an early death remained with him throughout his career.

"THE SAIL"

One of Lermontov's early lyrics, the short poem "Parus" ("The Sail"), became well known after his death. Written in three stanzas of iambic tetrameter, the most popular meter in Russian poetry at the time, the poem is wholly constructed on a strict scheme of parallels and repetitions. The first two lines of each stanza provide a description of a sea setting, while the second two depict the psychological condition of a person, perhaps a sailor, metonymically evoked by the image of the sail moving across the open sea (the word for "sail" in Russian is masculine, and the Russian pronoun *on* can be translated as either "he" or "it"). Within this framework of parallels, Lermontov uses a series of antitheses or oppositions that perhaps reflect the contradictory flux of emotions in the subject's soul. The poet asks in the first stanza: "What is it seeking in a distant land?/ What has it abandoned in its native region?" In the second stanza, however, he provides only negative answers: "Alas,—it is not seeking happiness/ And it does not flee from happiness!" Nor do the final lines provide a concrete resolution: "Rebellious one, it seeks the storm,/ As if in storms there is peace!" Lermontov's evocation of a rebellious spirit seeking peace through turmoil was given a political interpretation by some contemporary Russian readers, but the poem's generalized nature makes other interpretations possible, too. It is likely that Lermontov simply wanted to suggest the fundamental contradictions and confusion inherent in restlessness itself.

THE DEMON

Images of rebellion and negation occupied a prominent place among Lermontov's lyrics in the 1830's, and at the end of the decade he completed his most impressive portrait of a Romantic "spirit of negation"—the title character of the long narrative poem *The Demon*. Like many of Lermontov's other narrative poems, *The Demon* is less a tale involving several characters in a concrete setting than a forum for the lyric expression of the protagonist's emotional impulses. In its earlier versions, the poem was set in Spain, and the female protagonist was a nun, but Lermontov later shifted the setting to the Caucasus, and the austere mountain ranges of this region proved to be an excellent backdrop for his portrayal of human frailty and superhuman passion. The central character of the poem is the Demon, a dark spirit who becomes captivated by the beauty of a Georgian maiden, Tamara. After her fiancé has been killed, the Demon tries to persuade her to give her love to him, telling her that her love can restore him to goodness and reconcile him with Heaven. Having delivered his impassioned speech, he destroys her with a fatal kiss. As her soul is carried to Heaven by an angel, the Demon seeks to claim his victim, but the angel spurns him, and the furious Demon is left alone with his frustrated dreams.

The Demon is an enigmatic character. Lermontov does not provide the reader with a clear psychological portrait of his hero. He is not the stern, philosophizing rebel of Byron's verse drama *Cain* (1821) and of similar Western European treatments of the metaphysical Romantic hero. Rather, he resembles the protagonists of a number of Lermontov's other works in that he is a willful spirit motivated more by boredom than by Promethean ambitions. The Demon recalls happier times "When he believed and loved/ . . . And knew neither malice nor doubt," but his turn to evil is essentially unmotivated, and his speeches to Tamara are not logically structured arguments but rather dazzling torrents of charged phrases and images. When he identifies himself to her, he states: "I am the scourge of my earthly slaves,/ I am the tsar of knowledge and freedom,/ . . . And you see,—I am at your feet!"

When the Demon claims that he is ready to renounce evil and reconcile himself with the good, the reader is not sure how to gauge the Demon's sincerity. His attitudes are susceptible to instantaneous change. When he hears Tamara sing, he begins to enter her room "ready to love/ With a soul open to the good . . .," yet when an angel blocks his way, he flares up: "And again in his soul awoke/ The poison of ancient hatred." He tells Tamara that as soon as he saw her, he suddenly hated his immortality and power, but as he tries to convince her to love him, he offers her both of these gifts. Perhaps the best way to understand the Demon is to view him as a figure who has truly become bored with doing evil ("He sowed evil without enjoyment/ . . . And evil grew boring to him"), and therefore he allows himself to become caught up in his own rhetoric about renunciation of evil and reconciliation with the good. At the moment of his declarations, he may feel sincere, but at the core of his soul, he is cold and unfeeling. Tamara, on the other hand, is given little to say; she seems to serve merely as a pretext for Lermontov's hero to pour out his soul.

The interaction between the Demon and Tamara is played out against the forbidding landscape of the Caucasus. Lermontov's descriptions of the icy mountains that stand guard over small patches of inhabited land serve as an apt emblem of the cosmos itself. The universe of *The Demon* and of many other Lermontov works is an impersonal realm in which human activity plays but a small and insignificant role. Lermontov's readers, however, have been less moved by his descriptions of nature than by the glittering oratory of the Demon, and the work has left significant traces on the creative consciousness of later Russian artists. The painter Mikhail Vrubel painted a series of studies inspired by *The Demon*, and the composer Anton Rubinstein wrote an opera based on the work.

"THE DEATH OF A POET"

Lermontov's development beyond the narrow thematics of his early Romantic period is most apparent in his shorter lyric works, beginning with his famous poem on Pushkin's death, "Smert poeta" ("The Death of a Poet"). The poem can be divided into three parts. The first two parts were written immediately after Pushkin's death, while the third was composed several days later. Throughout the poem, Lermontov's talent for declamatory verse comes to the fore. The first section, written in lines of iambic tetrameter, is marked by frequent exclamations, rhetorical questions, and strong intonational breaks, as in the lines: "He rose up against the opinion of society/ Alone, as before . . . and was killed!/ Killed!" In an interesting form of homage to Pushkin, Lermontov draws on Pushkin's own poetry to depict the poet's death, echoing the images used by the earlier poet in his brilliant novel in verse, *Evgeny Onegin* (1825-1832, 1833; *Eugene Onegin*, 1881).

During the second part of the poem, which is written in iambic lines of varying lengths, Lermontov adopts an elegiac tone as he questions why Pushkin left the peaceful diversions of close friendships to enter into "this society, envious and suffocating/ To a free heart and fiery passions." In the final section, also written in iambic lines of varying lengths, Lermontov's elegiac tone gives way to a torrent of bitter invective. His charged epithets and complex syntax seem to boil over with the heat of his indignation. He begins with a harsh characterization of those who spoke ill of the dead poet—"You, arrogant offspring/ Of fathers renowned for notorious baseness"—and he continues with an attack on the court itself: "You, standing in a greedy crowd around the throne,/ The executioners of Freedom, Genius, and Glory." After reminding these villains of the inevitability of divine punishment, which cannot be bought off with gold, Lermontov concludes: "And you will not wash away with all your black blood/ The righteous blood of the poet!" "The Death of a Poet" heralded Lermontov's growing maturity as a poet. Although revealing his continued reliance on certain Romantic formulas, it indicated that he was beginning to find a workable poetic style for himself.

"MEDITATION"

Lermontov employed the declamatory style of "The Death of a Poet" with great success in his late period. A forceful poem of 1838, "Duma" ("Meditation"), for example, presents a concentrated indictment of the coldness and emptiness of Lermontov's entire generation. The poem begins, "I gaze on our generation with sadness!" and it contains such well-known lines as "We are disgracefully faint-hearted before danger/ And contemptible slaves before power." As Lidiya Ginzburg points out in her important study, *Tvorchesky put Lermontova* (1940), the lyric ego of Lermontov's early works had become a more generalized "we"; this shift perhaps reflected a greater objectivity on Lermontov's part as he soberly measured himself and the society in which he had come to maturity. Certainly the poet knew how to pinpoint the falsity and vanity of his peers. In a poem of 1840 that begins "How often, surrounded by a motley crowd . . .," Lermontov contrasts his feelings of boredom at a masquerade ball with his warm recollections of childhood and spontaneous dreaming. Noting that he hears "the wild whisper of speeches learned by rote" and is touched "with carefree audacity" by urban beauties' hands, "which long ago had ceased to tremble," the poet concludes by confessing an urge "to confuse their frivolity/ And to throw boldly into their faces an iron verse/ Steeped in bitterness and spite!"

MATURE WORKS

Lermontov's declamatory "iron verse," however, was only one style he used in his mature work. It is futile to look for sharp genre distinctions in his late verse, for he did not pay close attention to such distinctions, and one can find in individual poems a blending of features from various genres. Eikhenbaum identifies three categories of poetry in Lermontov's mature period: poems of an oratorical, meditational character; poems of melancholy reflection; and poems resembling lyric ballads with a weakened plot. Indeed, several of Lermontov's late poems resemble small verse novellas: "Uznik" ("The Prisoner"), "Sosed" ("The Neighbor"), "Kinzhal" ("The Dagger"), "Son" ("A Dream"), and "Svidanie" ("The Meeting"). In part, Lermontov's predilection for such brief verse "novellas" may have signified a dissatisfaction with the unrestrained confessional tenor of his early work and a desire to create works that displayed greater objectivity and universality. For the same reason, perhaps, Lermontov also favored short allegorical poems in which natural settings and objects convey human situations and feelings. One example of this type is "Utyos" ("The Cliff"), the first stanza of which depicts a cloud nestling for the night against the breast of a great cliff. In the morning, the cloud moves on, "gaily playing in the azure," but it has left behind a moist trace in a crack in the cliff. The poem concludes with a picture of the cliff: "Solitarily/ It stands, plunged deep in thought,/ And quietly it weeps in the wilderness." Again, one can contrast the restrained evocation of abandonment and isolation here with the unchecked egotism of Lermontov's early work . The "plot" of this poem is further enhanced by the fact that in Russian, the word for "cloud" is feminine while the word for "cliff" is masculine. Also noteworthy is the trochaic meter of the verse; Lermontov moved beyond the poetic models of his predecessors to develop new rhythmic patterns.

"It's Boring and Sad . . ."

At times, Lermontov's new rhythms produced an impression of ruggedness that aroused commentary from his readers. One such work is the poem "I skuchno i grustno. . ." ("It's Boring and Sad . . ."). Written in alternating lines of five-foot and three-foot amphibrachs, the poem stands out for its colloquial, almost prosaic diction, as at the beginning of the second stanza, where the poet writes: "To love . . . but whom? . . . for a short time—it's not worth the effort,/ But to love forever is impossible." After examining his situation and judging it dull, the poet concludes: "And life, if you look around with cold attentiveness,/ Is such an empty and foolish joke. . . ." The mood of pessimism and disillusionment is familiar from Lermontov's early work, but the detachment and impassivity of the verse are new. The poet is no longer swept away with the importance of his emotions. He surveys his own flaws and the flaws of his generation with an analytical eye that retains no illusions about the glamorous posturings of the Romantic hero. This detachment is precisely what makes Lermontov's portrait of Pechorin, the protagonist of *A Hero of Our Time*, so gripping and accurate.

"I Walk Out Alone onto the Road . . ."

Lermontov's innovative approach to rhythmic patterns was perhaps most influential in his reflective poem of 1841, "Vykhozhu odin ya na dorogu . . ." ("I Walk Out Alone onto the Road . . ."). This work, one of the last that Lermontov wrote, depicts the poet alone in the midst of nature on a quiet, starlit night. Within his soul, however, he is troubled. He wonders why he feels so pained, and he confesses that he no longer expects anything from life; he merely wants to fall into a deep sleep. Yet it is not the sleep of the grave that he seeks; rather, he would like to fall asleep in the world of nature, eternally caressed by a sweet song of love.

Of special interest in this poem is Lermontov's use of trochaic pentameter with a caesura after the third syllable of the line. This meter creates a special rhythmic effect in which the line seems to fall into two segments. The first segment is often anapestic, because the first syllable is frequently unstressed or weakly stressed, while the second part of the line seems to consist of three iambic feet. This structure creates an impression of an initial upsweep of movement, emphasizing the semantic charge of the poem's first word—"vykhozhu" ("I walk out")—followed by a more calm or stable interval over the rest of the line. Such a contrast or imbalance is itself emblematic of the poem's message, for despite the initial suggestion of movement conveyed by the poet's statement about walking out onto the road, he does not in fact go anywhere, and the poem concludes with images of passivity or stasis. This remarkable harmony between the rhythmic pattern of the poem and its message has had a lasting impact on the artists who followed Lermontov. Not only was the poem set to music and introduced to the general public as a song, but it also initiated an entire cycle of poems in which a contrast between the dynamic theme of the road or travel and the static theme of life or meditation is rendered in lines of trochaic pentameter. Among Lermontov's successors who wrote poems of this type were Fyodor Tyutchev, Ivan Bunin, Aleksandr Blok, Andrey Bely, Sergei Esenin, Boris Poplavsky, and Boris Pasternak.

OTHER MAJOR WORKS

LONG FICTION: *Geroy nashego vremeni*, 1839, serial (1840, book; *A Hero of Our Time*, 1854); *Knyaginya Ligovskaya*, 1935-1937 (wr. 1836-1837; in *Polnoe sobranie sochinenii v piati tomakh*; *Princess Ligovskaya*, 1965); *Vadim*, 1935-1937 (wr. 1832-1834; in *Polnoe sobranie sochinenii v piati tomakh*; English translation, 1984).

PLAYS: *Maskarad*, pb. 1842 (wr. 1834-1835; *Masquerade*, 1973); *Dva brata*, pb. 1880 (wr. 1836; *Two Brothers*, 1933); *Ispantsy*, pb. 1935 (wr. 1830; verse play); *Menschen und Leidenschaften*, pb. 1935 (wr. 1830); *Stranny chelovek*, pb. 1935 (wr. 1831, verse play; *A Strange One*, 1965); *Tsigany*, pb. 1935 (wr. 1830).

MISCELLANEOUS: *Sochtsnentsya M. Ya. Lermontova*, 1889-1891 (6 volumes); *Polnoe sobranie sochinenii v piati tomakh*, 1935-1937 (5 volumes; includes all his prose and poetry); *Polnoe sobranie sochinenii v shesti tomakh*, 1954-1957 (6 volumes; includes all his prose and poetry); *A Lermontov Reader*, 1965 (includes *Princess Ligovskaya*, *A Strange One*, and poetry); *Michael Lermontov: Biography and Translation*, 1967; *Selected Works*, 1976 (includes prose and poetry).

BIBLIOGRAPHY

Allen, Elizabeth Cheresh. *A Fallen Idol Is Still a God: Lermontov and the Quandaries of Cultural Transition.* Stanford, Calif.: Stanford University Press, 2007. In this volume, Allen takes a critical look at Lermontov's writing, applying literary theories, and placing it in the context of his time and culture. He is portrayed as a writer who defies categorization, straddling the line between Romanticism and Realism.

Briggs, A. D. P., ed. *Mikhail Lermontov: Commemorative Essays.* Birmingham, England: University of Birmingham, 1992. A collection of papers from a conference at the University of Birmingham in July, 1991, on Lermontov and his works. Bibliography and index.

Eikhenbaum, Boris. *Lermontov.* Translated by Ray Parrot and Harry Weber. Ann Arbor, Mich.: Ardis, 1981. A translation of the Russian monograph by a leading Russian critic of the 1920's, this thorough study of Lermontov's poetry and prose remains the seminal work on him. Many poems are offered in both Russian and English.

Garrard, John. *Mikhail Lermontov.* Boston: G. K. Hall, 1982. Presents Lermontov and his works meticulously in a concise, easy-to-understand fashion. Lays the foundation for more ambitious studies of Lermontov in any language.

Golstein, Vladimir. *Lermontov's Narratives of Heroism.* Evanston, Ill.: Northwestern University Press, 1998. Tackles the topic of heroism, prevalent in Lermontov's works, and how he presents and solves it. The emphasis is on "The Demon," "The Song," and Pechorin of *A Hero of Our Time.* Citations of works are in Russian and English translation.

Kelly, Laurence. *Lermontov: Tragedy in the Caucasus.* 1977. Reprint. New York: Tauris Park, 2003. Colorfully illustrated biography of Lermontov covers his childhood in the "wild" East, his education, the rise and fall in the society, and his attitudes toward war as reflected in his works.

Lermontov, Mikhail. *Major Poetical Works.* Translated with a biographical sketch, commentary, and an introduction by Anatoly Liberman. Minneapolis: University of Minnesota Press, 1983. A thorough detailing of Lermontov's life that takes good advantage of the previous works together with translations of more than one hundred of Lermontov's poems, not all of which have appeared in English previously. The translations have won much professional praise for their surprising poeticality that does not compromise accuracy. Includes more than fifty illustrations and is annotated and indexed.

Reid, Robert. *Lermontov's "A Hero of Our Time."* London: Bristol Classical Press, 1997. This analysis of the novel casts light on Lermontov's work as a whole. Includes bibliographical references.

Turner, C. J. G. *Pechorin: An Essay on Lermontov's "A Hero of Our Time."* Birmingham, England: University of Birmingham Press, 1978. A pithy discussion of various aspects of Lermontov's main character, of the relationship of the narrator and the reader, the narrator and the hero, the hero and himself, the hero and the author, and the hero and the reader.

Vickery, Walter N. *M. Iu. Lermontov: His Life and Work*. Munich, Germany: O. Sagner, 2001. A biography of Lermontov that examines his life and work. Includes a bibliography.

Julian W. Connolly

OSIP MANDELSTAM

Born: Warsaw, Poland, Russian Empire (now in Poland); January 15, 1891
Died: Vtoraya Rechka, near Vladivostok, Soviet Union (now in Russia); probably
December 27, 1938

OTHER LITERARY FORMS

Osip Mandelstam (muhn-dyihl-SHTAHM) was writing essays on Russian and European literature as early as 1913. Many of the theoretical essays were collected, some in considerably revised or censored form, in *O poezii* (1928; *About Poetry*, 1977). These, as well as his otherwise uncollected essays and reviews, are available in their original and most complete versions in *Sobranie sochinenii* (1955, 1964-1971, 1981; *Collected Works*, 1967-1969). Mandelstam's prose was not republished in the Soviet Union, with the exception of his single most important essay, "Razgovor o Dante" ("Conversation About Dante"), written in 1933 but not published until 1967, when an edition of twenty-five thousand copies sold out immediately and was not reprinted. Mandelstam's prose has been seen both as a key to deciphering his poetry and as a complex body of nonpoetic discourse of great independent value. All his prose has been translated into English.

ACHIEVEMENTS

Osip Mandelstam's poetry won immediate praise from fellow members of Russian literary circles, and he now holds an indisputable position as one of Russia's greatest poets. Like many of his contemporaries, however, Mandelstam experienced anything but a "successful" literary career. His work appeared often in pre-Revolutionary journals, but Mandelstam was not among the writers whom the Bolsheviks promoted after 1917. By 1923, the official ostracism of independent poets such as Mandelstam was apparent, though many continued writing and publishing whenever possible. Mandelstam did not write poetry between 1925 and 1930, turning instead to prose forms that were as inventive and as idiosyncratic as his verse. Attempts to discredit him intensified after 1928. He was arrested twice in the 1930's and is believed to have died while in transit to a Siberian labor camp.

Even during the "thaw" under Premier Nikita Khrushchev, Mandelstam's works were kept out of print, and it was not until 1973 that his "rehabilitation" was made credible by the publication of his poetry in the prestigious *Biblioteka poeta* (poet's library) series. That slim volume was reissued. During the Soviet era in Russia, scholarly writing about Mandelstam, although limited, appeared; his name was mentioned in many but by no means all studies of literature. Official publications, such as textbooks or encyclopedias, relegated him to minor status and often commented disparagingly on his "isolation" from his age. The deep respect commanded by his poetry in the Soviet Union was nevertheless measured by the evolution of scholarly interest in his work.

Mandelstam's reputation outside Russia was initially slow in developing because of the extreme difficulty in obtaining reliable texts of his works and because of the scarcity of information about the poet. As texts and translations became available, Mandelstam's reputation grew steadily. The single most important factor in making his work known in the West was the publication of two volumes of memoirs by his wife, Nadezhda Mandelstam. *Vospominania* (1970; *Hope Against Hope: A Memoir*, 1970) and *Vtoraya kniga* (1972; *Hope Abandoned*, 1974), issued in Russian by émigré publishers and translated into many Western languages, are the prime source of information concerning Mandelstam's life. Works of art in their own right, they also provide invaluable insights into his poetry.

BIOGRAPHY

Osip Emilievich Mandelstam was born in Warsaw, Poland, on January 15, 1891. His family moved almost immediately to St. Petersburg, where Mandelstam later received his education at the Tenischev School (as did Vladimir Nabokov only a few years later). Mandelstam's mother was a pianist; his father worked in a leather-tanning factory. Little is known about Mandelstam's childhood or young adulthood; he recorded cultural rather than personal impressions in his autobiographical sketch, *Shum vremeni* (1925; *The Noise of Time*, 1965).

Mandelstam took several trips abroad, including one to Heidelberg, where he studied Old French and the philosophy of Immanuel Kant at the University of Heidelberg from 1909 to 1910. He returned to St. Petersburg University's faculty of history and philology but seems never to have passed his examinations. Mandelstam had a highly intuitive approach to learning that foreshadowed the associative leaps that make his poetry so difficult to read. His schoolmate Viktor Zhirmunsky, later a prominent Formalist critic, said of Mandelstam that he had only to touch and smell the cover of a book to know its contents with a startling degree of accuracy.

Mandelstam had been writing in earnest at least as early as 1908, and he began publishing poems and essays in St. Petersburg on his return from Heidelberg. By 1913, his literary stance was defined by his alliance with the Acmeists, a group dedicated to replacing the murky longing of Russian Symbolism with a classical sense of clarity and with a dedication to the things of this world rather than to the concepts they might symbolize. Among the acquaintances made in the Acmeist Guild of Poets, Mandelstam formed a lifelong friendship with the poet Anna Akhmatova.

The ideological positions taken by poets were soon overwhelmed by the political upheavals of the decade. Mandelstam did not serve in World War I. He greeted the Revolution with an enthusiasm typical of most intellectuals; he grew increasingly disappointed as the nature of Bolshevik power became apparent. Mandelstam worked in several cultural departments of the young Soviet government, moving between Moscow and St. Petersburg (renamed Leningrad) in connection with these and other jobs. In May, 1919, he met and later married Nadezhda Yakovlevna Khazina. The civil war parted the Mandelstams at times, but they were virtually inseparable until Mandelstam's second arrest in 1938. Nadezhda Mandelstam became far more than her husband's companion and source of strength. She recorded his poems after he had composed them mentally; she memorized the poems when it became clear that written texts were in jeopardy; and she ensured her husband's poetic legacy many years after his death with her two volumes of memoirs and her lifelong campaign to have his poems published.

An early indication of Mandelstam's difficulties came in 1925, when the journal *Rossiya* rejected *The Noise of Time*. Living in or near Leningrad after 1925, Mandelstam busied himself with popular journalistic articles, children's literature, translations, and, by the end of the decade, hack editorial work. Although he published volumes of poetry, prose, and literary criticism in 1928, an attempt to entrap him in a plagiarism scandal the same year demonstrated the general precariousness of his status under the new regime. Nikolai Bukharin, who saved Mandelstam more than once, arranged a trip to Armenia and Georgia that proved crucial in ending his five years of poetic silence. Mandelstam wrote a purgative account of the plagiarism trial, *Chetvertaia proza* (1966; *Fourth Prose*, 1970), as well as poetry and prose inspired by the Armenian land and people.

After the journey, Mandelstam and his wife lived in near poverty in Moscow. Though he gave several readings, Mandelstam saw his prose work *Puteshestviye v Armeniyu* (1933; *Journey to Armenia*, 1973) denounced soon after its publication in the periodical *Zvezda*. On May 13, 1934, Mandelstam was arrested, ostensibly for a poem about Stalin's cruelty; the act of reciting such a poem even to a few friends was characteristic of his defiance of the authorities and of the Soviet literary establishment, which he openly despised. Bukharin again intervened, and the terms of exile were softened considerably. First sent to Cherdyn, the Mandelstams were allowed to select Voronezh, a southern provincial city, as the place where they would spend the next three years.

Mandelstam attempted suicide in Cherdyn and suffered intense periods of anxiety whenever Nadezhda Mandelstam was away, even briefly. He could find little work in Voronezh. Despite periods of near insanity, Mandelstam wrote (and actively sought to publish) three notebooks of poems in Voronezh. In May, 1937, the couple returned to

Moscow, where Mandelstam suffered at least one heart attack. Heart ailments had plagued him for years, and throughout his poetry, shortness of breath was always to be a metaphor for the difficulty of writing.

In the fall of 1937, a final respite from the hardships of Moscow was arranged. In the sanatorium in Samatikha, Mandelstam was again arrested in the early morning of May 2, 1938. In August, he was sentenced to five years' hard labor for counterrevolutionary activities. In September, he was sent to a transit camp near Vladivostock, from which he wrote to his wife for the last time. The actual circumstances of Mandelstam's death will probably never be known. The conditions of the camp almost certainly drove him, and not a few others, to the point of insanity. In 1940, his brother Aleksandr received an official statement that Mandelstam had died December 27, 1938, of heart failure.

Nadezhda Mandelstam lived another forty-two years, sustained by her friendship with Anna Akhmatova and by her commitment to preserving her husband's poems for a generation that could read them. As Mandelstam's works began appearing in print, Nadezhda Mandelstam published her two invaluable volumes of memoirs, *Hope Against Hope* and *Hope Abandoned*. On December 31, 1980, she achieved her great wish, an achievement rare enough for Russians of her generation: She died in her own bed.

ANALYSIS

In Osip Mandelstam's first published essay, "O sobesednike" (1913; "On the Addressee"), he describes the ideal reader as one who opens a bottle found among sand dunes and reads a message mysteriously addressed to the reader. Mandelstam's poetry, like the message in the bottle, has had to wait to find its reader; it also demands that a reader be aggressive and resourceful. His poems are intensely dependent on one another and are frequently comprehensible only in terms of ciphered citations from the works of other poets. The reader who wishes to go beyond some critics' belief that Mandelstam's lexicon is arbitrary or irrational must read each poem in the context of the entire oeuvre and with an eye to subtexts from Russian and European literature.

ACMEISM

Mandelstam's attempt to incorporate the poetry of the past into his works suited both the spirit and stated tenets of Acmeism, a movement he later defined as a "homesickness for world culture." Mandelstam always saw the Acmeist poets as the preservers of an increasingly endangered literary memory. "True" poetry could arise only from a celebration of its dependence on the old. Poetry plows up the fields of time, he wrote; his own poems bring forth rich layers of subsoil by their poetics of quotation. Apparently opaque lyric situations, when deciphered, yield transparent levels of meaning. Mandelstam especially loved the myths of Greece and Rome, though his quotations are most often from nineteenth and twentieth century Russian poets.

Using another metaphor, perhaps the most typical metaphor for the Acmeists, Mandelstam wrote in the early 1920's that Russian poetry has no Acropolis. "Our culture has been lost until now and cannot find its walls." Russia's words would build its cultural edifices, he predicted, and it is in the use of the word that one must seek the distinctive feature of Mandelstam's poetry.

"HAPPILY NEIGHING, THE HERDS GRAZE"

An example of Mandelstam's use of quotations will indicate how far interpretation of his poetry must stray from the apparent lyric situation. Referring to Mandelstam's first collection of poems, *Stone*, Kiril Taranovsky has noted that a line in the poem "S veselym rzhaniem pasutsia tabuny" ("Happily Neighing, the Herds Graze") quotes Alexander Pushkin's famous statement, "My sadness is luminous." Mandelstam's line is "In old age my sadness is luminous." Nineteen years later, Mandelstam wrote, in a poem memorializing Andrei Bely, "My sadness is lush." The epithet here comes from the *Slovo o polku Igoreve* (c. 1187; *The Tale of the Armament of Igor*, 1915), but the syntax still recalls Pushkin. Interpreting the stylized line "My sadness is lush" thus requires knowing Pushkin and *The Tale of the Armament of Igor*, to say nothing of Mandelstam's first quotation of Pushkin in "Happily Neighing, the Herds Graze" or the often ornate works of Andrei Bely.

In "Happily Neighing, the Herds Graze," Pushkin's presence is also felt in the poem's seasonal setting, his beloved autumn. The month mentioned, August, suggests Augustus Caesar, and the ancient Roman context is as significant as the Pushkinian overtones. The poem thus has more to do with the ages of human culture than with grazing herds; the poem contrasts the "classical spring" of Pushkin's golden age of Russian literature with the decline of Rome. The dominant color in the poem is gold, specifically the dry gold of harvest. Russia in 1915 resembled Rome during its decline, as the Romanov dynasty faced its end, so that three historical periods come to bear on an interpretation of this apparently pastoral poem. The rise and decline of civilizations do not upset this poet, for whom the cyclical nature of the seasons suggests that historical change is itself cyclical. As Mandelstam wrote in 1918, "Everything has been before, everything will repeat anew. What is sweet to us is the moment of recognition." To achieve such moments, the reader must allow Mandelstam's metaphors to acquire meaning in more than one context. The contexts will border on one another in surprising ways, but it is his peculiar gift to his readers that when they read his poems, they see past poets and past ages of man from new vantage points.

STONE

Mandelstam's first volume of poetry, *Stone*, was published in 1913, with successive enlargements in 1916 and 1923. *Stone* contains short lyrics, many of only three or four quatrains. The title evokes the volume's dominant architectural motifs. Aside from the well-known triptych of cathedral poems in *Stone*, there are also poems of intimate interiors, designs in household utensils, and seashells. The patterns of crafted objects or complex facades allow Mandelstam to write in *Stone* about the structures of language, about how poems may best be written. At times, his metapoetic statements emerge completely undisguised. A landscape is described by the technical language of poetics in "Est' ivolgi v lesakh" ("There Are Orioles in the Woods"), in which the birds' singing is measured by the length of vowel sounds, their lines ringing forth in tonic rhythms. The day "yawns like a caesura."

Mandelstam pursues the probable relationship between the oriole and the poet in "Ia ne slyxal rasskazov Ossiana" ("I Have Not Heard the Tales of Ossian"). Here, a raven echoing a harp replaces the oriole; the poem's persona intones, "And again the bard will compose another's song/ And, as his own, he will pronounce it." Mandelstam contrasts his own heritage with that of another land, as distinct as the singing of birds and men. Despite the differences between the battles of Russian soldiers and the feigned tales of Ossian, the poet's entire received heritage is "blessed," "the erring dreams of other singers" ("other" connotes "foreign" as well as "not oneself" in Russian). It is in making the dreams his own that the poet finds victory.

In "Est' tselomudrennye chary" ("There Are Chaste Charms"), Mandelstam concludes with an equally victorious quatrain. The poem has evoked household gods in terms derived from classical Rome and from eighteenth century poetry. After three quatrains of listening to ancient gods and their lyres, the poet declares that the gods "are your equals." With a careful hand, he adds, "one may rearrange them."

Among the poems that both assert and demonstrate Mandelstam's strength as an independent poet is "Notre Dame," the shortest and most clearly Acmeist of his three 1912 cathedral poems. The Acmeists consistently praised the Gothic optimism of medieval architecture and art, and they shared that period's devotion to art as high craft. In "Notre Dame," Mandelstam praises the church's "massive walls," its "elemental labyrinth." The cathedral becomes both that which the poet studies and that from which he is inspired to create something of his own. The outstretched body of Adam furnishes a metaphor for the opening description of the cathedral's vaulted ceiling. Adam's name, and his having been "joyful and first," had once provided an alternative name for Acmeism, Adamism, which never took hold. The name "Adam," nevertheless, invokes in "Notre Dame" the poetic principles of the movement, its clarity, its balance, its sense of the poem as something visibly constructed. "Notre Dame" is as close to a programmatic statement in verse as Mandelstam ever came; the poem does what a Gothic cathedral should do, "revealing its secret plan from the outside."

TRISTIA

Mandelstam's second volume, *Tristia*, appeared in 1922. Compared to the architectural poems of *Stone*, many drawing on the Roman tradition in classical culture, *Tristia* depends more on the myths of ancient Greece. It evokes the landscape of the Mediterranean or Crimean seas to frame tender, interiorized poems. The title is the same as that of a work by Ovid, written during his exile, and the connotations of *tristia*, both emotional and literary, resonate throughout the volume, though the title was not initially of Mandelstam's choosing. The title poem, "Tristia," addresses the difficulties of separation, the science of which the speaker says he has studied to the point of knowing it well. There are several kinds of separation involved, from women seeing men off to battle in stanza 1 to men and women facing their particular deaths in stanza 4. The poet feels the difficulty of moving from one kind of separation to another in stanza 3, where he complains, "How poor is the language of joy." Ovid's exile has been a continuous event since he wrote his *Tristia* (after 8 C.E.). There is joy in recognizing the repetition of historical and personal events; Mandelstam here performs his usual chronological sleight of hand in juxtaposing several ages in history, rising toward divinations of the future in the final stanza.

The moment of recognition or remembrance is sought after in vain in "Ia slovo pozabyl, chto ia khotel skazat'" ("I Have Forgotten the Word I Wanted to Say"). Like its companion poem "Kogda Psikheia-zhizn' spuskaetsia k teniam" ("When Psyche-Life Descends to the Shades"), the poem evokes the failure to remember poetic words as a descent into Hades. The close correspondence between these two psyche poems is characteristic of Mandelstam: The presentation of variants demonstrates his belief that the drafts of a poem are never lost. These poems also demonstrate the general Acmeist principle that there is no final or closed version of any work of literature.

PSYCHE POEMS

In the psyche poems, mythological figures are mentioned, such as Persephone or Antigone for their descent into the Underworld or for their devotion to the funeral ritual, respectively. The river mentioned in both poems is not Lethe, the river of forgetfulness, but Styx, the boundary of Hades. Forgetfulness plagues both poems, however; "I Have Forgotten the Word I Wanted to Say," a formula repeated in one poem, equates the fear of death's oblivion with the loss of poetry. The images of the dry riverbed, of birds that cannot be heard, of a blind swallow with clipped wings—all suggest an artist's sterility. It is the dead who revive an ability to remember (hence their avoidance of the river Lethe), to recognize meanings as significant as those of the divining women at the end of "Tristia." With the slowness so crucial to the entire volume, something develops in "I Have Forgotten the Word I Wanted to Say." In "When Psyche-Life Descends to the Shades," the soul is slow to hand over her payment for crossing the river. The "unincarnated thought" returns to the Underworld, but the black ice of its remembered sound burns on the poet's lips. For Mandelstam, lips (like breathing), suggest the act of composing poetry, so that these twin poems conclude with a kind of optimism, however fearful.

Several poems in *Tristia* treat the social causes of Mandelstam's fear of poetic failure, among them two of his most famous: "Sumerki svobody" ("The Twilight of Freedom") and "V Peterburge my soidomsia snova" ("In Petersburg We Shall Meet Again"). Both poems respond to the Revolution of 1917 ambiguously if not pessimistically. The sun both rises and sets in "The Twilight of Freedom," where the "twilight" of the title could mean "sunset" as well as "dawn." "In Petersburg We Shall Meet Again" also chooses an ambiguous source of light; the sun is buried and the "night sun" illuminates the final stanza.

Images from the psyche poems reappear with more pronounced political overtones. In "The Twilight of Freedom," there are immobilized swallows, bound into "fighting legions." The people appear as both powerful and restrained, expressing perfectly Mandelstam's perception of the Revolution as potentially empowering but finally overpowering. In "In Petersburg We Shall Meet Again," the "blessed, meaningless word" that the poet feared forgetting in the Psyche poems seems miraculously renewed. The poem displays terrifying sights and sounds, from ominous patrols to whizzing sirens, yet the speaker clings to his "word" as if oblivious of everything else. The poem closes with a crowd leaving a theater, where the end of the performance suggests the end of an entire culture. Yet, as in the exhortation to be brave in "The Twilight of Freedom," the poetic voice affirms its power to live beyond the threats of "Lethe's cold" or the "Soviet night." What endures in *Tristia*, though with difficulty, is what seemed immutable in *Stone*: faith in the word as the center of Russian culture.

POEMS

In 1928, Mandelstam published a volume of poems comprising revised versions of *Stone* and *Tristia*, as well as some twenty new poems. Several had appeared in the second edition of *Tristia*. These poems are even less optimistic than the ambiguous poems of *Tristia*; they are permeated by a fear of disorder that so threatened Mandelstam's voice that he ceased writing poems altogether from 1925 to 1930. The city arches its back threateningly in "In Petersburg We Shall Meet Again"; the back is broken in "Vek" ("The Age"). The age is dying in "Net, nikogda nichei ia ne byl sovremennik" ("No, I Was Never Anyone's Contemporary"), a poem whose first line discloses as well as any of his works Mandelstam's alienated state of mind. The source of light in these poems is not the sun, not even the occluded or nighttime sun, but stars that look down menacingly from the evening firmament. The air is steamy, foamy, dark, and watery, as impossible to breathe as the sky is to behold. Not being able to breathe, like not being able to speak, conveys Mandelstam's extraordinary difficulty in writing during this period.

"SLATE ODE" AND "THE HORSESHOE FINDER"

Two of Mandelstam's most startling and most difficult poems date from the early 1920's: "Nashedshii podkovu" ("The Horseshoe Finder") and "Grifel' naia oda"

("Slate Ode"). The poems test and affirm poetry's ability to endure despite the shifting values of the age. "The Horseshoe Finder" binds together long, irregular verse lines without rhyme (a new form for Mandelstam) by repeating and interweaving clusters of consonants. Rejecting the slow realizations of *Tristia*, the poem moves quickly from one metaphorical cluster to another. Finding the horseshoe, also a talismanic emblem for poetry in "Slate Ode," is like finding the bottled message in Mandelstam's essay "On the Addressee." The past can still be transmitted in "The Horseshoe Finder": "Human lips . . . preserve the form of the last spoken word," but these lips "have nothing more to say."

"LENINGRAD"

Mandelstam resumed writing poetry in 1930, and, had the official literary establishment not been forcing him out of print, there could easily have emerged a third volume of verse from the poems written in Moscow and Voronezh. A clear task unites many of these poems, a task of self-definition. The fate of the poet has become a metaphor for the fate of the culture, so that intensely personal poems avoid all solipsism. The triangular relationship "world-self-text" emerges as a conflict to be resolved anew in each poem. Mandelstam returned to Leningrad, "familiar to the point of tears." In his poem "Leningrad," Mandelstam proclaims against all odds, echoing the famous Pushkin line, that he does not want to die. Death moves inevitably through the poem, though, as his address book leads only to "dead voices"; the poet lives on back stairs, awaiting guests who rattle a ball and chain.

Mandelstam was arrested for the often-quoted epigram about Stalin; describing "cockroach whiskers" and "fat fingers, like worms," the poem was perhaps his angriest of the period. The secret police could have arrested Mandelstam, however, for any number of works from the early 1930's. Hatred of the "songs" with which the Soviets had supplied the new age, disgust at the ethos of the Socialist Utopia, and fear that Russia's genuine cultural heritage would perish are frequent themes. Mandelstam wanted no part of the changes around him; he names himself as the "unrecognized brother, an outcast in the family of man" in a poem dedicated to Anna Akhmatova, his dear friend and fellow poet who also suffered ostracism.

In the South and in Moscow, Mandelstam was befriended by several biologists. They inspired him to read Jean-Baptiste Lamarck, Charles Darwin, and other authors who in turn provided Mandelstam with a new metaphor for expressing his dislike of the age's paeans to "progress." In "Lamarck," Mandelstam chooses to occupy the lowest step on the evolutionary ladder rather than join in the false advances urged by the government. These steps bring humankind down in the evolutionary chain, observes the poet, toward species that cannot hear, speak, or breathe—toward those that do not produce poetry. The age, in copious images of the silence of deafness, has grown dumb; self-definition nears self-denigration as the surrounding cultural edifices crumble and threaten to bring the new Soviet literature down with them.

Destruction, pain, death, terror—these are the themes that dominate the post-1930 poems to a degree that would separate them from the poems written before 1925 even if there were no other distinctions. As Mandelstam wrote poems inspired by the chaos around him, so also the poems formally demonstrated the pervasiveness of chaos. Disintegration became both subject matter and structuring principle: The late poems demonstrate an openness, fragmentation, and avoidance of conventional poetic diction, meter, and rhyme that would have been inconceivable in the beautifully formed poems of *Stone* or *Tristia*. The early predilection for exact rhyme is reshaped by an admixture of near rhymes of all sorts. The poems grow rich in internal paronomasia, where interweavings of sounds create controlling structures in lines that seem otherwise arbitrarily ordered. The rhythms grow freer during the 1930's as well. Mandelstam had used free verse in the 1920's, as in "The Horseshoe Finder," and returned to it for longer, more complex works such as "Polnoch' v Moskve" ("Midnight in Moscow"). Conventionally metered poems include aberrant lines of fewer or more metrical feet or with entirely different schemes; conversely, the free verse of "Midnight in Moscow" permits interpolated lines of perfect or near-perfect meter.

The spontaneity that the late poems explore represents the final version of Mandelstam's longstanding commitment to the openness of the poetic text. Including fragments of conversation and unconventional constructions in these poems, Mandelstam was converting the destructive chaos around him to his own ends. Hence the fluidity of "cross-references" in his poetry, particularly in the late verse, where there are not only "twin" or "triplet" poems, as Nadezhda Mandelstam called them, but also entire cycles of variants, among them the poems on the death of Bely in 1934. Moving beyond the concrete referentiality of the early poems, the late Mandelstam dramatizes rather than describes the act of self-definition. The communicative act between poet and reader overrides the encoding act between poet and world, as the reader is drawn deeply into the process of decoding the poet's relationships with his world and his poems.

Mandelstam's confidence that a reader would someday seek to understand even his most labyrinthine poems shines through unexpectedly during the late period. There are love poems to his wife and others—among the most remarkable is "Masteritsa vinovatykh vzorov" ("Mistress of Guilty Glances")—as well as poems wherein renunciation yields extraordinary strength. Mandelstam's enduring gift, long after he had himself fallen victim to the society at odds with him, was to find strength in the deepest threats to his identity. Hence, the halfhearted desire to write an ode to Stalin, which might save his wife after his own death, gave rise instead to a host of deeply honest poems that were as hopeful as they were embattled. Though the simple longings of the late poems may be futile, the act of recording his desires into completely threatened poems represents Mandelstam's typical achievement in the late works.

OTHER MAJOR WORKS

SHORT FICTION: *Yegipetskaya marka*, 1928 (*The Egyptian Stamp*, 1965).

NONFICTION: *O prirode slova*, 1922 (*About the Nature of the Word*, 1977); *Feodosiya*, 1925 (autobiography; *Theodosia*, 1965); *Shum vremeni*, 1925 (autobiography; *The Noise of Time*, 1965); *O poezii*, 1928 (*About Poetry*, 1977); *Puteshestviye v Armeniyu*, 1933 (travel sketch; *Journey to Armenia*, 1973); *Chetvertaia proza*, 1966 (wr. 1930 or 1931; *Fourth Prose*, 1970); *Razgovor o Dante*, 1967 (*Conversation About Dante*, 1965); *Selected Essays*, 1977; *Slovo i kul'tura: Stat'i*, 1987.

CHILDREN'S LITERATURE: *Dva tramvaya*, 1925; *Primus*, 1925; *Kukhnya*, 1926; *Shary*, 1926.

MISCELLANEOUS: *Sobranie sochinenii*, 1955, 1964-1971, 1981 (*Collected Works*, 1967-1969); *The Complete Critical Prose and Letters*, 1979.

BIBLIOGRAPHY

Baines, Jennifer. *Mandelstam: The Later Poetry*. New York: Cambridge University Press, 1976. Scholarly treatment of Mandelstam's poems written in Moscow and Voronezh in the 1930's. The study of these poems has been somewhat neglected because of their enigmatic nature.

Brown, Clarence. *Mandelstam*. New York: Cambridge University Press, 1973. The best authority on Mandel stam in the English-speaking world presents his seminal work, covering all aspects of Mandelstam's life and work. Brown's analyses of Mandelstam's poems are particularly valuable.

Broyde, Steven. *Osip Mandelstam and His Age: A Commentary on the Themes of War and Revolution in the Poetry, 1913-1923*. Cambridge, Mass.: Harvard University Press, 1975. A detailed analysis of Mandelstam's poems inspired by, and centered on, war and revolution. There are many citations of poems, in Russian and in English.

Cavanagh, Clare. *Osip Mandelstam and the Modernist Creation of Tradition*. Princeton, N.J.: Princeton University Press, 1995. Places Mandelstam within the modernist tradition of T. S. Eliot and Ezra Pound of reflecting a "world culture" divorced from strict national or ethnic identity.

Glazov-Corrigan, Elena. *Mandel'shtam's Poetics: A Challenge to Postmodernism*. Toronto, Ont.: University of Toronto Press, 2000. Analyses Mandelstam's thoughts on poetry and art in the context of the major postmodern literary debates and traces their development throughout his writings. Describes Mandelstam's intellectual world and its effect on his evolution as a thinker, specifically, on differences in his attitude toward language.

Mandelstam, Nadezhda. *Hope Against Hope: A Memoir*. New York: Atheneum, 1970. The first volume of memoirs written by Mandelstam's wife, dealing with biographical details but also with the genesis of many of Mandelstam's poetms.

_____. *Hope Abandoned*. New York: Atheneum, 1974. The second volume of the memoirs.

Pollack, Nancy. *Mandelstam the Reader*. Baltimore: The Johns Hopkins University Press, 1995. A study of Mandelstam's late verse and prose. The two genres receive approximately equal treatment, but the analyses of poems tend to be deeper.

Prsybylski, Ryszard. *An Essay on the Poetry of Osip Mandelstam: God's Grateful Guest*. Translated by Madeline G. Levine. Ann Arbor, Mich.: Ardis, 1987. A noted Polish scholar treats Mandelstam's attraction to, and reflection of, Greek and Roman classicism, the musical quality of his poetry, his affinity to architecture and archaeology, and other features of the poetry. The author places Mandelstam in the framework of world literature.

Zeeman, Peter. *The Later Poetry of Osip Mandelstam: Text and Context*. Amsterdam: Rodopi, 1988. Detailed interpretations and analyses of Mandelstam's poems written in the 1930's. Zeeman uses primarily contextualization and historical reconstruction in his discussion of the poems, some of which are among the most difficult of all Mandelstam's poems .

Stephanie Sandler

VLADIMIR MAYAKOVSKY

Born: Bagdadi, Georgia, Russian Empire (now Mayakovsky, Georgia); July 19, 1893
Died: Moscow, Soviet Union (now in Russia); April 14, 1930

OTHER LITERARY FORMS

Vladimir Mayakovsky (muh-yih-KAWF-skee) was primarily a poet, but he also wrote several plays, some prose works, and numerous propaganda pieces. His first play, *Vladimir Mayakovsky: Tragediya* (pr. 1913; *Vladimir Mayakovsky: A Tragedy*, 1968), displayed the characteristics that would become associated with him throughout his career: audacity, bombastic exuberance, a predilection for hyperbole, an undercurrent of pessimism, and, above all, an uncontrollable egotism (underscored by the title). In *Misteriya-buff* (pr., pb. 1918, 1921; *Mystery-bouffe*, 1933), subtitled "A Heroic, Epic and Satiric Presentation of Our Epoch," which Helen Muchnic has termed "a cartoon version of Marxist history," Mayakovsky presents the events of World War I as a class struggle between the Clean (the bourgeoisie) and the Unclean (the proletariat). His best two plays, written in the last years of his life, contain sharp satirical attacks on Soviet society. *Klop* (pr., pb. 1929; *The Bedbug*, 1931) depicts a proletarian in the 1920's who forsakes his class by showing bourgeois tendencies. He perishes in the fire during his tumultuous wedding. Resurrected after fifty years, he finds himself forsaken in turn by the future Soviet society. Mayakovsky's warnings about the possibly pernicious direction of the development of Soviet society fell on deaf ears, as did his attacks on Soviet bureaucracy in his last major work, *Banya* (pr., pb. 1930; *The Bathhouse*, 1963). Both plays were complete failures when they were performed in the last year of the author's life. Among the best plays in Soviet literature, they met with greater approval three decades later.

ACHIEVEMENTS

Perhaps Vladimir Mayakovsky's greatest achievement as a poet was his incarnation of the revolutionary spirit in Russian literature. He was indeed the primary poet of the Russian Revolution: Right or wrong, he was able to instill the revolutionary spirit into his poetry and to pass it over to his readers. His hold on their fancy and admiration is still alive today. As a member of the Futurist movement, which he helped to organize in Russia, he brought new life into poetry by providing a viable alternative to Symbolism, which had been the dominant force in Russian poetry in the preceding two decades. Mayakovsky effected many innovations by following trends in other national literatures, thus bringing Russian poetry closer to the mainstream of world literature. He could not speak or read any foreign language, but he was always keenly interested in other literatures. His inimitable free verse set a standard for decades. He made the language of the street acceptable to the newly developing taste of both readers and critics, thus appealing to a wide audience despite his excesses. He has had many followers among poets, but none of them has been able to approximate his greatness.

BIOGRAPHY

Vladimir Vladimirovich Mayakovsky was born on July 19, 1893, in Bagdadi (a small town that was later renamed after him), where his father was a forester. From his early childhood, he showed himself to be independent and strong-willed. Although he was not a very good student, he possessed a remarkable memory for facts and long passages from poetry and other books. His childhood and early youth passed amid social unrest and rebellions. Because his entire family leaned toward the revolutionaries, Mayakovsky, too, participated in workers' demonstrations, giving his father's guns to the rebels, reading Socialist literature, and preparing himself for a lifelong revolutionary activism.

In 1906, after the death of Mayakovsky's father, the family moved to Moscow, where Mayakovsky entered high school and continued his association with the revolutionaries. He was accepted by the Communist Party when he was only fourteen and was arrested three times for his underground work. The last time, he was kept in jail eleven months, during which he read voraciously, becoming familiar with the classics of Russian literature for the first time. After his release, he decided to go back to school rather than devote all his time to political activity. Because of his activism, however, he was allowed to enroll only in an art school, where he fostered his natural talent for drawing and painting. There, he met David Burlyuk, an artist and poet who encouraged him not only in his artistic endeavors but also as a poet, after Mayakovsky's timid beginnings. Together they formed the backbone of the Russian Futurists, a group that had some affinities with Filippo Tommaso Marinetti's Futurism, although Russian Futurism originated independently from the Italian movement. In 1912, the Russian Futurists issued a manifesto, appropriately titled "Poshchechina obshchestvennomu vkusu" ("A Slap in the Face of the Public Taste"), which included a poem by Mayakovsky. He spent the years before the Russian Revolution writing and publishing poetry, making scandal-provoking public appearances, continuing his revolutionary activity, and impressing everyone with his powerful voice and imposing physique, especially the police. He was not called into the czarist army because of his political unreliability, but during the Revolution, as well as in its aftermath, he helped the cause by drawing posters and writing captions for them and composing slogans, marching songs, and propaganda leaflets.

After the Revolution, however, Mayakovsky began to voice his dissatisfaction with Soviet policies and to fight the burgeoning bureaucracy, which remained his greatest enemy for the rest of his life. He especially disliked the seeming betrayal of revolutionary ideals on the part of the new Soviet establishment. He fell in love with Lili Brik, the wife of his close friend, the critic Osip Brik. He traveled abroad often, including a four-month-long trip to the United States, to which he reacted both favorably and critically. During his visit to Paris, he fell in love with a young Russian émigré woman. His efforts to persuade her to return with him to the Soviet Union were fruitless. This failure, along with other disappointments, led to periods of depression. He had become one of the leading poets in Soviet literature and the poet of the Russian Revolution, yet he and the circle centered on the journal *LEF* (founded by Mayakovsky in 1923) fought protracted and bitter battles with the literary establishment.

LEF, an acronym standing for *Levy front iskusstva* ("left front of art"), was an independent movement of avant-garde artists and writers organized under Mayakovsky's leadership. As Soviet cultural policy, initially supportive of the avant-garde, turned more conservative, LEF was suppressed, and its eponymous journal was forced to cease publication. In January of 1930, an exhibition that Mayakovsky organized to celebrate his twenty years of writing and graphic work was boycotted by Soviet cultural officials and fellow writers. His increasing dissatisfaction with the regime, his repeated failures in love, a prolonged throat illness, the failure of his plays, and a deep-seated disposition toward self-destruction, which he had often expressed in the past, caused him to commit suicide in his Moscow apartment on April 14, 1930. His death stunned the nation but also provoked harsh criticism of his act. A few years later, however, he received his due as a poet and as a revolutionary, a recognition that is increasing with time.

ANALYSIS

Vladimir Mayakovsky's poetry can be divided into three general categories. In the first group are the poems with political themes, often written on ephemeral occasions as everyday political exigencies demanded. These poems represent the weakest and indeed some of the silliest verses in his opus and are, for the most part, forgotten. The second group contains his serious revolutionary poems, in which he expressed his loyalty to the Revolution as a way of life and as "the holy washerwoman [who] will wash away all filth from the face of the earth with her soap." There are some excellent poems in this group, for they reflect Mayakovsky's undying faith in, and need for, an absolute that would give him strength to live and create, an absolute that he found in communism. Undoubtedly the best poems from the aesthetic point of view, however, are those from the third group, in which Mayakovsky writes about himself and his innermost feelings. These poems, which are more revealing of his true personality than all the loudly proclaimed utterances that made him famous, are the most likely to endure.

Mayakovsky's development as a poet parallels closely his life experiences. As he was growing into a fiery young revolutionary, his early poetry reflected his ebullience and combative spirit. His first poems, contained in Futurist publications, revealed his intoxication with the enormous power of words, a spirit that informs his entire oeuvre. The Futurist movement offered Mayakovsky a suitable platform from which to shout his messages. Indeed, it is difficult to say whether he joined Futurism for its tenets or Futurism embraced his volcanic energy, both as a poet and an activist, for its own purposes. The Futurists conceived of art as a social force and of the artist as a spokesperson for his age. To this end, new avenues of expression had to be found in the form of a "trans-sense" language in which words are based not so much on their meaning as on sounds and form.

YA AND A CLOUD IN PANTS

Much of Futurist dogma found in Mayakovsky an eager practitioner and an articulate spokesperson. His first serious work, a collection of four poems under the title *Ya*, already shows his intentions of "thrusting the dagger of desperate words/ into the swollen pulp of the sky." His most important prerevolutionary work, the long poem *A Cloud in Pants*, begins as a lamentation about an unanswered love but later turns into a treatise on social ills, punctuated forcefully with slogans such as "Down with your love!" "Down with your art!" "Down with your social order!" "Down with your religion!" Such pugnacity corresponds closely to the irreverent rejection of the status quo in the Futurist manifesto "A Slap in the Face of the Public Taste":

> The past is stifling. The Academy and Pushkin are incomprehensible hieroglyphs. We must throw Pushkin, Dostoevsky, Tolstoy, etc. from the boat of modernity.

The title of the poem reveals Mayakovsky's predilection for a striking metaphor: The cloud symbolizes the poet flying high above everything, while the trousers bring him down to Earth.

150,000,000

The poems Mayakovsky wrote during the Revolution bear more or less the same trademarks. The most characteristic of them, *150,000,000*, was inspired by the American intervention in the Russian Civil War on the side of anti-Bolsheviks. It was published anonymously (the ruse did not work, though), as if 150 million Soviet citizens had written it. The central theme, the struggle between the East and the West, is depicted in a typically Mayakovskian fashion. The East is personified by Ivan (the most common Russian name), who has 150 million heads and whose arms are as long as the Neva River. The West is represented by President Woodrow Wilson, who wears a hat in the form of the Eiffel Tower. Undoubtedly the poet believed that the more grotesque the expression, the more effective the message. He sets the tone at the very beginning:

> 150,000,000 are the makers of this poem.
> Its rhythm is a bullet.
> Its rhyme is fire sweeping from building to building.
> 150,000,000 speak with my lips.
> This edition is printed
> with human steps
> on the paper of city squares.

The protagonist of the poem is in reality the masses, as in another work of this time, the play *Mystery-bouffe*, and in many other works by Mayakovsky. This tendency of the poet to lose himself behind the anonymity of collectivism runs alongside an equally strong tendency to place himself in the center of the universe and to have an inflated opinion of himself, as shown in "An Extraordinary Adventure," where he invites the sun to a tea as an equally important partner in the process of creativity.

SUPPORTING THE REVOLUTION

After the Revolution, Mayakovsky continued to help the regime establish itself, to contribute to the new literature in his country, and to feud with other literary groups. With the introduction of the New Economic Policy (NEP), however, which allowed a return to a modified, small-scale capitalism, Mayakovsky was among many supporters of the Revolution who felt that the ideals for which so much had been sacrificed were being betrayed. His opposition was somewhat muted; instead of attacking directly, he found a surrogate in the ever-growing bureaucracy. He also detected a resurgence of bourgeois and philistine habits, even among the party members and supporters of the regime, who, "callousing their behinds from five-year sittings,/ shiny-hard as washbasin toilets," worried more about their raises and ball attire than about society's welfare. In the poem "In Re Conferences," he lashes out at the new malaise in the Russian society—incessant conferences, actually an excuse to evade work. At the same time, in "Order No. 2 to the Army of the Arts," he exhorts artists to "give us a new form of art." When Vladimir Ilich Lenin died in 1924, Mayakovsky wrote a long poem eulogizing the great leader, using this opportunity to reaffirm his loyalty to pure communism as personified by Lenin.

ABOUT THAT

During this period, along with poetry on political themes, Mayakovsky wrote poems of an excruciatingly personal nature. The best illustration of this dichotomy in his personality, and one of the most dramatic and disturbing love poems in world literature, *About That*, reveals the poet's unhappiness in his love affair with Lili Brik. More important, however, it lays bare his "agony of isolation, a spiritual isolation," in the words of Helen Muchnic. Belaboring the nature of love, which he does on numerous occasions, the poet is forced to conclude that he is destined to suffer defeat after defeat in love, for reasons he cannot understand. He calls for help, he considers suicide, and he feels abandoned by all, even by those who are closest to him. In retrospect, one can see in these expressions of loneliness and despair signs of what was to come several years later.

BEYOND THE SOVIET UNION

For the time being, however, Mayakovsky found enough strength to continue his various activities and skirmishes with many enemies. A fateful decision was put off during his several trips abroad in the mid-1920's. In poems resulting from these journeys, he was remarkably objective about the world outside the Soviet Union, although he never failed to mention his pride in being a Soviet citizen. In addition to predictable criticism of the evils of capitalist societies, he expressed his awe before the technical achievements of Western urban centers:

> Here
> stood Mayakovsky,
> stood
> composing verse, syllable by syllable.
> I stare
> as an Eskimo gapes at a train,
> I seize on it
> as a tick fastens to an ear.
> Brooklyn Bridge—
> yes . . .
> That's quite a thing!

It was easy for Mayakovsky to voice such unrestrained praise for the "wonders" of the modern world, for he always believed that the urban life was the only way of life worth living.

The trips abroad, however, troubled Mayakovsky more than he acknowledged. In addition to another unhappy love affair, with the beautiful young Russian émigré Tatyana Yakovleva, he was disturbed by his firsthand experience of the West. After his return, he wrote several poems affirming his loyalty to the Soviet regime in a manner suggesting that he was trying to convince himself of his orthodoxy. It is difficult to ascertain, however, whether Mayakovsky was fully aware at this time of the depth of his obsequiousness and, if he was, why he wrote that way. Several years later, in *At the Top of My Voice*, which was written only three months before his suicide, he would admit the true nature of his submission: "But I/ subdued/ myself,/ setting my heel/ on the throat/ of my own song."

FINE!

Another long poem, *Fine!*, written to celebrate the tenth anniversary of the October Revolution, shows not only Mayakovsky's compulsive optimism but also the signs that his poetic power was diminishing: "Life/ was really/ never/ so good!" he exclaims unabashedly.

> In the cottages
> —farmer lads
> Bushy-beards
> cabbages.
> Dad's rest
> by the hearth.
> All of them
> crafty.
> Plough the earth,
> make
> poetry.

Such idyllic gushing may have reflected truthfully the poet's feelings and observations in 1927, but it is remarkable that only a year or two later he would unleash in his plays a scathing criticism of the same land where "gladness gushes." It is more likely that Mayakovsky wanted to believe what he had written or, more tragically, that he was writing in compliance with an order for a certain kind of poem.

DEPRESSION AND SUICIDE

Mayakovsky's suicide in 1930 showed that everything was not all right, either in his personal life or in his country. Although the act surprised many people, even those professing to have been very close to him, keen observers had felt that Mayakovsky was riddled with morbid pessimism throughout his mature life, his loud rhetoric notwithstanding. Indeed, one could go as far back as 1913 to find, in his very first poem, words such as these: "I am so lonely as the only eye/ of a man on his way to the blind." As early as 1916, in *The Backbone Flute*, he wondered whether he should end his life with a bullet. On another occasion at about that time, in "Chelovek" ("Man"), he stated bluntly:

> The heart yearns for a bullet
> while
> the throat raves of a razor

> . . . The soul shivers;
> she's caught in ice,
> and there's no escape for her.

In a poem discussed earlier, *About That*, he debates with himself whether he should follow the example of a member of the Communist Youth League who had committed suicide. In his last completed poem, *At the Top of My Voice*, he addresses his "most respected comrades of posterity" to explain what he had wanted to achieve in poetry, not trusting contemporary literary critics and historians to tell the truth. Among the incomplete poems found in his apartment after his death, there was a quatrain that may have been intended by Mayakovsky as a suicide note:

> And, as they say, the incident is closed.
> Love's boat has smashed against the daily grind.
> Now you and I are quits. Why bother then
> to balance mutual sorrows, pains, and hurts.

The word "love" in the second line was changed to "life" by Mayakovsky in a handwritten version of this stanza.

Whatever the reasons for his suicide, Mayakovsky's death brought to an end a promising career that symbolized for a long time the birth of the new spirit in Russian literature. The eminent literary critic Roman Jakobson saw in his death the work of an entire generation that had squandered its poets. Boris Pasternak brought into focus a virtue of many Soviet writers, both well known and unsung, when he speculated that Mayakovsky "shot himself out of pride because he had condemned something in himself or around himself with which his self-respect could not be reconciled." Placing the heavy hand of officialdom on the memory of the poet who had spent half of his life fighting insensitive officials, Joseph Stalin praised him belatedly: "Mayakovsky was and remains the best and most talented poet of our Soviet epoch. Indifference to his memory and his work is a crime."

VERSIFICATION AND NEOLOGISMS

The work of this great poet will survive both his human weaknesses and the vagaries of the time and place in which he had to create. Although Mayakovsky was not the first in Russian poetry to use free verse, he wrote it with a verve unequaled before or after him. He rhymes sparingly and unconventionally. He seldom divides verses into stanzas; instead, he breaks them into units according to their inner rhythm, producing a cascading effect.

Another strong feature of Mayakovsky's verse is the abundant use of neologisms; there is an entire dictionary of expressions created by him. Mayakovsky also used slang with abandon, deeming any expression acceptable if it suited his purpose; he is credited with bringing the language of the street into Russian poetry. The sound of his verse is richly textured—indeed, his poems are better heard than read.

When this richness of style is added to his original approach to poetry and to his thought-provoking subject matter, the picture of Mayakovsky as one of the most important and exciting poets of the twentieth century is complete.

OTHER MAJOR WORKS

PLAYS: *Vladimir Mayakovsky: Tragediya*, pr. 1913 (*Vladimir Mayakovsky: A Tragedy*, 1968); *Misteriya-buff*, pr., pb. 1918, 1921 (*Mystery-bouffe*, 1933); *A chto y esli? Pervomayskiye grezy v burzhuaznom kresle*, pr. 1920; *Chempionat vsemirnoy klassovoy borby*, pr. 1920 (*The Championship of the Universal Class*, 1973); *Pyeska pro popov, koi ne pobnimayut, prazdnik chto takoye*, pr. 1921; *Kak kto provodit vremya, prazdniki prazdnuya*, pr. 1922; *Radio-Oktyabr*, pr. 1926 (with Osip Brik); *Klop*, pr., pb. 1929 (*The Bedbug*, 1931); *Banya*, pr., pb. 1930 (*The Bathhouse*, 1963); *Moskva gorit*, pr. 1930 (*Moscow Is Burning*, 1973); *The Complete Plays*, 1968.

SCREENPLAYS: *Baryyshyna i khuligan*, 1918; *Ne dlya deneg rodivshiisya*, 1918 (adaptation of Jack London's novel *Martin Eden*); *Serdtse kino*, 1926; *Dekadyuvkov i Oktyabryukhov*, 1928.

NONFICTION: "Kak rabotaet respublika demokraticheskaya," 1922; "Kak delat' stikhi?," 1926 (*How Are Verses Made?*, 1970); *Moye Otkrytiye Ameriki*, 1926 (*My Discovery of America*, 2005).

BIBLIOGRAPHY

Aizlewood, Robin. *Two Essays on Maiakovskii's Verse*. London: University College London Press, 2000. Two short studies of selected poetic works by Mayakovsky.

Almereyda, Michael, ed. *Night Wraps the Sky: Writings by and About Mayakovsky.* New York: Farrar, Straus and Giroux, 2008. Filmmaker Almereyda gathers translations of Mayakovsky's poetry, along with memoirs, artistic appreciations, and eyewitness accounts to produce a profile of a man.

Brown, Edward J. *Mayakovsky: A Poet in the Revolution*. Princeton, N.J.: Princeton University Press, 1973. Discussion of Mayakovsky in his times and in relationship to artists, poets, critics, and revolutionaries including Vladimir Ilich Lenin and Joseph Stalin. Shows how Mayakovsky's work was shaped by events of his life and discusses his relationship to the Soviet state and Communist Party.

Cavanaugh, Clare. "Whitman, Mayakovsky, and the Body Politic." In *Rereading Russian Poetry*, edited by Stephanie Sandler. New Haven, Conn.: Yale University Press, 1999. Discusses the influence of the American poet Walt Whitman on Mayakovsky and the ways in which Mayakovsky sought to overcome this influence or to displace Whitman as a poet of the people and of self-celebration. This fresh, postmodern perspective emphasizes the body and sexuality in the work of Mayakovsky, in terms both literal and symbolic.

Stapanian, Juliette R. *Mayakovsky's Cubo-Futurist Vision*. Houston, Tex.: Rice University Press, 1986. Examines Mayakovsky from the perspective of the artistic movements of cubism and Futurism. Places Mayakovsky not simply within the social and political revolutionary movements of his day but also within the aesthetics of literary and artistic modernism.

Woroszylski, Wiktor. *The Life of Mayakovsky*. New York: Orion Press, 1970. The life of Mayakovsky as told through a variety of records, testimonies, and recollections, which are then arranged in accordance with the author's understanding of their place in Mayakovsky's life. Recollections include that of Boris Pasternak, Ilya Ehrenberg, Lily Brik, and Ivan Bunin. Includes copious illustrations and passages from Mayakovsky's poetry.

Vasa D. Mihailovich

ADAM MICKIEWICZ

Born: Zaosie, Lithuania; December 24, 1798
Died: Burgas, Turkey; November 26, 1855

OTHER LITERARY FORMS

In the last twenty years of his life, Adam Mickiewicz (meets-KYEH-veech), the national bard and prophet of Poland, wrote only a handful of poems, turning instead to religious and political works and to literary criticism. The messianic fervor of Mickiewicz's prose is exemplified by *Ksiegi narodu polskiego i pielgrzymstwa polskiego* (1832; *The Books of the Polish Nation and of the Polish Pilgrims*, 1833, 1925), a tract written in a quasi-biblical style. Mickiewicz's lectures given at the Collège de France in Paris, where from 1840 to 1844 he held the first chair of Slavic literature, fill several volumes of his complete works.

ACHIEVEMENTS

Adam Mickiewicz embodied in his work the soul of the Polish people. Through his poetry, he symbolized the land, history, and customs of Poland. Starting as a classicist and then quickly becoming a Romantic, he portrayed the everyday life of the Polish people and, at the same time, gave voice to visions and prophecies. His poems, written to be understood by the common man, brought him instant popular acclaim but also exposed him to attacks from many critics, who condemned his Romanticism and his provincial idioms.

The first volume of Mickiewicz's poetry was published in Wilno in an edition of five hundred copies. It contained ballads and romances, genres of poetry then unknown in Poland, and portrayed the common people in a simple but eloquent manner. A second volume followed in 1823, containing *Grażyna*, a tale in verse, and parts 2 and 4 of a fragmentary fantastic drama, *Forefathers' Eve*. With the publication of these works, followed by the narrative poem *Konrad Wallenrod*, set in medieval Lithuania, Mickiewicz became the founder of the Romantic movement in Polish literature. During his greatest creative period, in the years from 1832 to 1834, Mickiewicz published part 3 of *Forefathers' Eve*, which seethed with the eternal hatred felt by the Poles for their Russian conquerors. With its publication, Mickiewicz became a national defender, proclaiming that Poland was the Christ among nations, crucified for the sins of others. Like a prophet, he predicted that Poland would rise again. *Pan Tadeusz*, Mickiewicz's masterpiece, was also written during this period. An epic poem in twelve books depicting Polish life in Lithuania in 1811 and 1812, it is the greatest work of Polish literature and perhaps the finest narrative poem in nineteenth century European literature. Devoid of hatred or mysticism, it warmly and realistically depicts the Polish land and people and embodies a firm faith in their future.

BIOGRAPHY

Adam Bernard Mickiewicz was born on December 24, 1798, on the farmstead of Zaosie, near Nowogródek, a small town in Lithuania. After the Tartars' savage destruction of Kiev in 1240, the area previously known as Byelorussia and the Ukraine were annexed by the warlike Grand Duchy of Lithuania. In four centuries, however, the Lithuanian gentry was almost completely Polonized, and after the union with the Polish Crown in 1386, Lithuania's territory was greatly reduced. In the district of Nowogródek, while the gentry was predominantly Polish (old immigrants from Mazovia), the peasants were Byelorussian. Mickiewicz's father, Mikolaj, was a lawyer and a small landowner. His mother, Barbara (Orzeszko) Majewska , was also from the middle gentry. Both families had a strong military tradition.

It is noteworthy that Mickiewicz, the national bard of Poland, the ardent patriot who gave such superb literary expression to the life and aspirations of the Polish people, never even saw Poland proper nor its cultural centers, Warsaw and Krakow. Moreover, during his lifetime, Poland did not exist as a sovereign state, for Mickiewicz was born after the so-called Final Partition of 1795, when Poland was divided among Russia, Prussia, and Austria-Hungary.

Mickiewicz, one of five sons, started his education at home and then continued at the Dominican parochial school in Nowogródek. Later, he studied philology at the University of Wilno, where he excelled in Latin and Polish literature. He was greatly influenced by a liberal historian, Joachim Lelewel, who later became a leader in the Insurrection of 1830-1831. At the university, Mickiewicz was one of the six founders of the Philomathian Society, a secret society that emphasized Polish patriotism and tried to influence public affairs. After spending a short time in Kowno as a district teacher of Greek and Latin, Polish literature, and history, Mickiewicz returned to Wilno, where he maintained close relations with his friends in the Philomathian Society. In 1823, Mickiewicz and several of his friends were arrested by the Russian authorities for plotting to spread "senseless Polish nationalism" and were confined in the Basilian Monastery in Wilno, which had been converted to a prison. After their trial on November 6, 1824, Mickiewicz and his friend Jan Sobolewski were sent to St. Petersburg to work in an office.

In 1819, before his imprisonment and deportation, Mickiewicz met and fell in love with Maryla Wereszczaka, the daughter of a wealthy landowner. Maryla, however, complying with the wishes of her family, refused to marry Mickiewicz, who was only a poor student, and married the rich Count Puttkamer instead. Partially inspired by his unrequited love for Maryla, Mickiewicz turned to writing Romantic poetry and, with the publication of two small volumes of poetry in 1822 and 1823, became the founder of the Romantic school in Poland. His earlier writing shows the influence of the pseudo-classical style then prevalent in Poland.

Mickiewicz stayed in Russia almost four years and wrote his *Sonety* and *Sonnets from the Crimea* there as well as *Konrad Wallenrod* and "Faris," an Arabian tale. He lived in St. Petersburg, Odessa, and Moscow, where he was warmly accepted into literary circles, befriended by Alexander Pushkin and others, and made a welcome guest in the literary salon of Princess Zenaida Volkonsky (herself an accomplished poet, whom Pushkin called "tsarina of muses and beauty"). He often improvised there, gaining the admiration of Pushkin, who called him "Mickiewicz, inspired from above."

In 1829, Mickiewicz secured permission to leave Russia and lived for a time in Switzerland and then in Rome. The Polish Insurrection broke out in 1830, and Mickiewicz tried in vain to join the revolutionists in August, 1831. After the defeat of the insurrection, Mickiewicz settled in Paris, where he spent most of his remaining years. In 1834, he married Celina Szymanowski, the youngest daughter of Maria Szymanowski, a famous concert pianist, whom he had met while still in Russia. The marriage was unhappy because of her mental illness, and her early death left Mickiewicz with several small children. During this period, he wrote part 3 of *Forefathers' Eve*, a mystical and symbolic dramatic treatment of his imprisonment at Wilno by the Russian authorities. The poem embodied the anti-Russian feeling of the Polish people and intensified their hatred of their oppressor. Mickiewicz's next poem was his masterpiece, *Pan Tadeusz*, which glorifies the rustic life of the Polish gentry in picturesque Lithuanian Byelorussia and praises the Napoleonic invasion of Russia as symbolic of Poland's hope for liberation ("God is with Napoléon, Napoléon is with us"). *Pan Tadeusz* is a true national epic.

After the publication of his masterpiece, Mickiewicz fell under the influence of Andrzej Towianski, a charismatic figure who preached that a new period in Christianity was at hand and that he himself was its prophet. Unconditionally accepting Towianski's claims, Mickiewicz was compelled to give up his professorship at the Collège de France when he used his position to advance the doctrines of Towianski's sect. Mickiewicz spent his last years working for Polish independence and aiding fellow exiles. In 1855, following the outbreak in the previous year of the Crimean War, which he hailed as a prelude to the liberation of Poland, Mickiewicz went to Constantinople. He contracted cholera and died on November 26, 1855. His body was first sent to Paris; in 1890, it was brought to Wawel Castle in Krakow, where it now rests with Tadeusz Kościuszko and the Polish kings.

ANALYSIS

The Romantic movement had unique features in Poland, where it did not begin until the 1820's, some thirty years later than in England and Germany. The most prominent literary figure of Romanticism in Poland was Adam Mickiewicz, whose poetry grew out of his formative years in Lithuanian Byelorussia. Mickiewicz wrote poems that had universal as well as regional and national significance. A poet of genius, he raised Polish literature to a high level among Slavic literatures and to a prominent place in world literature.

Although he was in many respects the quintessential Romantic poet, Mickiewicz eludes categorization. There is a strong classical strain running throughout his oeuvre, evident in the clarity of his diction and the precision of his images. He combined meticulous observation of the familiar world with an evocation of spiritual realms and supernatural experience. His concerns as a poet went beyond poetry, reflecting a responsibility to his beloved, oppressed Poland and to humanity at large. As he was a spokesperson in exile for Polish freedom, so he remains a spokesperson for all those who share his hatred of tyranny.

FROM CLASSICISM TO ROMANTICISM

Mickiewicz's work in philology at the University of Wilno instilled in him the values of eighteenth century classicism. Accordingly, his first significant poem, "Oda do mlodości" ("Ode to Youth"), reflected the tradition of the Enlightenment, but it also contained some of the pathos of Romanticism. In the ballad "Romantyczność" ("The Romantic"), this pathos becomes the dominant tone. The poem concerns a woman who is mocked and regarded as insane because, in despair, she talks to the ghost of her beloved. Mickiewicz treats her sympathetically, concluding: "Faith and love are more discerning/ Than lenses or learning." Revealing a Slavic preference for faith and feeling rather than Western rationalism, Mickiewicz returned to these youthful ideas in his later, more complex works.

Mickiewicz's shift toward a thoroughgoing Romanticism was influenced by his reading of Italian, German, and English literature, by his study of early Lithuanian history, and by his love for Maryla Wereszczaka. With his first two volumes of poetry Mickiewicz raised the stature of Polish poetry. His first volume contained short poems, mainly a group of fourteen "ballads and romances" prefaced with a survey of world literature. "The Romantic," the programmatic poem of the Polish Romantic movement, expresses his faith in the influence of the spirit world on man.

FOREFATHERS' EVE, PARTS 2 AND 4

The second volume of Mickiewicz's poems contained the second and fourth parts of the incomplete fantastic drama, *Forefathers' Eve*; a short poem, "The Vampire," connected with that drama; and a short tale in verse, *Grażyna*. The genre of the fantastic drama was in fashion at the time. *Forefathers' Eve*, complete with ghosts and demons, was based on a folk rite that involved serving a meal to the spirits of the departed on All Souls' Day. Part 2 of *Forefathers' Eve* (the first part of the poem to be written) is an idealization of this rite, in which Mickiewicz probably had participated as a boy in Lithuanian Byelorussia. He explained that Forefathers' Eve is the name of a ceremony celebrated by the common folk in memory of their ancestors in many parts of Byelorussia, Lithuania, Prussia, and Courland. The ceremony, once called the Feast of the Goat, originated in pagan times and was frowned upon by the Church.

In the first part of *Forefathers' Eve*, for which he only completed a sketch, Mickiewicz appears in the guise of Gustav, a name taken from *Valérie* (1803), a sentimental novel by Baroness von Krüdener. Gustav kills himself, disappointed in his love for Maryla. In a revised version of part 2 of *Forefathers' Eve*, Mickiewicz added a section expressing his love for Maryla. He depicts Maryla as a "shepherdess in mourning dress" whose lover, Gustav, has died for her. His spirit appears and gazes on the shepherdess and then follows her as she is led out of a chapel. In the fourth part of the poem, his ghost appears at the house of a priest and delivers passionate, sorrowful monologues, pouring out his sad tale of disillusioned love while casting reproaches upon Maryla. He recommends to the priest the rites of Forefathers' Eve and finally reenacts his own suicide. Gustav is Mickiewicz's version of the self-dramatizing Romantic hero, but he is also a tragic hero in the Aristotelian sense, since he is defeated by a mistake in judgment—his overwhelming love for a person who proves to be unworthy.

GRAŻYNA

Mickiewicz wrote *Grażyna*, an impersonal narrative poem, at about the same time he wrote the highly personal and passionate *Forefathers' Eve*. *Grażyna* resembles the tales or "novels" in verse characteristic of the Romantic movement in Western Europe but lacks the supernatural elements and the exoticism that distinguish such works. The poem concerns the Lithuanians' struggle in the fourteenth century against the German

Knights of the Cross. Mickiewicz was inspired by the ruins of a castle near Nowo-gródek, by his study of early Lithuanian history, and by his reading of Torquato Tasso, Sir Walter Scott, and Lord Byron. In the narrative, the Lithuanian prince, Litavor, plans to join the Teutonic Knights against Duke Witold. These traitorous intentions are foiled by Grażyna, Litavor's brave and patriotic wife. Dressed in her husband's armor, she leads the Lithuanian knights in battle against the Teutons instead of accepting their help against her compatriots. Mickiewicz modeled his heroine on Tasso's Clorinda and Erminia, although the type goes back to Vergil's Camilla and ultimately to the Greek tales of the Amazons. This stately narrative reveals Mickiewicz's extraordinary gift for vivid characterization, even though the poet himself did not attach much importance to the work.

SONNETS FROM THE CRIMEA

At the end of 1826, Mickiewicz published his first cycle of sonnets, the so-called love sonnets. There were few Polish models in the sonnet form, and he turned for a model to the Petrarchan sonnet, with its elaborate rhyme scheme and rigid structure. His second cycle of sonnets, *Sonnets from the Crimea*, was vastly different in thought and feeling and was met with hostile criticism from Mickiewicz's classically minded contemporaries.

While in Russia, Mickiewicz had made a trip of nearly two months through the Cri-mea, and it was this journey that produced the eighteen poems that constitute the *Son-nets from the Crimea*. He made the trip with, among others, Karolina Sobanski, with whom he had an ardent love affair; critics have speculated that the three sonnets "Good Morning," "Good Night," and "Good Evening" reflect their relationship. With his *Son-nets from the Crimea*, Mickiewicz introduced to Polish literature the Romantic poetry of the steppe, the sea, and the mountains, as well as the Oriental elements of European Ro-manticism, represented by Byron and Thomas Moore in England and by Pushkin in Russia. The sonnets express an attitude toward nature that is characteristically Roman-tic and at the same time "modern": Nature is valued for its own sake as well as for its symbolic reflection of the poet's psychological states. The sonnets are further distin-guished by their exotic vocabulary, the fruit of Mickiewicz's study of Persian and Arabic poetry, mainly in French translation. (Near Eastern and Oriental literature was popular throughout Europe toward the end of the eighteenth century.) The rigid struc-ture demanded by the sonnet form enabled Mickiewicz to communicate his psycho-logical experiences with utmost conciseness, and these poems are among his finest.

KONRAD WALLENROD

Mickiewicz had conceived the idea of his next major work, *Konrad Wallenrod*, while in Moscow in 1825. Like *Grażyna*, the poem is set in medieval Lithuania during the conflict between the Lithuanians and the Knights of the Cross. *Konrad Wallenrod* is both longer and more powerful than *Grażyna*, however, and, although the poet modified and altered history to some extent, it is mainly based on actual historical events; Mickiewicz himself described the work as "a story taken from the history of Lithuania and Prussia." A tale in verse in the Byronic style, the poem relates the tragedy of a Lithuanian who is forced by fate to become a Teutonic Knight. The hero, in an effort to save his people from annihilation, sacrifices all that is dear to him, including his own honor. Mickiewicz changed the historical Wallenrod, an ineffective Grand Master of the Knights of the Cross, to a Lithuanian who, captured as a youth, has been reared by the Germans and then gains influence and authority over the Teutonic Knights in order to destroy them. To capture the aura of intrigue, Mickiewicz studied Machiavelli and read Friedrich Schiller's *Die Verschwörung des Fiesco zu Genua* (pr., pb. 1783; *Fiesco: Or, The Genoese Conspiracy*, 1796). The poem reverts to the somber and Romantic atmosphere that Mickiewicz had temporarily abandoned in his sonnets; it is Byronic in type, and Mickiewicz evidently used *The Corsair* (1814) and *Lara* (1814) for inspiration. Mickiewicz's Wallenrod, however, differs markedly from the Byronic hero: Above all, he is a patriot, rather than a mysterious outsider. Indeed, so clear is the political allegory that underlies *Konrad Wallenrod* that it is surprising that the Russian censors allowed the poem to be published.

"FARIS"

In St. Petersburg in 1828, Mickiewicz wrote "Faris ," a poem depicting an Arab horseman's extravagant ride through the desert. Mickiewicz had developed an interest in Arabic poetry through his contact with the Oriental peoples in the south of Russia. The Arabic word *faris* means "horseman" or "knight." Mickiewicz's special affection for the poem is often attributed to its story of a proud, strong will that triumphs over great obstacles; perhaps Mickiewicz saw himself in this light.

FOREFATHERS' EVE, PART 3

Mickiewicz wrote his greatest works, part 3 of *Forefathers' Eve* and *Pan Tadeusz*, in a brief period from 1832 to 1834. Part 3 of *Forefathers' Eve* is only loosely connected with parts 2 and 4, published almost ten years earlier. It is the longest, the most enigmatic, and certainly the most famous of the three parts. The poet went back for his subject matter to his Wilno days in 1823, when the Russian authorities arrested him and other members of the Philomathians. Using his personal experience in the Romantic manner, Mickiewicz sought to justify the actions of a loving God in allowing a devout Roman Catholic country such as Poland to be partitioned by three cruel neighbors, each "on a lower moral level than their victim."

While in Rome, Mickiewicz had been intrigued by Aeschyulus's tragedy *Prometheus desmōtēs* (date unknown; *Prometheus Bound*, 1777), with its presentation of the Titan who rebels against Zeus in the name of love for humanity, and Aeschylus's influence is apparent in part 3 of *Forefathers' Eve.* The story of Prometheus attracted many Romantic writers, including Percy Bysshe Shelley and Johann Wolfgang von Goethe. Mickiewicz, who had considered writing his own poetic drama about Prometheus, may have been influenced by these authors as well in composing the third part of *Forefathers' Eve.*

Part 3 of *Forefathers' Eve* consists of a prologue, nine scenes, and a final sequence of six long poems about Russia. This sequence, titled "Ustcp" ("Digression"), constitutes a second act or epilogue. In the prologue, Maryla's lover, Gustav, a young prisoner, is seen in his cell in the Basilian Monastery, watched over by good and evil spirits. He takes the name Konrad, suggesting an affinity with Konrad Wallenrod. The first scene, a description of the life of the student prisoners, is followed by the improvisation—the foundation of the whole drama—in which Konrad arrogantly challenges God's justice, charging him with an absence of feeling or love in spite of his strength and great intellect. Konrad declares that he himself is greater than God, since he loves his nation and desires her happiness. The improvisation and the following scenes reflect the fulfillment of Mickiewicz's previous plan of writing a tragedy with the Prometheus theme adapted to a Christian setting. Konrad's arrogant pride, although inspired by love for Poland and a sense of divinity within himself, is blasphemous. Father Peter, who represents mystic humility just as Konrad represents mystic pride, receives in a vision an understanding of the source of Konrad's torment—the problem of the fate of Poland, an innocent victim crushed by cruel foreign powers. He sees Poland as the Christ among nations, who, crucified by Prussia, Russia, and Austria, will rise again. The promised hero who will bring about the resurrection of Poland is probably Mickiewicz himself, although in the work there is reference only to a hero whose name is "Forty and Four." With this notion that Poland is the Christ among nations, Mickiewicz became the founder of Polish messianism, a mystic faith that helped to define "Polishness" for generations and that is not without influence in Poland even today.

PAN TADEUSZ

In November, 1832, Mickiewicz began work on *Pan Tadeusz*, a narrative poem that was to become his masterpiece. He worked on the poem until February, 1834. *Pan Tadeusz*, a stately epic of 9,712 lines, is a story of the Polish gentry. The poem's twelve books present the whole of Polish society in Lithuanian Byelorussia during a highly significant period of history, the time of Napoleon's campaign in Russia, in 1811-1812, a time when Polish society appeared to have achieved a temporary harmony, stability, and order. Mickiewicz stresses the value of ritual, order, and ceremony, and his characters are courteous, modest, and patriotic.

The subtitle of *Pan Tadeusz—Or: The Last Foray in Lithuania, a Tale of Gentlefolk in 1811 and 1812, in Twelve Books in Verse*—is significant: Mickiewicz's use of the word "tale" may indicate, as some critics have argued, that *Pan Tadeusz* is not an epic or narrative poem at all, although it is connected to these genres , but a blending together of a number of genres to achieve the poet's artistic purpose in a truly Romantic style. The word "last" in the subtitle implies the disappearance of a traditional way of life, as exemplified in the "foray" or ritualistic execution of justice. Mickiewicz's two main themes, the recapture of the past and the conflict between reality and appearance, are classic themes in Western literature, and the poem thus attains a certain universality in spite of its intense concern with a specific cultural and historical tradition.

The plot concerns Tadeusz, an impressionable young man recently graduated from the university; his love for Zosia; and a feud over a castle between the Soplicas and the Horeszkos: Tadeusz is a Soplica, while Zosia is a Horeszko (a premise that recalls William Shakespeare's *Romeo and Juliet*, pr. c. 1595-1596). To add to the conflict, the father of Tadeusz has killed Zosia's grandfather. The plot becomes more involved later in the work when an emissary of Napoleon turns out to be Tadeusz's father disguised as a monk, Father Robak. (In constructing his plot, Mickiewicz was influenced by Sir Walter Scott.) Mickiewicz chose for his setting rural Lithuanian Byelorussia, the land of his childhood, to which he longed to return. The real hero of the poem is Jacek Soplica, who wants to marry Eva, the daughter of an aristocrat, the Pantler Horeszko. When he is rejected, Jacek kills the Pantler in a fit of anger, under circumstances that falsely suggest collusion with the Russians. Jacek spends the rest of his life humbly serving his country. He becomes a monk and works as a political agent urging Poles to join Napoleon in his campaign against Russia and so to contribute to the restoration of Poland in an indirect manner. Mickiewicz united in Jacek the conflicting motives of pride and humility, represented in part 3 of *Forefathers' Eve* by Konrad and Father Peter. In *Pan Tadeusz*, Mickiewicz is no longer a prophet and teacher, appearing rather as a kindly, genial man who is proud of the glorious past of his country and has faith in her future. He is once more the jovial companion of his Wilno days and no longer the leader of Polish exiles who were haunted by their own misfortunes and those of Poland. He is a realist who sees the faults of his countrymen but still loves them.

It is difficult to believe that part 3 of *Forefathers' Eve* and *Pan Tadeusz* were written by the same poet within a period of two years. In the latter, the poet is moved by childlike wonder: He sees beauty in even the most commonplace scenes in Poland, such as a young girl feeding poultry in a farmyard. The period about which he was writing embodied the whole life of Old Poland—its people, its customs, and its traditions. While the action of *Pan Tadeusz* develops in the country among rural people, set against a background of vibrant descriptions of nature and animals, all classes of the gentry are described, including the wealthy, the aristocratic, the middle class, and the poor gentry, and there are representatives of a number of old offices, such as chamberlain, *voyevoda*, pantler, cupbearer, seneschal, judge, and notary. In addition, there are representatives of other classes and nationalities, including the peasants (rather incompletely presented, however), a Jew, and various Russians.

In *Pan Tadeusz*, Mickiewicz describes nature in a manner that has never been equaled in Polish literature. He paints verbal pictures of the forest, meadows, and ponds at different times of the day and night in different lights and in myriad colors; he describes sunrises and sunsets, and the world of plants and animals, all with acute perception. Mickiewicz also meticulously describes a mansion, a castle, a cottage of the provincial gentry, an inn, hunting parties, the picking of mushrooms, feasts, quarrels, duels, and a battle—an extraordinary range of settings and experiences.

The masterpiece of Polish literature, *Pan Tadeusz* is regarded by many as the finest narrative poem of the nineteenth century. "The smile of Mickiewicz" reflected in the kindly humor of the poem, the radiant descriptions, and the dramatic truth of the characters, all contribute to its excellence. *Pan Tadeusz* is known and loved throughout Poland, by peasants as well as university professors. With this masterpiece, Mickiewicz reached the summit of his literary career. It is unfortunate that the total effect of the poem, which is derived from a close interaction of diction, style, and word associations, the portrayal of marvelously drawn characters, the presentation of setting, and the creation of a dynamic atmosphere, cannot be conveyed in all its beauty in translation.

OTHER MAJOR WORKS

PLAYS: *Jacknes Jasinski, ou les deux Polognes*, 1836; *Les confédérés de Bar*, 1836.

NONFICTION: *Ksiegi narodu polskiego i pielgrzymstwa polskiego*, 1832 (*The Books of the Polish Nation and of the Polish Pilgrims*, 1833, 1925); *Pierwsze wieki historyi polskiej*, 1837; *Wyklady Lozanskie*, 1839-1840 ; *Literatura slowianska*, 1840-1844 (4 volumes).

BIBLIOGRAPHY

Debska, Anita. *Country of the Mind: An Introduction to the Poetry of Adam Mickiewicz.* Warsaw: Burchard, 2000. A biography of Mickiewicz that also provides literary criticism, particularly of *Pan Tadeusz.*

Gross, Irena Grudzinska. "How Polish Is Polishness: About Mickiewicz's *Grażyna.*" *East European Politics and Societies* 14, no. 1 (Winter, 2000): 1-11. Mickiewicz has been enshrined as an icon, his work classic and his vibrant presence is felt strongly in Polish culture. Gross examines Mickiewicz's poem *Grażyna* and the nationalism in it.

Kalinowska, Izabela. "The Sonnet, the Sequence, the Qasidah: East-West Dialogue in Adam Mickiewicz's Sonnets." *Slavic and East European Journal* 45, no. 4 (Winter, 2001): 641. Looks at Orientalism in the sonnets Mickiewicz published in 1826.

Koropeckyj, Roman. *Adam Mickiewicz: The Life of a Romantic.* Ithaca, N.Y.: Cornell University Press, 2008. This biography of Mickiewicz examines his entire life as well as his major works.

_____. *The Poetics of Revitalization: Adam Mickiewicz Between "Forefathers'*

Eve," Part 3, and "Pan Tadeusz." Boulder, Colo.: East European Monographs, 2001. This work focuses on two works, *Forefathers' Eve*, part 3, and *Pan Tadeusz*, and the author's development between them.

Welsh, David. *Adam Mickiewicz.* New York: Twayne, 1966. An introductory biography and critical study of selected works by Mickiewicz.

John P. Pauls and La Verne Pauls

BORIS PASTERNAK

Born: Moscow, Russia; February 10, 1890
Died: Peredelkino, near Moscow, Soviet Union (now in Russia); May 30, 1960

OTHER LITERARY FORMS

Besides poetry, Boris Pasternak (PAS-tur-nak) composed several pieces of short fiction. They include "Pisma iz Tuly" (1922; "Letters from Tula," 1945), "Detstvo Luvers" (1923; "The Childhood of Luvers," 1945), and *Rasskazy* (1925; short stories). He wrote two autobiographical works: *Okhrannaya gramota* (1931; *Safe Conduct*, 1949) and *Avtobiograficheskiy ocherk* (1958; *I Remember: Sketch for an Autobiography*, 1959). His novel *Doktor Zhivago* (*Doctor Zhivago*, 1958) was first published in Italy in 1957. An unfinished dramatic trilogy, *Slepaya krasavitsa* (*The Blind Beauty*, 1969), was published after his death, in 1969.

Among Pasternak's many translations into Russian are several of William Shakespeare's plays, including *Romeo and Juliet* (pr. c. 1595-1596) in 1943 and *Antony and Cleopatra* (pr. 1606-1607) in 1944. Most of these translations were published between 1940 and 1948. He also translated into Russian the works of several Georgian lyric poets, especially those works of his friends Titian Tabidze and Paolo Iashvili. His translation of Johann Wolfgang von Goethe's *Faust: Eine Tragödie* (pb. 1808, 1833; *The Tragedy of Faust*, 1823, 1838) appeared in 1953, and Friedrich Schiller's *Maria Stuart* (1800) in 1957. Other authors whose works he translated include Heinrich von Kleist, Lord Byron, and John Keats.

The best English editions of Pasternak's prose works are found in *Selected Writings*—which includes the short prose works, *Safe Conduct*, and selected poems— translated by C. M. Bowra et al.; *I Remember*, translated with preface and notes by David Magarshack; and *Doctor Zhivago*, translated by Max Hayward and M. Harari, with the poems translated by Bernard G. Guerney.

ACHIEVEMENTS

Known in the West mainly as the author of *Doctor Zhivago*, Boris Pasternak established his reputation as a poet in the Soviet Union in 1922 with the publication of *My Sister, Life*. He is regarded as a "poet's poet," and his contemporary Anna Akhmatova referred to him simply as "the poet," as if there were no other in his time. Indeed, Pasternak ranks as one of the foremost Russian poets of the twentieth century, if not the greatest. At the turn of the century, Symbolism, as in the works of Andrey Bely and Aleksandr Blok, dominated Russian poetry, and in the years before the Revolution more daring innovation and verbal experimentation occurred in the Futurist movement, as in the poetry of Vladimir Mayakovsky and Sergei Esenin. Pasternak inherited from both movements and yet was a part of neither. Like the Symbolists, he is able to see life in images; like the Futurists, he uses daring verbal combinations, intricate sound patterns, and a relaxed conversational vocabulary. In his verses, there is a simplicity and clarity that goes back to Alexander Pushkin, together with a freshness and originality that are timeless.

Pasternak's early poetry, especially *My Sister, Life*, is his most innovative and enigmatic. In these "rimes and riddles," as Robert Payne observes, Pasternak seemed to send the reader "in search of the key, until he realized that no key was necessary." Pasternak creates pure poetry, and the creation itself is the message. His poetry is music, like that of Paul Verlaine, whom he greatly admired; it is a search and a discovery, like Paul Valéry's; it is a perpetual celebration of the senses, as in Mikhail Lermontov; above all, it is a cosmic apotheosis of nature. It had a message of newness for the years of hope and optimism following the Revolution, and as Lydia Pasternak-Slater writes: "each reader discovered individually and for himself that these poems were the spontaneous outbursts of genius, of a 'poet' by the grace of God."

Pasternak was not a political poet. He seldom wrote of the Revolution or of reform.

At first glance, he seems to be unaware of events, as he states in the poem "About These Verses": "Dear friends . . . what millennium is it out there?" A. Lezhnev states that these lines might be considered the epigraph of Pasternak's entire work. Yet the throbbing rhythm of *My Sister, Life* incarnates the Revolution, as *The Year 1905* sounds an ominous yet hopeful note, and as the poems of the 1940's speak of the desolation of the war years. Contemporary events are both present and absent in Pasternak's verse. Their absence angered Soviet officials, yet Joseph Stalin himself spared Pasternak.

Pasternak's greatest poetry, *The Poems of Doctor Zhivago* and the poems of his last years, sheds the excessive imagery and startling verbal play of his earlier works. These poems reach a sublime simplicity in perhaps a single transparent image, and the music and the message are one. Such is "Winter Night," perhaps one of the greatest poems in all Russian literature. Into these later works, Pasternak has injected a profound Christian symbolism, very much evident in the *The Poems of Doctor Zhivago*, more subtle in *When the Skies Clear*. Many of these poems are probably among the best-known modern poems in the entire world for their simplicity, universality, and lyricism.

BIOGRAPHY

Boris Leonidovich Pasternak was born in Moscow on February 10, 1890 (January 29, Old Style). He was the first and most illustrious of four children born to the painter Leonid Osipovich Pasternak and the pianist Rosa Isidorovna Kaufman. A close family relationship and a deeply cultured atmosphere marked his childhood. The influence of the Russian Orthodox religion came to this child of predominantly Jewish roots through his nurse Akulina Gavrilovna and was to reappear during his later years. Leonid Pasternak's literary associations, particularly with Leo Tolstoy and Rainer Maria Rilke, were to prove very important to Pasternak's development, although perhaps the most powerful influence on him was exerted by the composer Aleksandr Scriabin. Scriabin was his idol from 1903 to 1909, when Pasternak also began composing. Disillusioned in 1909, he abandoned the pursuit of a musical career and turned to philosophy. A trip to Marburg in 1912, then the philosophical center of Germany, where he was to study under Professor Hermann Cohen, seemed to be the ultimate fulfillment of his dreams. Then a sentimental crisis, Ida Vysofskaya's refusal of his proposal of marriage, led him to abandon philosophy and to turn to poetry—without, however, his losing altogether the musical gift and the philosophical preoccupations that are evident in his works.

Upon his return to Moscow, Pasternak became involved in literary circles and devoted himself completely to poetry. The wife of his early protector, the Lithuanian poet Jurgis Baltrushaitis, rightly warned him that he would later regret the publication of his first volume, pretentiously called *Bliznets v tuchakh* (a twin in the clouds). Its title suggested the Futurist movement, which Pasternak was unable to integrate into his work. Exempted from the military draft because of a childhood leg injury, he tutored and worked at a chemical plant in the Urals from 1914 to 1917. The beauty of the Urals, which so impressed him, colors many of his works, from "The Childhood of Liuvers" to his poetry. When the Revolution broke out, he returned to Moscow enthusiastically, only to be disillusioned. This famous summer of 1917 is immortalized in the volume of poetry *My Sister, Life*, which was published in 1922, immediately assuring his reputation as a poet.

In 1922, Pasternak married Evgenia Vladimirovna Lourié, and their son Evgeny was born in 1923. The marriage, however, was not a happy one, and in 1930, he became enamored of Zinaïda Nikolaevna Neuhaus, whom he married in 1934. Their son Leonid was born in 1937. Although his second wife was to remain faithful to him until his death, their relationship was greatly strained by Pasternak's liaison with Olga Vsevolodovna Ivinskaya, which began in 1946. Ivinskaya showed a sensitive appreciation of Pasternak's literary works and aided him in much of his secretarial work. For her association with him, she was imprisoned and deported to Siberia twice, from 1949 until Stalin's death in 1953 and after Pasternak's death in 1960 until 1964. Pasternak himself was spared—miraculously, since the 1930's and 1940's saw the exile, death, or suicide of many of Russia's most gifted writers. Never hostile to the regime, he also never wrote according to the tenets of Socialist Realism and thus was in constant jeopardy.

During the difficult years of World War II and afterward, Pasternak supported himself and his family principally by translating, which he resumed later when he was unable to receive royalties from the West. After Stalin's death, he began working seriously on *Doctor Zhivago*, which he regarded as his most important work. Its refusal by the journal *Novy Mir* and subsequent publication in Italy by Petrinelli in 1957 placed him in a very dangerous position. When awarded the Nobel Prize in Literature in 1958, official pressures caused him to refuse. He died on May 30, 1960, at Peredelkino, the writers' village where he had spent almost all his summers and many of his winters since 1936.

ANALYSIS

Although Boris Pasternak would refuse to equate music with poetry, his verse is inseparable from the music it embodies. D. L. Plank has studied the music of Pasternak in great detail and speaks of his "sound symbolism" and "phonetic metaphors." With its unusual rhythms and internal rhymes, alliteration, and evocative word patterns, Pasternak's poetry has a resonance that most translators have despaired of capturing. At all times he uses classical patterns and regular meters, never attempting the free verse of the Futurists, whose daring use of vocabulary, however, he does share. Perhaps one of the best examples of Pasternak's sound patterns is "Oars at Rest," brilliantly analyzed by Plank and Nils Nilsson.

It is not surprising that Pasternak's last work should be called *Zhivago*, which means "life," for his entire literary creation is a celebration of life. In *My Sister, Life*, he wrote, "In all my ways let me pierce through into the very essence. . . ." Although his sensitive nature suffered greatly during the personal and national upheavals in which he participated, he was basically positive and optimistic, a poet of hope and exultation. He frequently wrote of birth; one of his volumes of verse is titled *Second Birth*; the sight of the Urals for the first time is the vision of the great mountains in the pangs of childbirth and joy of new life. He frequently wrote of the change of seasons, implying life and death, growth and change. The religious poems of the Zhivago cycle lead to the Resurrection, the ultimate symbol of life and hope.

NATURE

Nature is the subject of the majority of Pasternak's poems. Poet Marina Tsvetayeva said: "We have written about nature, but Pasternak has written nature." Nature is the actor in his poems, the doer, the hero. Traditional roles are reversed: the garden comes into the house to meet the mirror ("Mirror"); "Dust gulps down the rain in pellets" ("Sultry Night"); young woods climb uphill to the summit ("Vision of Tiflis"). Pasternak became the river or the mountain or the snow. He captured nature on the move. For him, says Payne, "All that happened was eternally instantaneous."

Pasternak lived in a world of linden trees and grasses, lilacs and violets, herbs and nettles. They were personified and became the poet and time and life. "Today's day looks about with the eyes of anemones" ("You in the Wind . . ."); "The storm, like a priest, sets fire to the lilacs" ("Our Thunderstorm"). Lilacs and linden trees seemed to have a mysterious but definite significance for him. Most of nature entered his works through rain or snow. Poet Tsvetayeva said that the entire book *My Sister, Life* swims. The mere titles of the poems reveal this love of rain: "Rain," "Spring Rain," "The Weeping Garden." The same theme is evident in *When the Skies Clear*, but here snow dominates. There are blizzards, blinding snow, like the passing of the years, but also "Flowers covered with surprise;/ Corners where the crossroads rise," for Pasternak was essentially a poet of hope, and for him drenching rains and snowy winters were signs of life and growth.

LOVE

Life for Pasternak was inseparable from love. *My Sister, Life* evokes a tumultuous love affair. *Second Birth* is the story of his love for Zinaïda Nikolaevna, with regrets and admiration for Evgenia Vladimirovna. The poems of the Zhivago cycle probably refer to Ivinskaya in the person of Lara. Pasternak seldom wrote of love in explicit terms but used rhythm and metonomy: the sleepy breast, elbows, willows ("Oars at Rest"); crossed arms and legs ("Winter Night"). Like Stéphane Mallarmé, Pasternak frequently combined love and artistic creation, especially in his earlier works .

IMAGERY

Pasternak's early method is associative and linear. Many brief themes follow in rapid succession, with only a tenuous link, if any. Lezhnev observes that Pasternak, like an Impressionist painter, was a better colorist than draftsman. In the early works, images cascade and overwhelm one another and the reader. "Definition of Poetry" moves from the crescendo of a whistle to a ringing icicle to a duel between nightingales. Andrei Sinyavsky notes that for Pasternak, the poet does not compose or write images; he gathers them from nature. The young Pasternak was overwhelmed by all that he saw in nature, and his early works are saturated with such imagery.

SPIRITUALITY

The religious theme is barely present in Pasternak's earlier works, which seem like a pantheistic celebration of nature. Even in *When the Skies Clear*, humanity's creative power is seen in the might of the elements ("Wind"). In the Zhivago cycle, however, the spiritual element dominates, corresponding to a maturing and broadening of Pasternak's talent as well as to an inner conversion. This development has been interpreted as a poetic conversion to another set of images, but it is evident that Pasternak's values have moved to another sphere. He reaches a metaphysical and spiritual plane that uplifts the reader and draws him into an atmosphere of hope and immortality.

MY SISTER, LIFE

My Sister, Life (or *Sister My Life*, as Phillip Flayderman prefers in his translation) consists of fifty short lyrics written by Pasternak in a single burst of creative energy in the summer of 1917. It was his third volume of verse, and his first really great poetic achievement, immediately establishing his reputation. In it, Pasternak writes of life, love, and nature in a cosmic yet a very personal sense. The book is dedicated to Mikhail Lermontov, the great nineteenth century Russian poet whom Pasternak greatly admired, and the first poem recalls Lermontov's magnificent *Demon* (1841; *The Demon*, 1875). Pasternak himself states that in the summer of 1917, Lermontov was to him "the personification of creative adventure and discovery, the principle of everyday free poetical statement." The book is broken up by twelve subtitles, such as "Isn't It Time for the Birds to Sing," "Occupations of Philosophy," "An Attempt to Separate the Soul," and "Epilogue," which give only a slight indication of the contents of the respective sections.

The summer of 1917 was unlike any other in Pasternak's lifetime or in Russian history. It was the summer between the February and October revolutions, when Pasternak returned to Moscow, near which, at the family *dacha* at Molodi, he composed the poems of this cycle. There is scarcely an echo of revolutionary events in the whole volume, yet Pasternak calls it "A Book of the Revolution." Tsvetayeva discerned "a few incontrovertible signs of 1917" in "The Sample," "Break-up," "The Militiaman's Whistle," "A Sultry Night," and the poem to Aleksandr Kerensky, "Spring Rain." Robert Payne sees the entire volume as poems "filled with the electric excitement of those days." The rhythm begins softly, as in "The Weeping Garden," and ends in stifling heat and thunderstorms, as in "Summer," "A Momentary Thunderstorm Forever," and "At Home."

Many of the poems refer directly to a love affair: stormy, tumultuous, and at times tender. Pasternak does not reveal the person or the circumstances but simply portrays the emotional impact. He does this mostly through images of nature and sonorous evocations that defy translation. The significance of the images is intensely personal, and although the sensitive reader can feel the emotion and identify with it, he cannot interpret it. There are playful and sensual images ("Your lips were violets") as well as serious ones: "You handed me life from the shelf,/ And blew the dust away" ("Out of Superstition"). The love affair seems to end on a note of farewell, like a song that has been sung and a moment immortalized in poetry.

As is usual in Pasternak's early poetry, images of nature saturate each poem. Gardens (especially drenched in rain), lilac branches, summer storms, and starry skies run through most of the poems. Pasternak does not create them; he gathers them up from the universe in a net as a fisherman gathers his fish. He does not evoke them; he becomes the river or the storm or the rain. There is a cosmic quality about his nature imagery which excites and exalts. At the same time, Pasternak uses simple conversational language. He writes of mosquitoes and cafés and trolleys along with more exotic themes. The short prose work "The Childhood of Liuvers" has been considered to be a companion piece to *My Sister, Life* and thus helps to clarify some of the more enigmatic images that many critics, including Pasternak's sister Lydia, see as "too complicated, too cryptic, with too many escapes into the brilliance of sound and word."

If there is a philosophical message in these early works, it is the absolute value of freedom. Pasternak remains above political involvement and above conventional images. Like Lermontov, he seeks sensual freedom as well. He expresses freedom in language as he creates new melodies independent of ordinary vocabulary and syntax. Although Pasternak had not yet achieved the realism of Pushkin's imagery, with its universal application, his subjective boldness stands out in *My Sister, Life* as a new and fresh voice in Russian poetry.

HIGH MALADY

Pasternak's greatest achievement is in lyric poetry, but in the 1920's, he attempted four longer poems of epic scope dealing with the Revolution. They are *High Malady*, *The Year 1905*, *Lieutenant Schmidt*, and *Spektorsky*—the latter was left unfinished. Although all these poems have the narrative quality that Pasternak was to develop in his prose works, they are colored predominantly by his lyricism and emotional response.

High Malady is the only epic directly connected with the Revolution. It is a debate about the nature of poetry, "the high malady that is still called song," and Moscow under Bolshevik rule. Under the shadow of the siege of Troy, Pasternak speaks of the suffering in Moscow during the early 1920's: the cold winter, the lack of food, the imminence of death. Into this somber atmosphere, he introduces Vladimir Lenin (Vladimir Ilich Ulyanov), whose "living voice pierced [us] with encircling flames like jagged lightning." He grows taller, his words are like the thrust of a sword, as alone "he ruled the tides of thought." Lenin is one with history and brings hope to the suffering people.

THE YEAR 1905

The Year 1905 is retrospective of twenty years, written by Pasternak in 1925 to 1926. As a young student, he had participated in some of the Moscow demonstrations in 1905, and the recollection remained with him all his life. The poem consists of six parts, of unequal lengths and varying meters. The first part, "Fathers," goes back to the roots of the Revolution in the 1880's, grouping together such diverse people as the anarchist Sergey Nechayev and the great novelist Fyodor Dostoevski. Part 2, "Childhood," is partially autobiographical and contains reminiscences of Pasternak's own student days, his father's study, and the music of Aleksandr Scriabin. Against a background of snow, Pasternak fuses and confuses events in both St. Petersburg (or Petrograd) and Moscow, as he is spiritually present in both. The third part, "Peasants and Factory Workers," short and perhaps the least successful, describes the Polish insurrection at Lodz.

"PRINCE POTEMKIN"

Part 4 describes the mutiny at sea aboard the *Prince Potemkin*. With classical overtones recalling Homer, Pasternak salutes the sea. With classical reticence, he avoids the direct description of violence. The hero, Afanasy Matushenko, is described in larger-than-life proportions, and as the section ends, the ship sails away "like an orange-colored speck." Part 5, "The Students," tells of the funeral procession of Nikolai Baumann, killed by an agent of the secret police. In the tone of a lament, Pasternak writes: "The heavens slept plunged in a silver forest of chrysanthemums." The last part, "Moscow in December," speaks of the famous strike of the railwaymen. Pasternak himself was very moved by this event and, perhaps in memory of it, frequently used the image of railways in his poetry. The entire poem is powerful in its lyricism, but, as J. W. Dyck observes, it is too diffuse and lacks a central focus.

LIEUTENANT SCHMIDT

Lieutenant Schmidt remedies this problem by evoking a single subject. Lieutenant Schmidt was a historical personage who led a mutiny among the sailors at Sebastopol and almost single-handedly seized one battleship. Ten other ships had already joined him when he was captured and condemned. His famous "Testament," in which he speaks about cherishing his country's destiny and sees himself as "happy to have been chosen," is one of the most sublime parts of the entire poem.

SPEKTORSKY

Spektorsky was never completed, but Pasternak planned it as a novel in verse. It is highly autobiographical and tells of the unsuccessful love affair of Olga and Spektorsky and his later meeting with her while she was a revolutionary. A second love affair, with the poetess Maria Ilyna, is equally disappointing. The poem is also symbolic of the spiritual submission of the poet, not yet characteristic of Pasternak. It reflects independence in the face of any given ideology. The handling of plot in *Spektorsky* is unsure, but the poem does present a very modern character and shows the development of Pasternak's lyric gifts.

THE POEMS OF DOCTOR ZHIVAGO

Although the epic poems do not constitute the highest form of Pasternak's literary expression, they pleased the general public because of their accessibility. They also show the fusion of Pasternak's lyric and narrative skills, anticipating the achievement of *Doctor Zhivago*. In his *I Remember*, Pasternak describes *Doctor Zhivago* as "my chief and most important work, the only one I am not ashamed of and for which I can answer with the utmost confidence, a novel in prose with a supplement in verse." The essential connection between the poetry and prose is evident to the sensitive reader, for Pasternak intended the poems to constitute the seventeenth and final chapter of his work. Donald Davie, Dmitri Obolensky, and George Katkov, among others, have provided valuable commentaries in English that help to interpret the poems and show their link with the novel.

The Poems of Doctor Zhivago represents the most mature phase of Pasternak's poetry. The musical quality is important here, as in all his works. The poems are inherently religious, a fact recognized by the editors of *Novy Mir*, who refused to print them. They speak of life and death, love and immortality, within a framework of the four seasons. The year begins in March, with a promise of spring, and ends with Holy Thursday and the hope of resurrection. The cycle begins and ends with Gethsemane and emphasizes the mission of Christ, of Hamlet, and of the poet "to do the will of him who sent me."

Obolensky divides the poems into three basic categories or themes: nature, love, and the author's views on the meaning and purpose of life. Although each of the twenty-five poems fits one of these categories better than the others, they overlap and the division is not absolute. The nature poems speak of all the seasons, but spring predominates: "March," "Spring Floods," "In Holy Week," "The Earth," and the religious poems that conclude the cycle. The nightingale, so frequent in Pasternak's poetry, is present here, and appears as the Robber-Nightingale of Russian folklore in "Spring Floods." The poems of spring point to the Resurrection, where "death finds its only vanquishing power."

The love poems are among the most intense in modern literature, yet they are remarkable for their restraint. The many women whom Pasternak knew and loved in his lifetime inspired the poems, yet there is a universality that applies to all human love, sublimated in the divine. The erotic "Intoxication," the tender "Meeting," and the mysterious "White Night" speak variously of the poet's passion. Perhaps the most successful is "Winter Night," which, by delicate repetitions of words and sounds (especially the letter *e*), by metonymic suggestions, and by the central image of the candle burning in a window, suggests the fateful passion and the consuming possession of love.

The love poems move imperceptibly into the religious cycle and form a part of it, underlining the deeply spiritual aspect of love and the ultimate meaning of life for Pasternak. "Christmas Star" introduces the series and recalls a medieval Russian icon and a Russian version of the Dutch *Adoration of the Magi* alluded to in *Safe Conduct*, Pasternak's first autobiography. "Daybreak" is addressed to Christ and emphasizes the importance of the New Testament to Pasternak, like a dawn in his own life. The other religious poems refer to the liturgical texts used in the Holy Week services in the Orthodox Church. They end with Christ in the Garden of Gethsemane and complete the cycle of death and resurrection, destruction and creation, sin and redemption—for Zhivago is a sinful man, yet one who has faith in life.

The Poems of Doctor Zhivago is a work of extraordinary simplicity. The use of religious imagery raises the poems above the purely personal symbols of *My Sister, Life*. Although Pasternak makes no effort to repeat the verbal brilliance and intricate sound patterns of his early years, the rhythm is clear and resonant. Each poem has a central focus around which the images converge. The cycle itself centers on the person of Hamlet, whom Pasternak considers to be a heroic figure, symbolizing Christ and, ultimately, resurrection. Pasternak's basic optimism, his celebration of life and exaltation of love, have their finest expression in this cycle of poems.

OTHER MAJOR WORKS

LONG FICTION: *Doktor Zhivago*, 1957 (*Doctor Zhivago*, 1958).

SHORT FICTION: "Pisma iz Tuly," 1922 ("Letters from Tula," 1945); "Detstvo Liuvers," 1923 ("The Childhood of Luvers," 1945); *Rasskazy*, 1925; *Sochineniya*, 1961 (*Collected Short Prose*, 1977).

PLAY: *Slepaya krasavitsa*, pb. 1969 (*The Blind Beauty*, 1969).

NONFICTION: *Okhrannaya gramota*, 1931 (autobiography; *Safe Conduct*, 1945 in *The Collected Prose Works*); *Avtobiograficheskiy ocherk*, 1958 (*I Remember: Sketch for an Autobiography*, 1959); *An Essay in Autobiography*, 1959; *Essays*, 1976; *The Correspondence of Boris Pasternak and Olga Freidenberg, 1910- 1 954*, 1981; *Pasternak on Art and Creativity*, 1985; *Pis'ma k gruzinskim*, n.d. (*Letters to Georgian Friends by Boris Pasternak*, 1968).

TRANSLATIONS: *Hamlet*, 1941 (of William Shakespeare); *Romeo i Juliet*, 1943 (of Shakespeare); *Antony i Cleopatra*, 1944 (of Shakespeare); *Othello*, 1945 (of Shakespeare); *King Lear*, 1949 (of Shakespeare); *Faust*, 1953 (of Johann Wolfgang von Goethe); *Maria Stuart*, 1957 (of Friedrich Schiller).

MISCELLANEOUS: *The Collected Prose Works*, 1945; *Safe Conduct: An Early Autobiography, and Other Works by Boris Pasternak*, 1958 (also known as *Selected Writings*, 1949); *Sochinenii*, 1961; *Vozdushnye puti: Proza raz nykh let*, 1982; *The Voice of Prose*, 1986.

BIBLIOGRAPHY

Barnes, Christopher. *Boris Pasternak: A Literary Biography*. New York: Cambridge University Press, 1989-1998. A two-volume comprehensive biography, scholarly but also accessible.

Ciepiela, Catherine. *The Same Solitude: Boris Pasternak and Marina Tsvetaeva*. Ithaca, N.Y.: Cornell University Press, 2006. Ciepiela examines the ten-year love affair between Pasternak and Tsvetayeva, whose relationship was primarily limited to long-distance letters. Included in this volume is the correspondence between the two authors along with letters from Rainer Maria Rilke, who completed the couple's literary love triangle. Ciepiela reveals the similarities between Pasternak and Tsvetayeva by painting a portrait of their lives and personalities. She scrutinizes their poetry and correspondence, finding significant links between them. This volume is written clearly and succinctly, making it easily accessible to all readers.

Conquest, Robert. *The Pasternak Affair: Courage of Genius*. London: Collins and Harvill, 1961. A detailed account of Pasternak's conflict with the state on his reception of the Nobel Prize. Conquest provides much valuable information about Pasternak as a man and a writer.

De Mallac, Guy. *Boris Pasternak: His Life and Art*. Norman: University of Oklahoma Press, 1981. An extensive biography of Pasternak. The second part is devoted to De Mallac's interpretation of the most important features of Pasternak's works. A detailed chronology of his life and an exhaustive bibliography complete this beautifully illustrated book.

Erlich, Victor, ed. *Pasternak: A Collection of Critical Essays*. Englewood Cliffs, N.J.: Prentice-Hall, 1978 . This skillfully arranged collection of essays covers all important facets of Pasternak's work, including short fiction, although the emphasis is on his poetry and *Doctor Zhivago*.

Fleishman, Lazar. *Boris Pasternak: The Poet and His Politics*. Cambridge, Mass.: Harvard University Press, 1990. An extensive study of Pasternak's life and works written under the oppressive political system. A must for those who are interested in nonliterary influences upon literary creations.

Ivinskaya, Olga. *A Captive of Time*. Garden City, N.Y.: Doubleday, 1978. Ivinskaya, Pasternak's love in the last years of his life, the model for Lara in *Doctor Zhivago*, and a staff member at the influential Soviet literary magazine *Novy Mir*, provides a wealth of information about Pasternak, his views and works, and Russia's literary atmosphere in the 1940's and 1950's.

Pasternak, Boris, Rainer Maria Rilke, and Marina Tsvetayeva. *Letters: Summer 1926*. New York: New York Review Books, 2001. The selected correspondence between the great Russian writers, scattered in the wake of the Bolshevik Revolution. This poignant record of a dreadful year for all three writers reveals their views on art, love, and sorrow.

Rudova, Larissa. *Understanding Boris Pasternak.* Columbia: University of South Carolina Press, 1997. A general introduction to Pasternak's work, including both his early poetry and prose and his later work; provides analyses of individual novels and stories.

Sendich, Munir. *Boris Pasternak: A Reference Guide.* New York: Maxwell Macmillan International, 1994 . This indispensable reference contains a bibliography of Pasternak editions with more than five hundred entries, a bibliography of criticism with more than one thousand entries, and essays on topics including Pasternak's poetics, relations with other artists, and influences.

Irma M. Kashuba

ALEXANDER PUSHKIN

Born: Moscow, Russia; June 6, 1799
Died: St. Petersburg, Russia; February 10, 1837

PRINCIPAL POETRY

Ruslan i Lyudmila, 1820 (*Ruslan and Liudmila*, 1936)
Gavriiliada, 1822 (*Gabriel: A Poem*, 1926)
Kavkazskiy plennik, 1822 (*The Prisoner of the Caucasus*, 1895)
Bratya razboyniki, 1824
Bakhchisaraiskiy fontan, 1827 (*The Fountain of Bakhchisarai*, 1849)
Graf Nulin, 1827 (*Count Nulin*, 1972)
Tsygany, 1827 (*The Gypsies*, 1957)
Poltava, 1829 (English translation, 1936)
Domik v Kolomne, 1833 (*The Little House at Kolomna*, 1977)
Skazka o mertvoy tsarevne, 1833 (*The Tale of the Dead Princess*, 1924)
Skazka o rybake ir rybke, 1833 (*The Tale of the Fisherman and the Fish*, 1926)
Skazka o tsare Saltane, 1833 (*The Tale of Tsar Saltan*, 1950)
Skazka o zolotom petushke, 1834 (*The Tale of the Golden Cockerel*, 1918)
Medniy vsadnik, 1837 (*The Bronze Horseman*, 1899)
Collected Narrative and Lyrical Poetry, 1984
Epigrams and Satirical Verse, 1984

OTHER LITERARY FORMS

Often considered the founder of modern Russian literature, Alexander Pushkin (POOSH-kuhn) was a prolific writer, not only of poetry but also of plays, novels, and short stories. His *malenkiye tragedii*, or "little tragedies"—brief, dramatic episodes in blank verse—include *Skupoy rytsar* (pr. 1852; *The Covetous Knight*, 1925), *Kamyenny gost* (pb. 1839; *The Stone Guest*, 1936), *Motsart i Salyeri* (pr. 1832; *Mozart and Salieri*, 1920), and *Pir vo vryemya chumy* (pb. 1833; *The Feast in Time of the Plague*, 1925).

Boris Godunov (pb. 1831; English translation, 1918) is Pushkin's famous historical tragedy constructed on the Shakespearean ideal that plays should be written "for the people." A story set in late sixteenth century Russia—a period of social and political chaos—it deals with the relationship between the ruling classes and the masses; written for the people, it, not surprisingly, gained universal appeal.

Pushkin's most important prose work, *Kapitanskaya dochka* (1836; *The Captain's Daughter*, 1846), is a historical novel of the Pugachev Rebellion. *Pikovaya dama* (1834; *The Queen of Spades*, 1858) is another well-known prose work, which influenced Fyodor Dostoevski's novels.

Alexander Pushkin
(Library of Congress)

With its emphasis on civic responsibility, Pushkin's works have been translated into most major languages. His letters have been collected and annotated in English by J. Thomas Shaw as *The Letters of Alexander Pushkin* (1963).

ACHIEVEMENTS

Alexander Pushkin was the first poet to write in a purely Russian style. Aleksandr Tvardovsky calls him "the soul of our people." Considered as one of Russia's greatest poets, if not the greatest, he does not hold the same place in foreign countries, because his greatest achievement is in his use of the Russian language, with a flavor impossible to capture in translation. His verses continue to be regarded as the most natural expression of Russian poetry. After a lengthy period of stiff classicism and excessive sentimentality in eighteenth century literature, as seen in Konstantine Batyushkov, Vasily Zhukovsky, and Nikolai Karamzin, Pushkin breathed freshness and spontaneity into Russian poetry. Zhukovsky, the acknowledged dean of Russian letters, recognized this new spirit when, after the publication of *Ruslan and Liudmila* in 1820, he gave Pushkin a portrait of himself with the inscription: "To the victorious pupil from the vanquished master on that most important day on which he completed *Ruslan and Liudmila*."

It was Pushkin who brought the Romantic spirit to Russia, although it is impossible to categorize him as a pure Romantic. Pushkin's Byronic heroes in *The Prisoner of the Caucasus* and Aleko in *The Gypsies* introduced a new type of character, proud, disillusioned, and in conflict with himself and society, which greatly appealed to the Russia of the 1820's. Pushkin also introduced a love for the primitive and the exotic, which he found especially in southern Russia, and a deep and personal appreciation of nature. In the Romantic spirit, Pushkin showed a fond appreciation of Russia's past, her heroes, her folklore, and her people, which Soviet critics saw as *narodnost*.

Pushkin was also a realist who maintained a certain detached objectivity and distance, never quite penetrating beneath the surface of his heroes or completely identifying with them. He documents even his most Romantic poems. Pushkin's last post permitted him access to the imperial archives, a privilege that he deeply cherished. His interest in history led him to works on Peter the Great, on the Pugachev Rebellion, and into his own family history in *Arap Petra velikogo* (1828-1841; *Peter the Great's Negro*, 1896).

Although Pushkin was primarily a lyric poet, he was accomplished in all genres. *Evgeny Onegin* (1825-1832, 1833; *Eugene Onegin*, 1881), the only Russian novel in verse, lacks the richness of plot and social commentary that Honoré de Balzac, Leo Tolstoy, and Fyodor Dostoevski were later to develop, but it does contain humor, satire, and tender lyricism, all presented in poetry of incomparable assurance and grace. The work was acclaimed by the great nineteenth century critic Vissarion Belinsky as "an encyclopedia of Russian life."

Pushkin aimed at revitalizing the Russian theater and saw William Shakespeare as a better model than Jean Racine or Molière. Although his major play *Boris Godunov* falls short of dramatic intensity in its failure to realize the tragic fate of the hero, it is a lyric masterpiece and a profound study of ambition and power. Never a success on the stage, Pushkin's play was the inspiration for operas by Modest Mussorgsky and Sergei Prokofiev. The "little tragedies" are models of concision and true classical concentration. Each highlights one main theme: covetousness (*The Covetous Knight*), envy (*Mozart and Salieri*), passion (*The Stone Guest*, on the Don Juan theme), and pleasure before death (*Feast in Time of the Plague*). These plays rank among Pushkin's finest achievements.

Pushkin's later years were devoted more to prose than to poetry, with the exception of *The Bronze Horseman*, the folktales in verse, and several lyric poems. Pushkin did for Russia what the Brothers Grimm did for Germany in folk literature. Although many of his sources were not specifically Russian, such as *The Tale of the Dead Princess*, Pushkin transformed them into authentic national pieces by his unaffected use of folk expressions, alliteration, and real feeling for the people. In all his work, his effortless rhymes, easy and varied rhythms, natural speech, and true identification with the spirit of his time make him beloved by the Russian people and the founder of all Russian literature.

Alexander Sergeyevich Pushkin was born in Moscow on June 6, 1799, the second of three children. His mother, Nadezhda Osipovna Hannibal, was of African descent through her grandfather, Abram Hannibal, who was immortalized by Pushkin in *Peter the Great's Negro*. His father, Sergei Lvovich, and his uncle, Vasily Lvovich, were both writers. His father frequently entertained literary friends and had an excellent library of French and Russian classics, in which Pushkin by the age of twelve had read widely but indiscriminately. Pushkin's childhood was marked by the lack of a close relationship with his parents, although he formed lasting ties with his maternal grandmother, Marya Alexeyevna, and his nurse, Arina Rodionovna, who was responsible for his love of folklore. The family could boast of very ancient aristocratic roots but suffered from a lack of money.

In 1811, Pushkin was accepted into the newly founded *lycée* at Tsarskoe Selo, designed by the czar to give a broad liberal education to aristocrats, especially those destined for administrative posts in the government. He remained there until his graduation in 1817, where he distinguished himself less by diligence than by natural ability, especially in French and Russian literature. Always of uneven temperament, he was not the most popular student in his class, but he did form lasting friendships with schoolmates Ivan Pushchin, Wilhelm Küchelbecker and Baron Anton Delvig; he also formed ties with such great literary figures as Zhukovsky and Karamizin, as well as bonds with the hussar officers, notably Pyotr Chaadayev. Pushkin began writing his earliest verses in French but soon turned to Russian.

After completing the *lycée*, Pushkin was appointed to the Ministry of Foreign Affairs in St. Petersburg. From 1817 to 1820, he led a dissipated life in the capital, much like that of Onegin in chapter 1 of *Eugene Onegin*. He became involved in liberal causes, though not as a member of the more revolutionary secret societies, and began to circulate his liberal verses. This alarmed the authorities, who proposed exile in Siberia, but because of the intercession of prominent personalities, among them Zhukovsky and the former principal of the *lycée*, Egor Englehardt, Pushkin was simply transferred to the south under the supervision of the paternal General I. N. Inzov.

Pushkin's first months in the south were spent traveling with the family of General Nikolai Raevsky through the Caucasus and the Crimea. Overwhelmed by the beauty of nature and the simplicity of the people, it was here that he wrote most of his so-called southern poems. The Raevskys introduced him to an appreciation of Lord Byron, which was reflected in his works of this period. Their daughters, especially Marya, were among Pushkin's many passions. Between 1820 and 1823, a productive literary period, he remained mostly in Kishinev. This peaceful existence was to end when Pushkin was transferred to Odessa under the stern General Vorontsov, whose wife, Elisa, became the object of Pushkin's attentions after Amalia Riznich. For this and other offenses, Pushkin was dismissed from the service in 1824 and sent to his mother's estate at Mikhailovskoe near Pskov. Here he was placed under the direct supervision of his father and the local authorities. He quarreled constantly with his family, so that all of them withdrew and left him alone from 1824 to 1826. He had few companions other than the aged nurse Arina Rodionovna. This enforced isolation proved very productive, for it was here that he composed a great deal of *Eugene Onegin*, wrote *Boris Godunov* and many short poems, and drew his inspiration for later *skazki* (tales).

The death of Alexander I in 1825 provoked the Decembrist Revolt on December 26 of the same year. Pushkin's sympathies were with the revolutionaries, but his exile fortunately prevented him from participating. He took the opportunity of the new czar's accession to the throne, however, to make a successful plea for liberation. After 1826, he was permitted to travel to Moscow and, with reservations, to the capital, although his supervisor, Count Benkendorf, was not amenable to his requests. The years between 1826 and 1830 were a period of maturing and searching; they were also rich in literary output, especially of lyric poetry and the "little tragedies."

In 1830, Pushkin became engaged to the Moscow beauty Natalia Nikolayevna Goncharova, whom he married in 1831. It was an unsuccessful match, though not a completely disastrous marriage. Pushkin's wife had no interest in literature and had social aspirations far beyond either her or her husband's means. Four children were born to them, but Natalia's dissipation and Pushkin's jealousy eventually led him to melancholy and resentment. Financial worries and lack of advancement added to his problems. When Baron Georges d'Anthès, a young Alsatian, began paying undue attention to Pushkin's wife and the entire affair became a public scandal, Pushkin challenged d'Anthès to a duel. Pushkin was mortally wounded and died on February 10, 1837.

ANALYSIS

Alexander Pushkin's first verses were written in the style of French classicism and sentimentalism. His models were Voltaire and Evariste Parny, Gavrila Derzhavin, Zhukovsky, and Batyushkov. He wrote light, voluptuous verses, occasional pieces, and epigrams. Even in his early works, of which the most important is *Ruslan and Liudmila*, he shows restrained eroticism, always tempered by his classical training, which led him from the very beginning into excellent craftsmanship, brevity, and simplicity.

WIT, HUMOR, AND SATIRE

The lively wit, humor, and satire that were evident from the first continued to characterize Pushkin's work. *Ruslan and Liudmila* is a mock-epic, and the same strain appears in chapters 1 and 2 of *Eugene Onegin*. *Gabriel*, a parody on the Annunciation, which caused Pushkin a great deal of embarrassment with the authorities, has many witty passages, such as Satan's ensnarement of Adam and Eve by love. Pushkin achieves his humor by the use of parody, not hesitating to use it in dealing with the greatest authors such as Shakespeare and Voltaire, and with his friend and master Zhukovsky. Like Molière, however, he never really offends; his satire and dry irony produce a generally good-natured effect.

POLITICAL POEMS

Pushkin first became known in St. Petersburg as a writer of liberal verses, and this—coupled with charges of atheism—made him a constant target of the imperial censors. His famous "Vol'nost': Oda" ("Ode to Freedom") is severe on Napoleon and condemns the excesses of the French Revolution, yet it reminds monarchs that they must be subservient to the law. In "Derevnya" ("The Countryside"), he longs for the abolition of serfdom, yet looks to the czar for deliverance. Pushkin did not conceal his sympathy for the Decembrists, and in his famous "Vo glubine sibirskikh rud" ("Message to Siberia"), he reminds the exiled revolutionaries that "freedom will once again shine, and brothers give you back your sword." His later poems address more general issues, and in 1831 during the Polish Uprising, he speaks out clearly in favor of the czar in "Klevetnikam Rossii" ("To the Slanderers of Russia"). Finally, *The Bronze Horseman* addresses the very complex theme of the individual in conflict with the state.

HEROINES AND LOVE POETRY

Pushkin knew many passions in his brief lifetime, and several women inspired both his life and poetry. Marya Raevskaya became the model for many of his heroines, from the Circassian girl in *The Prisoner of the Caucasus* to Marya in *Poltava*. Amalia Riznich, destined to die in Italy, reappears in "Dlya beregov otchizny dal'noy" ("Abandoning an Alien Country") in 1830. Elisa Vorontsova, the wife of Pushkin's stern superior in Odessa, was a powerful influence who haunted the poet long after his return to the north. The ring she gave him is immortalized in "Khrani menya, moy talisman" ("Talisman") and "The Burned Letter," where the ashes recall her memory. Anna Kern was the inspiration for the almost mystical "Ya pomnyu chudnoye mgnoven'ye" ("I Remember a Wonderful Moment"). Natalya Goncharova, while still Pushkin's fiancé, likewise assumes a spiritual role in "Madona" ("Madonna"). Pushkin's love poetry, while passionate, is also delicate and sensitive, and even the most voluptuous evocations concentrate on images such as those of eyes and feet.

NATURE

In Romantic fashion, Pushkin was one of the first to introduce nature into his works. First inspired by the trip to the south, where the beauty of the Caucasus overwhelmed him, he sees freedom in the wide expanses and steep mountains. Later, on a second trip—as described in "Kavkazsky" ("The Caucasus")—he evokes the playful rivers, the low clouds and the silver-capped mountains. He feels that the sight of a monastery brings him to the neighborhood of Heaven. The north also has its charms, particularly the Russian winter. There are exquisite verses on winter in the fifth chapter of *Eugene Onegin*, and in his lyrics about the swirling snowstorm in "Zinniy Vecher" ("Winter Evening") or the winter road that symbolizes his sad journey through life. Both city and country come alive in the crisp cold of winter in the prologue to *The Bronze Horseman*.

MELANCHOLY

Despite ever-recurring wit, irony, and gentle sensitivity, Pushkin's poetry is fundamentally melancholy and often tragic. This dichotomy corresponds to the division of his personality: dissipated yet deep. The southern poems all end tragically, his plays are all tragedies, and *Eugene Onegin* ends with the death of Lensky and the irremediable disappointment of Tatyana and Onegin. Pushkin frequently writes of the evil and demoniac forces of nature (as in Tatyana's dream), of madness (Eugene in *The Bronze Horseman*), and of violence (in "Zhenikh," "The Bridegroom"). A melancholy vein permeates his lyrics as well. Like the Romantics, Pushkin speaks frequently of death, perhaps foreseeing his own. The hour of parting from a loved one, a frequent subject of his lyrics, foreshadows death. As early as 1823, in "Telega zhizni" ("The Wagon of Time"), he sees the old man as the one who calmly awaits eternal sleep. Pushkin's tragic vision is complicated by the absence of a Christian worldview with a belief in life after death. Unlike Dostoevski, Pushkin writes of unmitigated, not of redemptive, suffering. S. M. Frank, who does admit a spiritual dimension in Pushkin, compares his work to Mozart's music, which seems gay but is in fact sad. Yet it is this very sadness which puts him in the tradition of Russian literature, anticipating Nikolai Gogol's "laughter through tears."

RUSLAN AND LIUDMILA

Pushkin's first major work, *Ruslan and Liudmila*, was published in 1820. It is now usually placed in a minor category, but it was important at the time as the first expression of the Russian spirit. Witty and ironic, the poem is written in the style of a mock-epic, much in the tradition of Ariosto's *Orlando Furioso* (1516, 1521, 1532; English translation, 1591). It also echoes Voltaire, and the fourth canto parodies Zhukovsky's "Spyaschaya carevna" ("Twelve Sleeping Maidens"). In fact, the whole plot resembles Zhukovsky's projected "Vladimir." It consists of six cantos, a prologue added in 1828, and an epilogue. Pushkin began the poem in 1817 while still in school, and he was already in exile in the south when it was published.

Ruslan and Liudmila, in Walter Vickery's words, transports the reader to the "unreal and delightful poetic world of cheerful unconcern," returning to the legendary days of ancient Kiev, where Prince Vladimir is giving a wedding feast for his daughter

Liudmila. The fortunate bridegroom Ruslan is about to enjoy the moment he has so voluptuously awaited, when a clap of thunder resounds and his bride is snatched away from him by the dwarf enchanter Chernomor. Prince Vladimir promises half of his kingdom and Liudmila as a bride to the man who rescues her. Ruslan sets off with his three rivals, Ratmir, Rogdai, and Farlaf. Ratmir eventually chooses a pastoral life, Rogdai is slain, and Farlaf reappears at the moment when Ruslan is about to return with Liudmila. In true knightly fashion, Ruslan saves Kiev from an attack by the Pechenegs, kills his last rival, and marries the princess.

Pushkin's poem captures many exaggerated scenes from the *byliny* or heroic tales, such as the death of the giant head, and ends with a full-scale epic battle. It is a gentle mockery of chivalry, sorcery, and love. Critics from Zhukovsky to the Soviets hailed it as a true folk-epic in the spirit of *narodnost* (nationalism) although many of Pushkin's contemporaries were shocked at his unfaithfulness to classical antiquity and his trivial subject. The public, however, welcomed it, seeing in it a new inspiration for the times. The prologue, especially, captures the popular spirit with its learned cat on a green oak who recites a folktale when he turns to the left and a song when he moves to the right.

As in all of Pushkin's works, the language is the most important feature, offsetting the many flaws of Pushkin's still immature talent. His choice of vocabulary is very Russian, even popular, and his rhythms and rhymes are graceful and effortless. Henri Troyat refers to him as "a virtuoso of rime" and says that this talent alone announced possibilities for the future.

EUGENE ONEGIN

Eugene Onegin, Pushkin's novel in verse, was begun in 1823 in Kishinev and completed in 1830. It is composed of eight cantos or chapters, as Pushkin preferred to call them. There are projects and fragments for two other parts, including Onegin's journey. Each chapter contains forty to fifty-four stanzas of fourteen lines each, in four-foot iambic, and with a special rhyme scheme called the "Onegin stanza": *AbAbCCddEffEgg* (small letters indicating masculine and capitals feminine rhymes). Pushkin did not return to this stanza form and it has rarely been used since. The novel itself resembles sentimental types such as Jean-Jacques Rousseau's *La Nouvelle Héloïse* (1761; *Julia: Or, The New Eloisa*, 1773) and Benjamin Constant's *Adolphe* (1815; English translation, 1816). It is also a type of bildungsroman or the *éducation sentimentale* of Tatyana and Onegin. It is in reality a combination of several genres: novel, comic-epic, and above all poetry, for it is inseparable from the verse in which it is written.

The first two chapters, the product of Pushkin's youth, show the greatest absence of structure. They abound in digressions and poetic ruminations ranging from the ballet to women's feet. They introduce us to the hero Eugene Onegin, a St. Petersburg dandy, who spends his life in boredom until an inheritance brings him to an equally boring life in the provinces. Here he meets the dreamy poet Lensky, in love with a neighbor, Olga

Larin. It is at this point that the tone of the poem changes, as Olga's older sister, Tatyana, immediately develops an intense passion for Onegin, and in her simplicity reveals her love for him in her famous letter. Onegin politely refuses her and continues his aimless existence, interrupted by a flirtation with Olga, thus provoking a duel with Lensky in which the poet is killed.

Years pass, and Tatyana is married against her will to an elderly and unattractive general. Onegin meets her in Moscow and falls passionately in love with her. He declares his love, but this time it is Tatyana in her mature serenity who informs him: "I love you . . . but I have become another's wife; I shall be true to him through life." Here the poem ends abruptly yet fittingly as Tatyana emerges as the tragic heroine in this tale of twice-rejected love.

The poem maintains an internal unity through the parallel between Onegin's rejection of Tatyana and her refusal of him. *Eugene Onegin* is, however, essentially a lyric poem about the tragic consequences of love rather than a pure novel with a solid substructure. Pushkin draws poetry out of a samovar, the wrinkled nanny who is modeled on Arina Rodionovna, and the broken-hearted resignation of Tatyana. The changing of the seasons indicates the passage of time as Pushkin sings of the beautiful Russian countryside. He likewise enters into his characters, and makes of Onegin a realistic hero and the first of a long line of "superfluous men" to appear in Mikhail Lermontov, Ivan Goncharov, and Ivan Turgenev. Tatyana is perfectly consistent as her youthful naïveté changes into a controlled maturity. She has often been described as the purest figure in the whole of Russian literature, and has become the prototype of Russian womanhood. Pushkin's contemporaries read his poem with enthusiasm, and today it is still one of the great classics of Russian literature. Foreign readers may know it better through Pyotr Ilich Tchaikovsky's opera; again, this results from the fact that it is essentially a poem, defying translation.

POLTAVA

Pushkin always showed a great deal of interest in Peter the Great, and refers to him in his lyric poetry, in longer poems, and in his prose (*Peter the Great's Negro*). It is in *Poltava* and *The Bronze Horseman* that he reaches his height. *Poltava*, written in three weeks in 1828, has an epic quality but also draws on the ballad, ode, and oral tradition. It recalls Sir Walter Scott's *Marmion* (1808), since it places historical characters in a Romantic background. Lord Byron in *Mazeppa* (1819), drew on the same sources but used instead an apocryphal account of the hero's youth.

The main focus of *Poltava* is the battle of 1709, in which the Russians under Peter the Great defeated the Swedes under Charles XII. Poltava was the turning point in the Russo-Swedish War. Against this historical backdrop is set the romance of the aged Ukrainian Cossack hetman Mazepa with the young and beautiful Marya, daughter of Kochubey, who refuses to allow the marriage. The two marry in spite of him, and

Kochubey seeks revenge by revealing, to Peter, Mazepa's plan of revolt against him. His project miscarries, however, when Peter believes Mazepa's denials. Kochubey is taken prisoner by Mazepa and is about to be executed when Marya learns about her husband's treachery against her father. Arriving too late to save him, she leaves, returning to her husband only briefly as a madwoman before Mazepa's flight with Charles XII after leading an unsuccessful revolt against the victorious Peter.

Although Pushkin has interwoven much historical material into his tale, he has been charged with excessive melodrama by critics from Belinsky to the present day, who see in Mazepa a kind of Gothic villain. Pushkin is likewise charged with unsuccessfully fusing the historical and the Romantic, and more recently, by John Bayley, for the gap "between two kinds of romance, the modern melodrama and the traditional tragic ballad." Mazepa is one of Pushkin's few dark and villainous characters, but Marya has been acknowledged as truly *narodnaya* by Belinsky and Soviet critics. Peter is the all-pervading presence, larger than life, who symbolizes the growing importance of Russia.

THE BRONZE HORSEMAN

In *The Bronze Horseman*, Peter reappears in retrospect. Pushkin wrote *The Bronze Horseman* in 1833 partially in response to the Polish poet Adam Mickiewicz, who had attacked the Russian autocracy. It consists of an introduction and two parts, 481 lines in all, and is rightly considered one of Pushkin's greatest masterpieces. It combines personal lyricism and political, social, and literary themes and raises philosophical questions in paradoxical fashion. The title refers to the equestrian statue of Peter the Great by E. M. Falconet that still stands along the Neva River. The historical incident that inspired the poem was the devastating flood that struck St. Petersburg on November 7, 1824.

In the introduction, Peter the Great stands looking over the Neva, then a deserted swamp with a few ramshackle huts. He plans to build a city there, which will open a window to the West and terrify all his enemies. A hundred years pass, and the young city is the pride of the north, a cold sparkling gem of granite and iron, the scene of royal balls, military reviews, and winter sports. Suddenly, the picture changes as Pushkin begins his sad tale. Eugene, a poor government clerk (whose last name is not important), is making plans to marry Parasha. That very night, the Neva whirls and swirls and rages like an angry beast; the next day Parasha's home is destroyed, and she is lost. Eugene visits the empty spot, and goes mad from the shock. Life continues as usual, but poor Eugene wanders through the city until one day he shakes his angry fist at the Bronze Horseman, who gallops after him down the streets of St. Petersburg. Later, a dilapidated house is washed up on one of the islands; near it Eugene's corpse is found.

Pushkin's poem shows complete mastery of technique. In lines starkly terse yet rich with onomatopoeic sounds, Pushkin conjures up the mighty flood, the proud emperor, and the defenseless Eugene. In the last scene, Peter and Eugene come face to face, and seemingly the emperor wins, yet Pushkin is far from being reconciled to the notion that individual destiny must be sacrificed to historical necessity. Indeed, Eugene is the first of a long line of downtrodden Russian heroes, such as Akakiy Akakyevich and Makar Devushkin, possessing dignity and daring to face authority. Peter is the human hero, contemplating greatness; he is also the impassive face of destiny. The poem itself poses the problem of Pushkin's own troubled existence as well as the ambiguous and cruel fate of all human beings.

OTHER MAJOR WORKS

LONG FICTION: *Evgeny Onegin*, 1825-1832, 1833 (*Eugene Onegin*, 1881); *Arap Petra velikogo*, 1828-1841 (*Peter the Great's Negro*, 1896); *Kirdzhali*, 1834 (English translation, 1896); *Kapitanskaya dochka*, 1836 (*The Captain's Daughter*, 1846); *Dubrovsky*, 1841 (English translation, 1892); *Yegipetskiye nochi*, 1841 (*Egyptian Nights*, 1896); *Istoriya sela Goryu khina*, 1857 (*History of the Village of Goryukhino*, 1966).

SHORT FICTION: *Povesti Belkina*, 1831 (*Russian Romance*, 1875; better known as *The Tales of Belkin*, 1947); *Pikovaya dama*, 1834 (*The Queen of Spades*, 1858).

PLAYS: *Boris Godunov*, pb. 1831 (wr. 1824-1825; English translation, 1918); *Motsart i Salyeri*, pr. 1832 (*Mozart and Salieri*, 1920); *Pir vo vryemya chumy*, pb. 1833 (*The Feast in Time of the Plague*, 1925); *Rusalka*, pb. 1837 (*The Water Nymph*, 1924); *Kamyenny gost*, pb. 1839 (wr. 1830; *The Stone Guest*, 1936); *Skupoy rytsar*, pr. 1852 (wr. 1830; *The Covetous Knight*, 1925); *Stseny iz rytsarskikh vryemen*, pr., pb. 1937 (wr. 1835); *Little Tragedies*, 1946 (includes *The Covetous Knight*, *The Stone Guest*, *Mozart and Salieri*, and *The Feast in Time of the Plague*).

NONFICTION: *Istoriya Pugacheva*, 1834 (*The Pugachev Rebellion*, 1966); *Puteshestviye v Arzrum*, 1836 (*A Journey to Arzrum*, 1974); *Dnevnik, 1833-1835*, 1923; *Pisma*, 1926-1935 (3 volumes); *The Letters of Alexander Pushkin*, 1963 (3 volumes); *Pisma poslednikh let 1834-1837*, 1969.

MISCELLANEOUS: *The Captain's Daughter, and Other Tales*, 1933; *The Poems, Prose, and Plays of Pushkin*, 1936; *The Works of Alexander Pushkin*, 1936; *Polnoye sobraniye sochineniy*, 1937-1959 (17 volumes); *The Complete Prose Tales of Alexander Pushkin*, 1966; *A. S. Pushkin bez tsenzury*, 1972; *Pushkin Threefold*, 1972; *Polnoye sobraniye sochineniy*, 1977-1979 (10 volumes); *Alexander Pushkin: Complete Prose Fiction*, 1983.

BIBLIOGRAPHY

Bethea, David M. *Realizing Metaphors: Alexander Pushkin and the Life of the Poet.* Madison: University of Wisconsin Press, 1998. Bethea illustrates the relation between the art and life of Pushkin and shows how he speaks to modern times.

_____, ed. *The Pushkin Handbook.* Madison: University of Wisconsin Press, 2005.

A collection of essays by Pushkin scholars in the Soviet Union and North America that looks at his life and legacy. Includes essays on his poetic works.

Binyon, T. J. *Pushkin: A Biography.* New York: Knopf, 2004. An extensive biography of Pushkin, Russia's national poet.

Debreczeny, Paul. *Social Functions of Literature: Alexander Pushkin and Russian Culture.* Stanford, Calif.: Stanford University Press, 1997. Debreczeny divides his study into three parts: the first is devoted to selected readers' responses to Pushkin; the second explores the extent to which individual aesthetic responses are conditioned by their environment; and the third concerns the mythic aura that developed around Pushkin's public persona.

Evdokimova, Svetlana. *Pushkin's Historical Imagination.* New Haven, Conn.: Yale University Press, 1999. An examination of the range of Pushkin's fictional and nonfictional works on the subject of history. Evdokimova considers Pushkin's ideas on the relation between chance and necessity, the significance of great individuals, and historical truth.

Feinstein, Elaine. *Pushkin: A Biography.* London: Weidenfeld & Nicolson, 1998. Drawing on newly discovered documents, Feinstein explores the life of one of nineteenth century Russia's greatest writers.

Kahn, Andrew, ed. *The Cambridge Companion to Push kin.* New York: Cambridge University Press, 2006. Looks at his works and their legacy. Contains several chapters on his poetry.

Ryfa, Juras T., ed. *Collected Essays in Honor of the Bicentennial of Alexander Pushkin's Birth.* Lewiston, N.Y.: Edwin Mellen Press, 2000. A selection of scholarly essays devoted to various works by Pushkin and his influence on his literary descendants.

Shaw, J. Thomas. *Pushkin's Poetics of the Unexpected: The Nonrhymed Lines in the Rhymed Poetry and the Rhymed Lines in the Nonrhymed Poetry.* Columbus, Ohio: Slavica, 1993. This is a highly specialized study of Pushkin's poetic technique that will be of most use to specialists.

Vitale, Serena. *Pushkin's Button.* Translated by Ann Goldstein and Jon Rothschild. New York: Farrar, Straus and Giroux, 1999. A cultural history and narrative of the last months of Pushkin's life before his fatal duel. Vitale brings to life the world of St. Petersburg in the 1830's using her own research with information gleaned from secondary literature and the memoirs and letters of Pushkin's contemporaries.

Irma M. Kashuba

EDITH SÖDERGRAN

Born: St. Petersburg, Russia; April 4, 1892
Died: Raivola, Finland; June 24, 1923

PRINCIPAL POETRY

Dikter, 1916 (*Poems*, 1980)
Septemberlyran, 1918 (*The September Lyre*, 1980)
Brokiga iakttagelser, 1919 (*Motley Observations*, 1980)
Rosenalteret, 1919 (*The Rose Altar*, 1980)
Framtidens skugga, 1920 (*The Shadow of the Future*, 1980)
Landet som icke är, 1925
Min lyra, 1929
Edith Södergrans dikter, 1940 (*The Collected Poems of Edith Södergran*, 1980)
We Women: Selected Poems of Edith Södergran, 1977
Love and Solitude: Selected Poems, 1916-1923, 1980, 1985
Poems, 1983
Complete Poems, 1984

OTHER LITERARY FORMS

Edith Södergran (SUH-dur-grahn) died of tuberculosis at the age of thirty-one, and many of her works were published posthumously. She left behind a remarkable collection of letters to Hagar Olsson, a critic and novelist whose favorable review of Södergran's *The September Lyre* led to a close friendship between the two young women. Södergran's correspondence with Olsson was published under the title *Ediths brev: Brev från Edith Södergran till Hagar Olsson* (Edith's letters: letters from Edith Södergran to Hagar Olsson) in 1955. The letters appeared in translation in *The Poet Who Created Herself: The Complete Letters of Edith Södergran to Hagar Olsson with Hagar Olsson's Commentary and the Complete Letters of Edith Södergran to Elmer Diktonius* (2001).

ACHIEVEMENTS

Edith Södergran's poetry met with a baffled and even hostile reception in her own day, with a few notable exceptions, and even caused a journalistic debate as to her sanity. Writing in a period when Nordic verse still supported traditional values of regular meter and rhyme, Södergran espoused free verse and arrived—apparently on her own initiative—at something like the "doctrine of the image" laid out by Ezra Pound in 1912, derived by him in part from his study of the first poems of H. D. Therefore, shortly before her death, Södergran was hailed in the Finno-Swedish journal *Ultra* as the pioneer of Finnish modernism.

By the 1930's, Södergran's home in Raivola (later Rodzino) had become an unofficial shrine for younger poets, and Södergran's work was revered by a number of successors, among these Gunnar Ekelöf, the Swedish poet, and Uuno Kailas, the Finnish writer. Her courageous rejection of verse conventions inspired later poets to do the same. Her canon makes clear the expressionistic elements in the modernist temper, and in granting pride of place to irrational forces, Södergran (wittingly or not) aligned herself with such contemporaries as D. H. Lawrence, James Joyce, and André Breton. In the words of George Schoolfield, "Her simple directness, enlivened by her genius for the unexpected in language, is seen to best advantage when [she] is overwhelmed by forces outside herself." This primordial and homespun receptivity has proved to be a highly prospective stance, and accounts for Södergran's continuing popularity, enhanced by the feminist movement's reexamination of women's writing, spreading far beyond the boundaries of Norden, and gaining momentum more than sixty years after her death.

BIOGRAPHY

Edith Södergran was born on April 4, 1892, in the cosmopolitan city of St. Petersburg (called Leningrad during the years of the Soviet Union), the principal Baltic seaport and then capital of Russia. Her father, Mattias Södergran, came from a family of farmers who, while they lived in northwestern Finland, were of Swedish stock. Her mother, Helena Holmroos, Mattias's second wife, was the daughter of a prosperous industrialist, also of Finno-Swedish descent. When she was three months old, Södergran's family moved to Raivola, a village in the Finnish province of Karelia, close to the Russian border. Thenceforth, the family divided their time between St. Petersburg, where they wintered, and Raivola. Södergran received a sound education at a German church school, studying the literature of France, Russia, and Germany. Her apprentice verse was written in German, which she learned not only in school but also at the sanatorium in Davos, Switzerland; she was a patient there from 1912 to 1913 and again from 1913 to 1914. Heinrich Heine provided the model for much of Södergran's early writing.

Södergran's father died of tuberculosis in 1907, after which his family ceased to reside in St. Petersburg. In 1908, Södergran was discovered to be tubercular, and between 1909 and 1911, she was on several occasions confined to a sanatorium at Nummela, in Finland. Nummela was the only place she lived where Swedish was the primary language; otherwise, Södergran spoke Swedish mainly with her mother.

It is believed that the philologist Hugo Bergroth was instrumental in persuading Södergran to write in Swedish. Nevertheless, she had very little knowledge of the literature of that language, beyond the work of two nineteenth century authors, C. J. L. Almqvist, whose novel *Drottningens juvelsmycke* (1834; *The Queen's Diadem*, 1992) she found fascinating, and Johan Ludvig Runeberg, with his aphoristic lyrical poems. Her interest, rather, lay elsewhere—in such German expressionists as Else Lasker-

Schüler and Alfred Mombert, in Victor Hugo (whose *Les Misérables*, 1862; English translation, 1862; captured her attention), in Rudyard Kipling (particularly his *The Jungle Book*, 1894), in Maurice Maeterlinck, in Walt Whitman, and in the Russians Konstantin Dmitrievich Balmont and Igor Severyanin.

A turning point in Södergran's life was her love affair, during her early twenties, with a married man, an affair of the kind customarily known as unhappy. Presumably it was not consistently so. For a poet so able to live with paradox, the relationship may have been, after all, deeply inspirational. Certainly, the affair virtually coincided with an intense period of production, during which she wrote the first of her mature works. Södergran's sense of her own poetic powers had been waxing throughout these two years, 1915 and 1916, and had given her the impetus to visit Helsinki to show her manuscripts to Arvid Mörne, the poet, and Gunnar Castrén, the critic. The literary world of Helsinki was unreceptive to her work; her first book, *Poems*, prompted one reviewer to wonder whether her publisher had wanted to give Swedish Finland a good laugh, and in general, reactions ranged from amused bewilderment to open ridicule. Södergran appears to have been taken completely aback by such uncomprehending hostility; her naïveté, one of the strengths of her poetry, was in this respect a major weakness of her person, and it caused her many painful passages.

However, resilience was hers in equal measure, and before long, Södergran regained equilibrium, coming to think of herself (indeed, quite properly) as a literary pioneer. Her sense of mission grew with her reading of Friedrich Nietzsche, whose influence may be traced throughout her subsequent work. Will in the sense of libido becomes a fundamental drive that her poetry not only acknowledges but also would advance. In "Mitt liv, min död och mitt öde" ("My Life, My Death, My Fate," composed in 1919, published in *Landet som icke är*), Södergran writes:

> I am nothing but a boundless will,
> a boundless will, but for what, for what?
> Everything is darkness around me.
> I cannot lift a straw.
> My will wants but one thing, but this thing I don't know.
> When my will breaks from me, then shall I die:
> All hail my life, my death and my fate!

She praises the moment when these three abstract, powerful forces unite into the one action, the moment of discovery, when the alienation of categories is banished by the wholeness, the good health, of choice, when the will to choose and the will to be chosen fuse, banishing both subjective and objective, to disclose the truth: that life, death, and one's fate are all of a piece, compose one single motion. The "I" one was until that moment "dies" and is replaced by the "I" who has chosen, having discovered that "thing" which until then one had not known.

Resilient though she was, however, Södergran was increasingly ill. More than her personal world was in turmoil. World War I, in which Russia was then engaged, led to the Russian Revolution of 1917. Raivola, astride a trunk line of the railroad from St. Petersburg, witnessed both troop transports and refugee trains passing through, and with the revolution, Södergran and her mother found themselves destitute, for St. Petersburg had been their source of funds. In this same year, 1917, Finland declared its independence from Russia, and the ensuing civil war resulted in near starvation for the poet and her family. At the same time, however, to behold so many other substantially afflicted persons helped Södergran place her own hardships in perspective. She learned quickly from her experiences. Huge, irrational forces had been unleashed, yet Södergran had the grace to recognize her world. In her introduction to *The September Lyre*, she observes:

> My poems are to be taken as careless sketches. As to the contents, I let my instincts build while my intellect watches. My self-confidence comes from the fact that I have discovered my dimensions. It does not behoove me to make myself smaller than I am.

To some extent, this was surely a whistling in the dark. Two further books of poetry were met with tremendous hostility. There was one favorable review, however, by Olsson, and to this Södergran responded with incredulous joy. The two became fast friends, albeit mainly through correspondence. (Invited to visit Olsson in Helsinki, Södergran declined: "Insomnia, tuberculosis, no money. We live by selling our furniture.") They met only a few times, but their correspondence flourished.

Södergran became a convert to anthroposophy, the belief of Rudolf Steiner, and thence to a primitive Christianity, which replaced for her the writing of poetry. She returned to poetry, however, shortly before her death, on June 24, 1923, at Raivola. The posthumous publication of her previously uncollected poems from 1915, under the title *Landet som icke är* (the land which is not), established her as a major poet. Subsequent collections and volumes of selected poems continue to appear, enhancing Södergran's reputation and securing for her an ever-widening audience.

ANALYSIS

The power of Edith Södergran's poetry stems from the complex mixture of its elements. She gives the impression of being very straight-spoken, yet for all that, most of her poems are deeply enigmatic. Her choice of subjects is usually appropriate to this technique. One is reminded of a child at that stage where puberty startles it out of one kind of consciousness into another. This is the age when the "big" questions come up: What is outside the universe? What was before time began? What is death? What shall be my destiny? And love—what is love?

Somehow, Södergran survived the subsequent stages of her life to produce virtually intact poems of a childlike naïveté wedded to a maturity that feels precocious—the precocious intelligence of the thirteen-year-old who has recently realized that she is more far-seeing than her elders and that she sees more clearly into the heart of adult life because she is so new to it. This image, subliminal in so many of her poems, of a gravely joyous child gazing directly into adulthood and finding it at once wanting and yet (wisely) sufficient, wreathes her poetry in an aura of heartbreak. All the mysterious grand abstractions—death, life, love, pain, happiness, grief, instinct, hell—framed by the pubescent as essential questions to be answered are answered in Södergran's poetry, as in life, with an image that may at first appear as basically haphazard but which one then comes to apprehend as intuitively adequate. Life proves to be not the wondrous thing one had at thirteen thought it to be; it turns out, however, in its difference from the ideal, to be something (a state of affairs that is recognized, by a sudden twist of maturity, to be in itself wondrous).

Södergran does not incorporate undigested personal experience into her work. Her experience is nearly always universalized, through either a symbol or (more interestingly) some less predicated distancing technique—or a combination of both, as at the end of part 2 of "Dagen svalnar . . ." ("The Day Cools . . . ," from *Poems*, 1980):

> You cast your love's red rose
> into my white womb—
> I hold it tight in my hot hands,
> your love's red rose that will shortly wilt . . .
> O thou master, with the icy eyes,
> I accept the crown you give me,
> that bends my head towards my heart.

This passage demonstrates Södergran's ability to qualify the symbol with realism and realism with its own stylization: "head" being a symbol for thought, rationality, as distinct from feeling, impulse, symbolized by heart, yet at the same time as she is using this symbolic language to imply that, in love, the head is brought nearer to the heart, she is also stating the fact that, in the act of love, the neck can bend the head forward, bringing it literally closer to the heart, but perhaps only literally. The physical undoes the symbolic, even as the latter transcends the physical. The same double movement is present throughout this poem: The presence of the physical both renders the symbolism ironic ("red rose" is so obviously a penis) and accounts for it, explains away its symbolism, even while the symbolic is raising the sad physical facts to a transcendent plane, as though from lust to love.

"DISCOVERY"

In this technique, the essential ambiguity of such a situation is preserved intact, preserved from the poet's intentions and from the reader's everlasting demand for assurance. Is the "master" subject only to "higher" motives? That one may doubt this is suggested in "Upp täckt" ("Discovery," from *The September Lyre*):

Your love darkens my star—
the moon rises in my life.
My hand is not at home in yours.
Your hand is lust—
my hand is longing.

Here, Södergran lays out neatly the two halves of the picture, the "fifty-fifty" of the heterosexual fix. His love, although desired (in fact, "longed for"), threatens to overwhelm the woman, who senses that her own "star" (her own sense of self and particular destiny) is being obscured by the male presence, no doubt filled with assumptions and demands, obscured in the way that the light of a star is blocked when the full moon rises. Panicked, she retreats: "My hand is not at home in yours." Presumably she had felt otherwise about this man. Thus she leads herself to her "discovery": He lusts, while she longs. He also longs, as no doubt she also lusts; it is a question of which emotion is primary. Enlightened, however sadly, the poet, through observing this dynamic, gives herself back to herself and finds her star. Able to describe the process, she finds a power within herself to withstand it. It is noteworthy that Södergran is not deterred from her use of natural imagery by preexisting symbolic meaning: that the moon, for example, is customarily a symbol of the female.

"FOREST LAKE"

Such nature imagery permeates Södergran's work from start to finish. Whole poems are built from observations of the landscape and weather of Raivola. "Skogssjön" ("Forest Lake," from *Poems*, 1980) is a striking example of this:

I was alone on the sunny strand
by the forest's pale blue lake,
in the heavens floated a single cloud
and on the water a singl`e isle.
The ripening summer's sweetness dripped
in beads from every tree
and into my opened heart ran
down one little drop.

Nature burgeons on all sides in supernumerous abundance, while in the felt middle of it all, the human singularity (which remarks not only the various signs of its own condition—cloud, island, lake, each one a singular—but also, the signs of its opposite state—the "beads" that drip from "every tree") inevitably, inescapably one feels, selects for itself that which most speaks to it of itself from out of the swarming possibilities. One senses at once the rightness of this as well as the sadness. In the phrase "one little drop," a pathos inheres: Why so little, when one is offered so much? However, the poem offers also a sense of this as sufficient; it is characteristic of Södergran's poetry to play between senses of pathetic inadequacy and grateful, if humble, plenitude.

"THE DAY COOLS . . ."

Sometimes the speaker senses herself as the source of the inadequacy, as in part 4 of "The Day Cools . . .":

> You sought a flower
> and found a fruit.
> You sought a well
> and found a sea.
> You sought a woman
> and found a soul—
> you are disappointed.

The irony of the situation, which she sees and names so clearly, does not completely expunge the guilt of the speaker. Somehow, one feels, she holds herself to blame for being so much more than the seeker expected to find. She is caught in the patriarchal trap, even as she would, with her vision and fluency, transcend it. Indeed, for her to testify otherwise would be an impossible distortion of reality, one that would demean her import and that of her fellow sufferers.

The simple symmetry of this poem reminds one of Södergran's courage in discarding so many of the conventional signs of verse. Perhaps it was as much a blind plunge forward as a reasoned decision; no matter, the result is the same. Whether the reader indeed interprets her poems, as she advised, as "careless sketches," or, disregarding that phrase as one born of a strictly temporary bravado, one views them as finished pieces is irrelevant. Certainly, she did not abjure regular meter and rhyme out of inability; while still a schoolgirl, she composed hundreds of verses in the manner typical of Heine.

While at Davos, Södergran learned something of the current furor and ferment at work in European art and letters, and possibly of free verse. Above all, however, her writing is instinct with craft; Södergran has no need to make a display of her talent in more conventional terms because so many of her poems bear this out at the microscopic level.

"NOTHING"

If there are infelicities in Södergran's poetry, they are those inherent in writing poetry whose rhythms are at times those of prose. One notes the occasional deafness to the echoes of what is being said. In "Farliga drömma" ("Dangerous Dreams," from *Landet som icke är*), she inquires, "Have you looked your dreams in the eye?" her own eye on the object of her poem, distracting her from the faintly ridiculous literal picture presented. Because both "dreams" and "look in the eye" are clichés, it is not easy to remember that they allude to specifics. Her practice of personifying abstractions gets her into trouble sometimes, "My soul can only cry and laugh and wring its hands," as in "Min själ" ("My Soul," from *Poems*, 1980), or "Will fate throw snowballs at me?" as in "Hyacinten" ("The Hyacinth," from *The Shadow of the Future*). However, there is a charm of sorts in these minor ineptitudes, some echo of the child just learning to put words together; surely this is one with her ingenuousness and directness. The person who senses her soul as real, as real as her body, is blind to the unintended image offered of a pair of bodiless hands "wringing" each other; this is the same person who can write of the abstraction nothing, in "Ingenting" ("Nothing," from *Landet som icke är*):

> We should love life's long hours of illness
> and narrow years of longing
> as we do the brief instants when the desert flowers.

In this poem, Södergran is reminiscent of John Keats in "To Autumn"—the spiritual definition of "iron" circumstance which allows one room to live. It is a wonderful benignity, won at what cost from malign condition, and not at all ironic. There are certainly poems of less mitigated bitterness, but even with these, one feels that in the act of naming the enemy, Södergran has won the only release truly possible from the shadow of death and death-in-life. Through the storms within her own organism, as through the storms without (war, revolution, poverty, and hunger) she looked steadily into the heart of things. In a very late and striking poem, "Lander som icke är" ("The Land That Is Not," from *Landet som icke är*), she wrote

> I long for the land that is not,
> because everything that is, I'm too weary to want.
> The moon tells me in silvery runes
> of the land that is not.
> The land where all our wishes shall be wondrously
>   fulfilled,
> the land where our shackles drop off,
> the land where we cool our bleeding forehead
> in moon-dew.
> My life was a feverish illusion.
> But one thing I have found and one I have really won—
> the way to the land that is not.

The poem has a further stanza but should have ended here. Södergran's gift for discerning the positive in the negative has seldom been more strongly realized. Through her genius, the reader comes to understand how the negative is so qualified, somewhat as "faery lands forlorn" in Keats's "Ode to a Nightingale," and that a simple act of the imagination may transform nothingness into a vision more sustaining than anything that blank materialism affords.

OTHER MAJOR WORKS

NONFICTION: *Ediths brev: Brev från Edith Södergran till Hagar Olsson*, 1955; *The Poet Who Created Herself: The Complete Letters of Edith Södergran to Hagar Olsson with Hagar Olsson's Commentary and the Complete Letters of Edith Södergran to Elmer Diktonius*, 2001 (translated and edited by Silvester Mazzarella).

BIBLIOGRAPHY

Jones, W. Glyn, and M. A. Branch, eds. *Edith Södergran*. London: University of London Press, 1992. A collection of nine biographical essays dealing with Södergran's life and works. Includes bibliographical references and indexes.

Katchadourian, Stina. Introduction to *Love and Solitude: Selected Poems, 1916-1923*, by Edith Södergran. 3d ed. Seattle, Wash.: Fjord Press, 1992. Katchadourian's introduction to this translation of a selection of Södergran's poetry offers some biographical and historical background for her life and works.

Lindqvist, Ursula. "The Paradoxical Poetics of Edith Södergran." *Modernism/Modernity* 13, no. 1 (2006) : 813-818. Examines the paradoxical nature of Södergran's poetry, which contains a complex mix of themes.

Schoolfield, George C. *Edith Södergran: Modernist Poet in Finland*. Westport, Conn.: Greenwood Press , 1984. A biography of Södergran detailing the historical background of her life and works. Includes bibliographic references and an index.

Södergran, Edith, and Hagar Olsson. *The Poet Who Created Herself: The Complete Letters of Edith Södergran to Hagar Olsson with Hagar Olsson's Commentary and the Complete Letters of Edith Södergran to Elmer Diktonius*. Translated and edited by Silvester Mazzarella. Chester Springs, Pa.: Dufour Editions, 2001. These letters to Södergran's critic and friend Olsson and to the poet and composer Diktonius reveal a great deal about the poet's thoughts. Olsson's commentary provides additional background.

Valtiala, Nalle. "Edith Södergran: When Karelia Was the Centre." In *Centring on the Peripheries: Studies in Scandinavian, Scottish, Gaelic, and Greenlandic Literature*, edited by Bjarne Thorup Thomsen. Norwich, England: Norvik Press, 2007. This essay looks at the innovations of Södergran and her influence on subsequent Scandinavian literature.

Witt-Brattstrom, Ebba. "Towards a Feminist Genealogy of Modernism: The Narcissistic Turn in Lou Andreas-Salomé and Edith Södergran." In *Gender, Power, Text: Nordic Culture in the Twentieth Century*, edited by Helena Forsås-Scott. Norwich, England: Norvik Press, 2004. Examines Södergran and the mistress of Rainer Maria Rilke, looking at the development of modernism from a feminist perspective.

David Bromige

MARINA TSVETAYEVA

Born: Moscow, Russia; October 8, 1892
Died: Yelabuga, Tatar Autonomous Soviet Republic, Soviet Union (now in Russia);
August 31, 1941
Also known as: Marina Tsvetaeva

PRINCIPAL POETRY
Vecherny albom, 1910
Volshebny fonar, 1912, 1979
Iz dvukh knig, 1913
Razluka, 1922
Versty I, 1922
Stikhi k Bloku, 1922, 1978
Psikheya, 1923
Remeslo, 1923
Posle Rossii, 1928 (*After Russia*, 1992)
Lebediny stan, 1957 (*The Demesne of the Swans*, 1980)
Selected Poems of Marina Tsvetayeva, 1971
Poem of the End: Selected Narrative and Lyrical Poetry, 1998

OTHER LITERARY FORMS

Marina Tsvetayeva (tsvih-TAH-yuh-vuh) wrote a number of plays, including *Konets Kazanovy* (pb. 1922; the end of Casanova), *Metel* (pb. 1923; the snowstorm), *Fortuna* (pb. 1923; fortune), *Priklyuchenie* (pb. 1923; an adventure), *Tezey* (pb. 1927; Theseus), and *Fedra* (pb. 1928; Phaedra). Several of these were later expanded or combined and reissued under different titles. Tsvetayeva's prose is extensive. Parts of her diaries and her many memoirs have appeared in journals and newspapers, mostly abroad. Some of these prose pieces, together with literary portraits, critical essays, and letters, were collected in *Proza* (1953). A prose collection in English, *A Captive Spirit: Selected Prose*, appeared in 1980. Tsvetayeva also translated poetry, prose, and drama into French, and from French into Russian. Some of her letters, notes, and individual poems remain unpublished and unlocated, but émigré publishers continue to search for material. A modest number of plays and prose pieces have been printed in Soviet journals.

ACHIEVEMENTS

Recognition came to Marina Tsvetayeva late in life, following decades of critical neglect, official Soviet ostracism, and émigré hostility. Her suicide during World War II, not known to the world for a long time, engendered critical fascination with the details of her life, eventually followed by publication, republication, and scholarly evaluation of her work. The creative variety and quality of Russian writing in the first quarter of the twentieth century created a situation in which many talented poets, among them Tsvetayeva, escaped public attention. Her adherence to the old orthography and to pre-Revolutionary values, cast into unconventional, awkward-seeming syntax, caused her work to appear disjointed. Only the subsequent careful study of her form and language has revealed the verbal and stylistic brilliance of a unique poetic voice. Political events forced Tsvetayeva to live in exile with artistically conservative Russians who did not understand her poetic experiments. She courageously developed her style, despite exclusion from émigré publishing houses and Soviet rejection of new forms, proudly suffering the ensuing material deprivation. Many of her themes are so closely linked to events in her life that it is difficult to comprehend them without biographical information; the publication of several critical and biographical studies has made her verse more accessible. Translations into English have appeared, and literary scholars now acknowledge her as a major Russian poet.

BIOGRAPHY

Marina Ivanovna Tsvetayeva's birth on October 8, 1892, into an educated, artistic family, augured well for her poetic future. Her mother, a talented amateur pianist, instilled in her an appreciation for the fine arts and insisted on rigorous musical training, while her father's respected position as a professor of art at Moscow University provided exposure to the creative community in Russia. Nicolas II himself, with his family, attended the opening of Professor Tsvetayeva's lifelong project, the Moscow Fine Arts Museum. This august event impressed Tsvetayeva and is reflected in both her poetry and prose, possibly contributing to the unswerving loyalty she displayed toward the imperial family, even when the expression of such sympathies proved dangerous. At age six, Tsvetayeva performed at a public piano recital and tried her hand at versification. Her mother's illness in 1902 necessitated a four-year stay abroad, during which Tsvetayeva developed her interest in literature at Swiss and German boarding schools. After the death of her mother in 1906, she reluctantly entered the Moscow *gimnaziya*, where she treated her courses rather casually. No longer attracted to music, she drifted in and out of schools, devoting all her time to the writing of poetry. She barely managed to complete secondary education, lagging two years behind her graduating class. A collection of poems written in her teens, *Vecherny albom* (evening album), was privately published in 1910 in an edition of five hundred copies. Several critics generously noted artistic promise in the volume, and the poet-painter Max Voloshin introduced Tsvetayeva to Moscow's literary world.

Tsvetayeva's independent, sometimes provocative demeanor—she smoked, bobbed her hair, traveled alone abroad—coupled with a budding literary reputation, brought a measure of local fame. At Voloshin's Crimean house, which served as an artists' colony, she met and shortly thereafter, in 1912, married the eighteen-year-old Sergey Efron, member of a prominent Jewish publishing family. In the same year, she issued her second book of verse, *Volshebny fonar* (the magic lantern), dedicated to her new husband. Neither this collection nor her third, *Iz dvukh knig* (from two books), caused much of a critical stir, with public attention diverted by an abundance of other talented writers and the imminent war. When Tsvetayeva's daughter Ariadna was born in 1912, she immediately became a frequently mentioned star in her mother's verse. Tsvetayeva's writings during the next ten years, disseminated primarily through public readings and occasional journal printing, also failed to receive critical acclaim. These pieces saw publication only in 1922 under the title *Versty I* (milestones I).

The Bolshevik Revolution found the poet in Moscow, nursing her second daughter, Irina, while Efron fought with the White Army in the south. Tsvetayeva coped poorly with the hardships of the Civil War. Unwilling to waste time at nonliterary jobs, she lived on the edge of starvation, and Irina died of malnutrition in a government orphanage in 1920. These years, however, were poetically Tsvetayeva's most productive. Between 1917 and 1921, she completed work that was eventually assembled into "Versty II" (unpublished), *The Demesne of the Swans*, *Razluka* (separation), and *Remeslo* (craft), and she developed friendships with the foremost poets of the time, among them Aleksandr Blok, Vladimir Mayakovsky, Osip Mandelstam, and Boris Pasternak. By 1921, Efron had made his way to Prague, where Tsvetayeva joined him with their surviving daughter a year later. During the following years, much of her work was printed by émigré houses in Berlin, Paris, and Prague. In 1925, having expanded her range to epic poems and plays, and following the birth of her son Georgy, Tsvetayeva set up residence in Paris, where a large colony of anti-Communist Russians had gathered. While her contact with foreign writers remained limited, she corresponded regularly with Marcel Proust and Rainer Maria Rilke. The latter, deeply impressed by her talent, addressed a long elegy to her in 1926.

Tsvetayeva's poetic style developed in exile, heavily reflecting Futurist trends. Its experimental nature did not find favor with conservative émigré writers or the public, and her 1928 collection, *After Russia*, largely escaped notice. Reluctantly, Tsvetayeva turned to prose to support herself but never managed a comfortable existence. Her romantic involvements testify to a growing estrangement from Efron, who changed his political outlook in the 1930's and became a Soviet agent. This step had disastrous consequences for the poet. In 1937, her daughter, a confirmed Communist, returned to the Soviet Union. Later that year, Efron was implicated in several political murders, but he escaped to the Soviet Union before he could be brought to trial. Tsvetayeva, now ostracized by fellow exiles and in desperate financial straits, decided to follow her family back to the Soviet Union in 1939. Before her departure, she wisely left her manuscripts in several safe places. This collection later facilitated a Tsvetayeva revival by Western researchers.

The poet returned home to a chilly reception. Tsvetayeva's émigré status and well-known pre-Revolutionary sympathies precluded publication of her work. Only one poem appeared in print after her return, and no record of subsequent work exists or has been made public. Instead, a series of tragic events—the aftermath of Joseph Stalin's purges—drove her to record thoughts of suicide in her diary. Within months of her arrival, Ariadna was sent to a labor camp, where Tsvetayeva's sister, Anastasia, also spent the last decade of Stalin's rule. Efron disappeared and was executed some time later. Fellow Russians, fearing political contamination, shunned Tsvetayeva. By 1941, wartime evacuation found her with her teenage son in the Tartar Autonomous Republic, east of Moscow. The village of Elabuga could offer the penniless poet only a job as kitchen maid. Proud and stubborn as always, she insisted on a more dignified occupation. When an appeal to establishment writers quartered nearby failed, she hanged herself. The villagers, unaware of her artistic credentials, buried her without ceremony in an unmarked grave. Her son Georgy joined the army and is presumed to have been killed in action. When the "Thaw" began after Stalin's death, Ariadna returned from prison and, with the aid of no-longer-silent poets, devoted herself to promoting her mother's literary heritage. In 1956, a Soviet edition of selected poems appeared, followed by public readings and further publication, always in moderate proportion, carefully chosen to avoid anti-Soviet allusions. In 1980, the Moscow Excursion Bureau instituted a tour of places associated with Tsvetayeva, during which the guide recites generous excerpts of her poetry. This revival, accompanied by an intense interest in her remarkable life, has led to a Tsvetayeva cult in the Soviet Union and a lively black market in her work, finally giving her the recognition so long withheld.

ANALYSIS

Marina Tsvetayeva's poetry is notable for its stylistic innovations, peculiarity of language, political sympathies, and autobiographical intensity. She did not immediately achieve mastery of style. Her early work shows that she was searching for a voice of her own, re-creating the language of Moscow's high society in a rather stilted, overly elegant fashion, punctuated by allusions to childhood and romantic longings that do not always mesh with her aristocratic tone. By the time she composed the poems collected in *Versty I,* the ornate phrasing had developed into a simpler language, but one reflecting old, already archaic Russian usage, thus evoking the poetic diction of earlier centuries. At the same time, Tsvetayeva destroyed this historic illusion by incorporating deliberately incongruous colloquialisms and by placing sacred Church Slavonic phrases in coarse contexts. This stylistic violence is redeemed by the expressive, sometimes whimsical quality of her language, which became the trademark of her later work. She selects significant words, often creating new ones by building on familiar roots, which can evoke extended images or form connections to the next phrase without any grammatical links. One of her favorite devices is the verbless stanza: She achieves the necessary cohesion by clever juxtaposition of sharply delineated nouns, producing a brittle, succinct, almost formulaic precision of line. Her lexical and phonetic experiments, especially her neologisms, evoke the work of Mayakovsky and other Futurists, but she manages to maintain a voice peculiarly her own, which is partially the result of her skill in combining archaisms with colloquialisms to produce an incongruous but striking blend of tradition and novelty.

In much of Tsvetayeva's later work, she also shifts the stress within the poetic line, carefully selecting her vocabulary to accommodate such prosodic deformation. Depending on the desired effect, Tsvetayeva drops unstressed syllables, adds dashes to represent syllables, or adds syllables to words, occasionally generating such awkward sequences that she feels it necessary to give intonation or pronunciation information in footnotes. Intensely interested in language expansion, she delighted in pushing poetic devices beyond existing limits. When employing enjambment, she broke the very word in half, creating odd, internal rhymes. These metric innovations, combined with her highly unusual diction, were responsible in part for the relative neglect that Tsvetayeva's work suffered for some time.

Theoretically, Tsvetayeva favored lost causes and failures. The most prominent example is *The Demesne of the Swans*, a cycle of mourning for the defeated White Army. The same compassion appears in the 1930 cycle on Mayakovsky, following his suicide, and in the poems condemning the German invasion of Czechoslovakia. Her loyalty to and love for the past led her again and again to reinterpret motifs from classical literature, with a particular emphasis on Russia's old epics and folklore.

A knowledge of Tsvetayeva's life does not merely enhance an understanding of her work; it is vital to it. Her poetry is a kind of diary in verse, a chronological account of her experiences, often inaccessible without further elucidation. When preparing her work for safekeeping before returning to Russia, she recognized the hurdles facing the reader and provided explanatory footnotes for many pieces. Even so, her verse demands time and attention before it yields its richness, and she is generally considered to be a difficult poet. The phonetic and semantic interplay that characterizes much of her work poses formidable challenges to the translator. Her inability or unwillingness to exist harmoniously with her surroundings—she continually stressed her otherness—led to a crippling isolation long before political exigencies forced her to extremes. While this withdrawal from the general community nourished her talents, it also lost her publishers, readers, friends, and family. In a December 30, 1925, letter to A. Tesková, she confessed that she had no love for life as such, caring only for its transformation into art. When that was no longer possible, she chose to end her existence.

VECHERNY ALBOM

Tsvetayeva's first book of verse, *Vecherny albom*, already shows the talent and originality of the later perfectionist, although it is still dominated by the immature, conventionally romantic confessions of a young girl. The poems are grouped around two thematic centers: hero worship and childhood feelings. She admires those who achieve a measure of exaltation and personal glory despite handicaps and mundane origin, among them Napoleon, Sarah Bernhardt, and Huck Finn. A special series is devoted to the doomed nobles featured in Edmond Rostand's works. When Tsvetayeva treats her early family life, she is equally idealistic, expressing impatience with the ways of the world: "I thirst for miracles/ Now, this minute, this very morning." The nursery verses also contain a fairy-tale dimension, filled with endearing diminutives, storytelling, the figure of her mother, and her own fear of leaving this shelter for adulthood. The metrical line and strophe are still traditional, although occasionally enlivened by flashes of lexical innovation.

VOLSHEBNY FONAR

Tsvetayeva's second collection, *Volshebny fonar*, dedicated to her bridegroom, does not differ significantly in theme and style. The desire to linger in the safe haven of childhood remains strong. She implores Efron to honor these sentiments: "Help me to remain/ A little girl, though your wife," so that the marriage will proceed "From one fairytale into another." Family, friends, and husband are celebrated in sad and joyful verses. While a few snatches of brisk dialogue point to her later telegraphic style, rhyme and meter are strictly conventional. Forty-one poems from her first two volumes were collected in *Iz dvukh knig*, concluding Tsvetayeva's idealistic, romantic period.

VERSTY I

Versty I (milestone I) represents the maturing of Tsvetayeva's poetry—hence the title. In this collection, she trims her lexical material to a minimum, focusing on sharply delineated images to produce an aphoristic style, and her rigid metrical design gives way to the more contemporary mixed meter, called *dolniki*, with which she had begun to experiment. The book serves as a poetic chronicle of 1916. Its unifying theme is the city of Moscow, to which she pays homage in every group of poems. She connects writers, friends, and family with various places in town, and employs diverse poetic personae (tavern queens and beggars) and a range of colorful, lower-class expressions. Among those poets singled out are Anna Akhmatova, Blok, and Mandelstam. In cycles dedicated to the first two, Tsvetayeva cleverly rephrases the artists' own poetic idiom and adapts their metrical peculiarities to her own compositions, giving the reader the strange impression of two simultaneous poetic voices. A brief infatuation with Mandelstam resulted in an exchange of dedications. Finally, there are personal poems, walks around the city with Ariadna, and the poet's first separation from her daughter. In one striking composition, she envisions her own grand funeral procession winding through the streets of Moscow, quite unlike the pauper's burial for which she was destined. The voice of alienation, of being out of place, so dominant in her later verse, already prevails in a number of poems in this volume.

THE DEMESNE OF THE SWANS

The Demesne of the Swans, Tsvetayeva's most controversial book, saw its first publication only in 1957, with a later edition in 1980 featuring English translations facing the original. The printings in the West evoked protest in the Soviet Union, where the work had not been published. Although Tsvetayeva's expressionistic technique and verbal brilliance are particularly evident in these cycles, the provocative theme of a noble, courageous White Army overrun by vile Bolshevik hordes dominates the book. Tsvetayeva's outrage at the destruction of venerated tradition by reincarnated Tartar hordes screams from almost every page. In chronicling the downfall of czarism, starting with Nicolas II's abdication and ending with the Communist victory in 1920, the poet reaches into Russia's epic past for motifs. She compares the White Army to the doomed troops of Prince Igor's campaign, whose defeat at the hands of looting Asiatics foreshadowed Russia's long suffering under the Tartar yoke. Conversely, the Red Army is depicted as an unseemly mob, stampeding all that is sacred and precious into the dust. Tsvetayeva's anguish concerning the unknown fate of Efron is evident but is overshadowed by the national tragedy, which she describes in dramatic effusion: "White Guard, your path is destined to be high/ . . . Godlike and white is your task/ And white is your body that must lie in the sands." Even the more personal poems in the volume are saturated with her hatred of the new regime. The intensity attending Tsvetayeva's treatment of the Civil War is in marked contrast to the poet's customary nonpolitical, disinterested stance.

The remainder of Tsvetayeva's lyric output continues the driving rhythm, the aphoristically compressed line, and the discordant sound patterns introduced in *Versty I*. Rejection of the environment and notes of despair appear ever more frequently in her verse. Following the Revolution, she also produced epic narratives, adding new dimensions to her style but still basing the narrative on private experience or reaching into Russian history to re-create its heroic legacy.

Tsvetayeva's verse is part of the general poetic flowering and experimentation of the early twentieth century. Her approaches reflect the innovations of Russian Futurists, but she manages to preserve a voice of her own. Despite isolation and hardship in exile, she continued to explore new means of poetic expression, maintaining an artistic link with developments in the Soviet Union. When her extensive output was finally collected and published, she began to emerge as a major Russian poet.

OTHER MAJOR WORKS

PLAYS: *Konets Kazanovy*, pb. 1922; *Fortuna*, pb. 1923; *Metel*, pb. 1923; *Priklyuchenie*, pb. 1923; *Tezey*, pb. 1927 (also known as *Ariadna*); *Fedra*, pb. 1928.

NONFICTION: *Proza*, 1953; *Izbrannaia Proza v Dvukh Tomakh, 1917-1937*, 1979; *A Captive Spirit: Selected Prose*, 1980; *Art in the Light of Conscience: Eight Essays on Poetry*, 1992.

MISCELLANEOUS: *Izbrannye proizvedeniya*, 1965 (selected works).

BIBLIOGRAPHY

Ciepiela, Catherine. *The Same Solitude: Boris Pasternak and Marina Tsvetaeva.* Ithaca, N.Y.: Cornell University Press, 2006. Ciepiela examines the ten-year love affair between Boris Pasternak and Tsvetaeva, whose relationship was primarily limited to long-distance letters. Included in this volume is the correspondence between the two authors along with letters from Rainer Maria Rilke, who completed the couple's literary love triangle. Ciepiela reveals the similarities between Pasternak and Tsvetaeva by painting a portrait of their lives and personalities. She scrutinizes their poetry and correspondence, finding significant links between them. This volume is written clearly and succinctly, making it easily accessible to all readers.

Cixous, Hélène. *Readings: The Poetics of Blanchot, Joyce, Kafka, Kleist, Lispector, and Tsvetayeva.* Translated by Verena Andermatt Conley. Minneapolis: University of Minnesota Press, 1991. A comparative analysis of a variety of innovative writers, including Tsvetayeva, by a noted French feminist thinker, geared toward a scholarly audience.

Feiler, Lily. *Marina Tsvetaeva: The Double Beat of Heaven and Hell.* Durham, N.C.: Duke University Press, 1994. This psychological biography draws on both classical and postmodernist psychoanalytic theory—Sigmund Freud's notion of pre-Oedipal narcissism and Julia Kristeva's concept of depression as "the hidden face of Narcissus"—to explain the contradictory impulses evident throughout Tsve tayeva's work.

Feinstein, Elaine. *A Captive Lion: The Life of Marina Tsvetaeva.* London: Hutchinson, 1987. A popular biography with annotation and a selected bibliography, this work draws on material from scholars and presents Tsvetayeva as a humanist and feminist interested in art, not politics.

Karlinsky, Simon. *Marina Tsvetaeva: The Woman, Her World, and Her Poetry.* New York: Cambridge University Press, 1985. A revised, updated, and definitive biography based on the poetry and prose of Tsvetaeva as well as the memoirs of her relatives. Material about her life and her writing are integrated in the text. Includes an excellent bibliography and notes.

Kudrova, Irma. *The Death of a Poet: The Last Days of Marina Tsvetaeva.* Translated by Mary Ann Szporluk. Woodstock, N.Y.: Overlook Press, 2004. A harrowing look at the conclusion of Tsvetayeva's life, pieced together using KGB documents.

Makin, Michael. *Marina Tsvetaeva: Poetics of Appropriation.* Oxford, England: Clarendon Press, 1993. Eschewing biographical interpretation, Makin stresses Tsvetayeva's reliance on literary antecedents. The text is well documented, contains a comprehensive source list, and provides original translations of the poetry discussed.

Pierpont, Claudia Roth. *Passionate Minds: Women Rewriting the World.* New York: Knopf, 2000. A collection of evocative interpretive essays on the life paths and works of twelve women, including Tsvetayeva.

Proffer, Ellendea, ed. *Tsvetaeva: A Pictorial Biography*. Translated by J. Marin King. Introduction by Carl R. Proffer. Ann Arbor, Mich.: Ardis, 1980. An excellent collection of annotated photographs of Tsvetayeva throughout her life.

Schweitzer, Viktoria. *Tsvetaeva*. Translated by Robert Chandler and H. T. Willetts. New York: Farrar, Straus and Giroux, 1992. This biography portrays Tsvetayeva as alienated from the world since early childhood by her poetic sensibilities. The author argues that a compulsive "need to be needed" kept Tsvetaeva grounded in events of the real world. Includes bibliography, chronology, index, and biographical notes.

Margot K. Frank

ANDREI VOZNESENSKY

Born: Moscow, Soviet Union (now in Russia); May 12, 1933
Died: Moscow, Russia; June 1, 2010

PRINCIPAL POETRY

Mozaika, 1960
Parabola, 1960
Treugol'naya grusha, 1962
Antimiry, 1964 (*Antiworlds*, 1966)
Akhillesovo serdtse, 1966
Voznesensky: Selected Poems, 1966
Antiworlds and the Fifth Ace, 1967
Stikhi, 1967
Ten' zvuka, 1970 (*The Shadow of Sound*, 1975)
Dogalypse, 1972
Little Woods: Recent Poems by Andrei Voznesensky, 1972
Nostalgia for the Present, 1978
Soblazn, 1978
Stikhotvoreniia: Poemy, 1983
An Arrow in the Wall: Selected Poetry and Prose, 1987
Rov, 1987 (*The Ditch: A Spiritual Trial*, 1987)
On the Edge: Poems and Essays from Russia, 1991
Gadanie po knige, 1994

OTHER LITERARY FORMS

Andrei Voznesensky (voz-nuh-SEHN-skee) is known primarily for his lyric poetry; however, he produced a body of experimental work that challenges the borders between literary forms. For example, his long work "Oza" (1964) is a literary montage alternating verse with prose passages and incorporating several points of view. *Avos* (1972; *Story Under Full Sail*, 1974), based on the life of the Russian diplomat and explorer Nikolai Petrovich Rezanov, is sometimes classified as poetry, sometimes as prose. Voznesensky's prose writings include a short memoir, "I Am Fourteen," which sheds light on his friendship with the famed Russian writer Boris Pasternak; "O" (about), which appears in *An Arrow in the Wall*, a critical commentary on art and literature; and "Little Crosses," an essay on spirituality. In addition, he wrote a play, *Save Your Faces* (pr. 1971), and collaborated on musical and theatrical pieces such as the "rock opera" *Iunona i Avos* (pr. 1983; *Juno and Avos*).

ACHIEVEMENTS

During the early 1960's, Andrei Voznesensky, like his contemporary Yevgeny Yevtushenko, enjoyed enormous popularity in what was then the Soviet Union. His books sold hundreds of thousands of copies as soon as they were published, and fans flocked to public readings held in athletic stadiums to accommodate audiences of ten thousand and more.

His poetry, which is intellectually demanding, drew critical acclaim internationally as well as within the Soviet Union. His literary awards spanned three decades. *Antiworlds* was nominated for the Lenin Prize in literature in 1966, and "The Stained Glass Panel Master" won the State Literature Prize in 1978. He was awarded the International Award for Distinguished Achievement in Poetry in 1972, and his collection *An Arrow in the Wall*, edited by William Jay Smith and F. D. Reeve, received the *New York Times* Editor's Choice Award in 1987.

BIOGRAPHY

Born in Moscow in 1933 to a well-educated family, Andrei Andreyevich Voznesensky was exposed to art and literature at an early age. His mother, a teacher, read him poetry and inspired his interest in major Russian writers. His father, a professor of engineering, introduced him to the work of the Spanish artist Francisco de Goya, which would later inspire "I Am Goya," one of Voznesensky's best-known poems. While growing up, Voznesensky pursued interests in the arts, especially painting, but he did not focus on poetry until 1957, the year he completed a degree from the Moscow Institute of Architecture. Then, in a strange twist of fate, a fire at the institute destroyed his thesis project. For Voznesensky, this was a sign that his future lay not in architecture but in poetry.

In the same year, he met the famed Russian writer Boris Pasternak, with whom he had been corresponding. Pasternak served as a mentor for Voznesensky, but the younger poet quickly found his own voice. The similarities between the work of the two authors lie in their moral vision and their goals as writers to revive Russian literature after years of oppression under the dictatorship of Joseph Stalin. An essential difference is in their fates. In spite of an easing of government censorship following Stalin's death in 1953, Pasternak was expelled from the powerful Soviet Writers' Union for the 1957 publication of *Doktor Zhivago* (*Doctor Zhivago*, 1958). The novel's free-thinking protagonist criticizes Soviet Communism. However, in the changing literary-political climate of the time, Voznesensky quickly became one of the best-known poets in the Soviet Union. In 1960, his first collection, *Mozaika* (mosaic), appeared in print, and he published a number of collections in rapid succession, as audiences responded enthusiastically to the freshness of his work.

The success of Voznesensky, his contemporary Yev tushenko, and other "liberal" writers created a backlash within the Writers' Union. By 1963, Voznesensky had come under attack from the more orthodox literary establishment, the government-controlled press, and Soviet premier Nikita Khrushchev. Unlike Pasternak, who was censored for the content of his writing, Voz nesensky was denounced for his innovative style, which critics claimed produced a decadent, superficial art, devoid of meaning. Charges of formalism and obscurantism resurfaced throughout the 1960's and into the following decade.

In response, Voznesensky addressed his critics directly in his poetry, and he began to produce verse on the subject of creative freedom and the nature of art. He defended the complexity and ambiguity of his work, asserting, "if the poems are complicated, why then, so is life." He also spoke out against government censorship. In 1967, he openly supported fellow writer Aleksandr Solzhenitsyn, who had been expelled from the Writers' Union and later exiled from the Soviet Union for his attack on Soviet censorship. In 1979, Voznesensky participated in the publication of an independent literary journal.

In spite of recurring conflicts with government and the conservative literary establishment, Voznesensky incurred only minor punishment. Throughout his career, he was able to travel abroad, live comfortably, and publish regularly. He remained committed to innovative and experimental art forms, producing a body of work that challenges conventional classification. Married to the writer and critic Zoya Boguslavskaya, he had one son. He died in Moscow, at the age of seventy-seven, on June 1, 2010.

ANALYSIS

The American poet W. H. Auden remarked that Andrei Voznesensky is a writer who understands that "a poem is a verbal artifact which must be as skillfully and solidly constructed as a table or a motorcycle." Voznesensky was well known for his technical virtuosity and structural innovation. His metric and rhyme schemes varied, often determined by the aural and visual aspects of the work. He paid close attention to surface patterning and sound play—assonance, alliteration, shaped text, stepped lines, palindromes—and often startled the reader with shifts in perspective, incongruous juxtaposition of images, and unexpected rhyme created by inserting slang or colloquial language into a line. He confronted the reader with a staggering array of metaphor, historical reference, and cultural allusion. Evidence of his early training in painting and architecture abounds in his work, which has been described as cubist, Surrealist, and Futurist. Voznesensky acknowledged, "As a poet I have been more profitably influenced by ancient Russian churches and by the works of Le Corbusier than by other poets."

Voznesensky's concern with technique and experimentation related directly to the content of his writing and his central concern with human destiny, which he viewed as dependent on interconnectedness. For him, without a sense of connection to one another, to culture and tradition, and to the planet, humanity might fall into a destructive spiral. In a mechanized, technological world, the potential for fragmentation and alienation is great. The responsibility of the artist is to expose relationships, to "peel the skin from the planet."

Voznesensky sought to achieve his goal by breaking away from habitualized methods of seeing, from routines that limit and fragment vision. His wordplay, his seemingly bizarre selections of imagery, his multiple perspectives, and his blurring of genres were all designed to defamiliarize the world, allowing the reader to discover the spiritual ecosystem of existence. While Voznesensky's themes are universal, his innovativeness, particularly his sound play, makes his work difficult to translate. Effective English versions of his work are the Haywood/Blake 1967 edition *Antiworlds and the Fifth Ace* and the award-winning collection *An Arrow in the Wall*, edited by Smith and Reeve.

"I AM GOYA"

One of the earliest and best-known of his poems, "I Am Goya" (1959), exemplifies Voznesensky's skill in creating new forms to examine broad themes. He framed the poem by opening and closing with the same line, "I am Goya." In identifying with Goya, a nineteenth century Spanish painter known for his harsh depictions of war, Voznesensky established an immediate link across time, space, and artistic genres. He reinforced these links in each of the four stanzas with an eclectic range of images and allusions and by the repetition of the first line. The horrors of war belong to all ages, and the artist's role is to transcend the immediate and speak to the universal, "hammer[ing] stars into the unforgetting sky—like nails."

Voznesensky composed "I Am Goya" aloud rather than writing it on paper in order to develop fully the aural qualities of the verse. He described it as "picking the words, so that they would ring out" like the bells of an ancient monastery playing "the music of grief." To this end, Voznesensky combined repetition of sounds with an uninterrupted beat that tolls throughout the poem. The rhythms of the poem anticipate the powerful image "of a woman hanged whose body like a bell/ tolled over a blank square," then embed it in a synesthetic format.

"PARABOLIC BALLAD"

Voznesensky considered "Parabolic Ballad" (1960) one of his best poems. Citing the career of the French painter Paul Gauguin as a model, Voznesensky justifies the ambiguity and experimental nature of his own work and reasserts his aesthetics. Like Gauguin, who "To reach the royal Louvre,/ Set his course/ On a detour via Java and Sumatra," the poet must not take the direct route, choose the ready-made symbol, or speak in clichés. Rather, the artist must follow the trajectory of a rocket, a parabola, to escape "the earth's force of gravitation" and explore the far side of the universe.

"OZA"

Written in 1964, a year after Voznesensky was denounced for formalism and obscurity, "Oza" was a bold response to his critics. This complex narrative poem contemplates the fate of humanity in a technological society and continues the poet's experiments with poetic structure. Sections of prose alternate with poetry, themes intersect, and point of view shifts. The work is rich in literary and historical allusion. One section parodies Edgar Allan Poe's poem "The Raven"; another satirizes former Soviet dictator Stalin.

Introduced as a diary found in a hotel in Dubna, the site of a Soviet nuclear research facility, "Oza" describes a world rearranged by technology. The protagonist, Zoia, is a well-meaning scientist transformed through her own arrogance and complacency into an automaton named Oza. Zoia means "life" in Russian, but in the rearrangement of letters of her name, the "I" has been lost, suggesting the loss of self in a rigidly mechanized culture. Like Zoia/Oza, the poet risks losing his identity. In a scene described sometimes comically from the perspective of a ceiling mirror, the poet is invisible, immune to the inversion of the reflecting surface, and alienated from his fellow beings. Although unseen, he makes himself heard, proclaiming "I am Andrei; not just anyone/ All progress is regression/ If the progress breaks man down."

THE DITCH

This long narrative poem explores human greed. The actual ditch is the site of a massacre near Simferopol, a city on the Crimean Peninsula, where in 1941, twelve thousand Jews were executed by Nazis. In the 1980's, grave robbing occurred at the site. Although several men were convicted and received prison sentences in 1985—and it is to this event that the "trial" of the subtitle alludes—the looting continued. On a visit to the site two years after the trial, Voznesensky observed skulls that had been excavated and smashed for the bits of gold in the teeth.

As in earlier works, Voznesensky employed contrasting imagery, shifts in perspective, and inversions. A prose "afterword" introduces the work, suggesting an inversion of values. The mixture of voices and genres and the range of references take the subject beyond the specific crime into an examination of human nature.

GADANIE PO KNIGE

Inspired by traditional Russian fortune-telling, *Gadanie po knige* (telling by the book) examines the interconnectedness of chance and design. In this collection, Voznesensky took his wordplay to a new level, creating complex, multilingual meanings. Like a fortune-teller, he shuffled language and laid it out in patterns: circles, palindromes, anagrams. At times, he mixed English words with Russian ones, switching between the Cyrillic and Roman alphabets as well; he fragmented words from both languages and rearranged the syllables. What may initially appear random, pointless, or merely amusing surprisingly yields meaning, as when he exploited phonetically MMM, the name of a financial institution involved in a costly scandal. He connected MMM with the English word "money," the Russian word for "mania," and finally, the Russian slang for "nothing."

OTHER MAJOR WORKS

LONG FICTION: *Avos*, 1972 (*Story Under Full Sail*, 1974).

PLAYS: *Save Your Faces*, pr. 1971; *I Am Goya*, pr. 1982 (music by Nigel Osborne); *Iunona i Avos*, pr. 1983 (music by Alexei Rybnikov).

BIBLIOGRAPHY

Airaudi, Jesse T. "Hard to Be a God: The Political Antiworlds of Voznesensky, Sokilov, and the Brothers Strugatsky." In *Visions of the Fantastic: Selected Essays from the Fifteenth International Conference on the Fantastic in the Arts*, edited by Allienne R. Becker. London: Greenwood Press, 1996. Airaudi provides a sound rationale for Voznesensky's use of the fantastic to escape from the false, primary world imposed by governments and ruled by ideologies. Airaudi places Voznesensky in the tradition of the Russian writer Nikolai Gogol, yet suggests Western readers can best understand Voznesensky in terms of Surrealism.

Anderson, Raymond. "Andrei Voznesensky, Russian Poet, Dies at Seventy-seven." *The New York Times*, June 1, 2010, p. A23. Obituary of Voznesensky recalls his experimental poetry, his problems with the Soviet authorities, and his popularity as a poet.

Brown, Deming. *Soviet Russian Literature Since Stalin*. New York: Cambridge University Press, 1978. This well-documented literary history provides a good overview of the complex and ever-fluctuating relationship between literature and politics in the two decades following the death of dictator Joseph Stalin. Voznesensky is referred to throughout the book and is a key figure in the fifth chapter, "The Younger Generation of Poets."

Carlisle, Olga. *Poets on Street Corners: Portraits of Fifteen Russian Poets*. New York: Random House, 1968. In this collection of biographical sketches, Carlisle, the granddaughter of noted Russian writer Leonid Andreyev, has included poets who write about and for ordinary Russians living ordinary lives. Her chapter on Voznesensky features lengthy quotations from interviews with the poet between 1963 and 1967. Voznesensky's comments on the significance of poetry and the role of the poet are particularly illuminating.

Jason, Philip K., ed. *Masterplots II: Poetry Series*. Rev. ed. Pasadena, Calif.: Salem Press, 2002. This set contains summaries and analyses of the Voznesensky poems "Foggy Street" and "The Last Train to Malkhovka."

Plimpton, George, ed. *Beat Writers at Work: "The Paris Review."* New York: Random House, 1999. Conversations between Voznesensky and American poets Allen Ginsberg and Peter Orlovsky provide an entertaining, behind-the-scenes look at the writers as they discuss the poet's craft.

Porter, Robert, ed. *Seven Soviet Poets*. London: Gerald Duckworth, 2000. Porter's slender collection provides a thoughtful introduction, bibliographies, a historical reference guide, annotations, and biographical time lines for Voznesensky as well as other twentieth century Russian poets. These sections are in English, but the poetry is in Russian. For readers who are new to the language, the collection provides a good starting point with a supplemental vocabulary.

K Edgington

YEVGENY YEVTUSHENKO

Born: Stantsiya Zima, Siberia, Soviet Union (now in Russia); July 18, 1933

<small>PRINCIPAL POETRY</small>
Razvedchicki gryadushchego, 1952
Tretii sneg, 1955
Shossye entuziastov, 1956
Stantsiya Zima, 1956 (*Zima Junction*, 1962)
Obeshchaniy, 1957
Luk i lira, 1959
Stikhi raznykh let, 1959
Yabloko, 1960
Nezhnost, 1962
Vzmakh ruki, 1962
Selected Poetry, 1963
Bratskaya GES, 1965 (*Bratsk Station, and Other New Poems*, 1966)
The Poetry of Yevgeny Yevtushenko 1953-1965, 1965
Kachka, 1966
Yevtushenko: Poems, 1966
Poems Chosen by the Author, 1967
Idut belye snegi, 1969
Stolen Apples, 1971
Doroga Nomer Odin, 1972
Poyushchaya dambra, 1972
Otsovskiy slukh, 1975
From Desire to Desire, 1976
Ivanovskiye sitsi, 1976
V Polniy Rost, 1977
Golub' v Sant'iago, 1978 (novel in verse; *A Dove in Santiago*, 1983)
Tyazholive zemli, 1978
The Face Behind the Face, 1979
Ivan the Terrible and Ivan the Fool, 1979
Invisible Threads, 1981 (poems and photographs)
The Poetry of Yevgeny Yevtushenko, 1981
Ty na planete ne odin, 1981
Early Poems, 1989
Grazhdane, poslushaite menia, 1989
Stikhotvoreniya i poemy, 1990

The Collected Poems, 1952-1990, 1991
Pre-Morning: A New Book of Poetry in English and Russian, 1995
Walk on the Ledge = Progulki po karnizu: A New Book of Poetry, 2005 (in English
　and Russian)
Yevtushenko: Selected Poems, 2008

OTHER LITERARY FORMS

The prose works of Yevgeny Yevtushenko (yehv-tuh SHEHNG-koh) include
Primechaniya k avtobiografii (1963; *A Precocious Autobiography*, 1963), first published in the Paris periodical *L'Express*; *Talant est' chudo nesluchainoe: Kniga statei*
(1980; talent is not an accidental wonder), a collection of essays that are mainly on poetry but also on music, film, and prose; *Yagodnye mesta* (1981; *Wild Berries*, 1984), a
novel; and *Pod kozhey statuey sbobody* (pr. 1972; under the skin of the Statue of Liberty), a poetic drama. Yevtushenko also published the novel *Ne umirai prezhde smerti*
(1993; *Don't Die Before You're Dead*, 1995), which is based on the failed 1991 coup
d'etat attempted by old-school communists who opposed the government of Mikhail
Gorbachev. Yevtushensko was the compiler and wrote the introduction for a one-thou-
sand-page poetry anthology, *Twentieth Century Russian Poetry: Silver and Steel*
(1993). The massive anthology ranges over the entire corpus of Russian poetry in the
twentieth century and had to be smuggled out of the country in sections beginning in
1972.

ACHIEVEMENTS

Yevgeny Yevtushenko's appeal to a popular audience began with his first verses,
which appeared in a sports magazine, *Sovjetskiy sport*, in 1949. His early publications,
full of autobiographical revelations, charmed his audiences by their freshness and sincerity.
After Joseph Stalin's death in 1953, Yevtushenko began to address deeper social and political issues and became known as a dissident voice in Soviet literature. During the period of
liberalization under Nikita Khrushchev in the late 1950's and early 1960's, Yevtushenko's
personal and political poetry appeared in numerous Soviet journals and newspapers, including *Sovjetskiy sport, Yunost, Komsomolskaya pravda, Molodaya gvardiya, Literaturnaya
gazeta, Pravda, Znamya, Ogonyok, Rossiya, Novy mir*, and *Oktyabr*. When *Stikhi raznykh
let* (poems of various years) appeared in 1959, twenty thousand copies were sold immediately. The 1962 collection *Vzmakh ruki* (a wave of the hand) enjoyed a sale of 100,000
copies.

Not all of Yevtushenko's poetry, however, was so widely appreciated. When the
controversial "Babii Yar" was published in *Literaturnaya gazeta* in 1961, many hostile
articles appeared in the Soviet press, such as that of D. Starikov in *Literatura i zhizn*. It
was during this same period that Yevtushenko wrote the script for Dmitri Shostakovich's moving *Thirteenth Symphony* (1962), a work that uses the Babii Yar incident

as its principal motif. As a tribute to the poem's power, "Babii Yar" was inscribed in the Holocaust Memorial Museum in Washington, D.C. The New York Philharmonic made a recording of the Shostakovich work featuring Yevtushensko reciting "Babii Yar." In the early 1960's, Yevtushenko began to travel abroad, to France, England, and the United States. This exposure made him one of the most popular Soviet poets. Articles about him, as well as his poems, appeared in *Paris-Match, London Observer, Der Spiegel, Time, Saturday Review, Holiday, Life, Harper's Magazine*, and many others. Known as a dynamic performer and reciter of poetry, Yevtushenko gave many poetry readings both in the Soviet Union and abroad in a vibrant, declamatory style. He claims to have given 250 in 1961 alone.

Yevtushenko has been recognized throughout his career for both his literary and political achievements. He was given the U.S.S.R. Commission for the Defense of Peace award in 1965, the U.S.S.R. state prize in 1984, and an Order of Red Banner of Labor. His novel *Wild Berries* was a finalist for the 1985 Ritz Paris Hemingway award for best novel published in English. He has traveled widely and incorporated his observations and reactions into poetry, photography (*Invisible Threads*), film, drama, essays, and fiction.

BIOGRAPHY

Yevgeny Alexandrovich Yevtushenko was born in Stantsiya Zima, Siberia, in the Soviet Union, on July 18, 1933, of mixed Ukrainian, Russian, and Tartar blood. In his famous poem "Stantsia Zima" ("Zima Junction"), he describes in detail this remote Siberian town on the Trans-Siberian Railway about two hundred miles from Irkutsk and not far from Lake Baikal. Both his grandfathers were victims of Stalinist purges, a fact that helps to explain Yevtushenko's attitude toward Stalin. Yevtushenko's father was a geologist, and between the ages of fifteen and seventeen, young Zhenya, as he was familiarly called, accompanied his father on geological expeditions to Kazakhstan and the Altai. His mother, of modest peasant stock, worked as a singer in Moscow during and after the war. His parents' careers gave Yevtushenko a broad appreciation for common working people and the day-to-day struggles to survive in an authoritarian state.

As a young boy in Moscow, Yevtushenko began to read Russian and foreign classics, familiarizing himself not only with the works of Leo Tolstoy and Anton Chekhov, but also those of Alexandre Dumas, père, Gustave Flaubert, Friedrich Schiller, Honoré de Balzac, Dante, and many other foreign authors. In 1941, he was evacuated to Zima Junction, where he developed his love for the Siberian taiga and his impassioned opposition to war. When his parents were separated in 1944, he returned to Moscow with his mother. His education from 1944 to 1948 was very desultory, and when he was expelled from school at fifteen, he ran off to join his father in Siberia for two years.

Among Yevtushenko's many interests was sports, and it was not accidental that his first verses were published in a sports magazine. He met the editors Tarasov and Barlas, who became his first mentors, although his continued interest in reading led him to other models, especially Ernest Hemingway, Aleksandr Blok, Sergei Esenin, and Vladimir Mayakovsky. Yevtushenko wrote in the style of the times, paying lip service to Stalin until the latter's death in 1953.

The year 1953 was a turning point in Yevtushenko's life, for along with many other Russians, he experienced disillusionment with the Stalinist regime. With the coming of the Khrushchev "Thaw" in 1956, he began to write poetry against the former rulers and, gradually, advocating for human rights and expressive freedom. In 1954, he married Bella Akhmakulina, whom he himself describes as Russia's greatest living woman poet, although the marriage was doomed to failure. Yevtushenko's meeting with Boris Pasternak in 1957 brought him into contact with his greatest mentor.

In 1962, Yevtushenko began to travel abroad. His great success and popularity was temporarily interrupted by the publication in Paris of *A Precocious Autobiography* without the permission of the Soviet authorities, for which infraction his travel was curtailed. He subsequently made trips abroad, however, including one to the United States in 1966, where he gave many poetry readings and charmed audiences with his engaging and dynamic personality. He also visited Cuba, which he admired greatly as exemplary of the revolutionary ideal. Later travels to Rome, Vietnam, Africa, Japan, Alaska, California, and Florida also inspired poems. He lists sixty-four countries that he visited up to 1981. His second marriage, to Galina Semyonovna, and the birth of a son greatly inspired his life and work. He later would marry Jan Butler (1978) and Maria Novika (1986).

Since the 1970's, he has been active in many fields of culture, writing novels and engaging in acting, film directing, and photography. His first novel, *Wild Berries*, was a finalist for the Ritz Paris Hemingway prize in 1985, and his first feature film, *The Kindergarten* (1984), played in the Soviet Union, England, and the United States. Yevtushenko wrote and direced the film *Stalin's Funeral* (1990), which featured Vanessa Redgrave and Claus Maria Brandauer. Yevtusheko was appointed honorary member of American Academy of Arts and Sciences in 1987. He continued to be politically outspoken during this period as well, supporting author Aleksandr Solzhenitsyn and other Russian writers who were exiled or imprisoned.

With the advent of glasnost (a term used to refer to the gradual opening of Soviet culture and politics under Gorbachev) in the late 1980's, Yevtushenko became a leading activist in the struggle to reform Soviet society. In 1989, Yevtushenko became a member of the Congress of People's Deputies, and he was appointed vice president of Russian PEN in 1991. From 1988 to 1991, Yevtushenko worked against censorship and for freedom of expression when he served in the first freely elected Russian Parliament. When the old Soviet stalwarts attempted to derail Gorbachev's new government in 1991, Yevtushenko shouted his poetry from the balcony of the Russian White House in front of a huge crowd. In 1993, he received a medal as Defender of Free Russia, which was given to those who took part in resisting the hard-line Communist coup in August, 1991. However, in 1994, Yevtushenko refused to accept President Boris Yeltzin's tribute of The Order of Friendship Between Peoples as an expression of his opposition to the Russian war against Chechen rebels. In 1996, Yevtushenko joined the faculty at Queens College, New York; he later began teaching Russian and European poetry and cinema at the University of Tulsa, Oklahoma. Although critical and popular reception of Yevtushenko's work has mostly depended on the Soviet political climate, critics have generally praised the multicultural quality of his writings and regard Yevtushenko as Russia's premier but unofficial cultural emissary to the world.

ANALYSIS

Although not the most original poet of the post-Stalinist era in the Soviet Union, Yevgeny Yevtushenko has shown himself to be one of the most significant. This is essentially because he has been able to put his finger on the pulse of the times. He became the spokesperson for a new generation, not only in his native land but also all over the world. Unflinchingly honest and sincere, he has spoken with clarity and courage on issues that threaten freedom. He is best known for his poems of protest such as "Babii Yar" and "Stalin's Heirs." In the tradition of Russian poetry, Yevtushensko sees himself invested with a mission and a message, and he proclaims it fearlessly. He directs his criticism not only against the cult of personality, anti-Semitism, and oppression in his own land, but also against the same abuses in other countries, especially in the United States. Images of Martin Luther King, Jr., John and Robert Kennedy, and Allison Krause of Kent State University appeared in his work in the 1970's; the perils of television and advertising, war in Northern Ireland, and the threat of nuclear weapons in poems of the late 1970's. "Freedom to Kill," "Flowers and Bullets," and "Safari in Ulster," among others, explore these themes.

Yevtushenko knows how to combine the social with the personal and how to move effortlessly from one to the other. His poetry is extremely autobiographical, and one can read his life by exploring his verse. He tells whimsically of his Siberian childhood in Zima Junction, in the poem by the same name; of his youth in Moscow; of his travels and disappointment in love; and of his family and children. He reflects on the idealism of youth and the fears of impending old age. He is especially sensitive to childhood and can frequently combine his own experiences, a universal theme of childhood, and social observation. A typical poem is "Weddings," which recounts his folk dancing at ill-fated wartime weddings in Siberia.

A child of the North, Yevtushenko speaks best of nature when evoking the taiga, the lakes, and the rivers of Siberia; or the smell of fresh berries or the blue glow of fresh snow in "Zima Junction," "Monologue of the Fox," and "The Hut." He is close to the sea and often associates it with love ("The Sea"), with women ("Glasha, Bride of the Sea"), and with contemporary problems, as in "Kachka" ("Pitching and Rolling"). Nature, however, is not the most common source of images for this contemporary poet, who prefers the city with its neon lights, the sound of jazz, and the smell of smog. He is especially fond of New York and records his impressions in many poems such as "New York Elegy," "Smog," and *Pod kozhey statuey sbobody.*

People, more than nature, dominate Yevtushenko's poetry. In the tradition of Fyodor Dostoevski, Anton Chekhov, and Maxim Gorky, the lowly and the downtrodden occupy an important place. Socialist Realism places an emphasis on the "people." Yevtushenko adopts this attitude, but he goes even further, showing genuine sympathy for the worker and the peasant, especially evident in *Bratsk Station, and Other New Poems,* in which he also speaks of the unmarried mother ("Nushka"). While extolling the humble and the poor, he manifests hatred for the cruel overseer, the bully, or the compromiser. Such characters appear in "Babii Yar," "Zima Junction," and "Song of the Overseers" and in *Bratsk Station, and Other New Poems.* He detests hypocrisy and slavery in any form and denounces it loudly in the Soviet Union, the United States, South Africa, and anywhere else in the world.

Women occupy an important place in Yevtushenko's verse. In keeping with his sympathy for the peasant and workers, he dedicates many poems to the hardworking Russian woman, as in "The Hut." Old women in particular are among his favorites, such as the one who brings the red flowers of the taiga to the workers of Bratsk Station. The young innocent girl in love, such as "Masha"; the mothers who work for their young children and are never appreciated; the dancer; the singer: All these are living people who impart to Yevtushenko's works a strong dramatic quality.

The narrative, along with the lyric, is an important feature of Yevtushenko's poetry. He prefers the epic style, and "Zima Junction," *Bratsk Station, and Other New Poems,* and *Ivan the Terrible and Ivan the Fool* illustrate this tendency, although he often falls short of his goals. All his verse is dynamic rather than static. Many of his shorter works have a balladlike quality; among these are "Glasha, Bride of the Sea," "Rhythms of Rome," and "Nushka" in *Bratsk Station, and Other New Poems.* Dialogue occurs frequently and enhances the dramatic effect of his verse. *Pod kozhey statuey sbobody,* partially prose and partially verse, was staged in Moscow as a play in 1972; it satirized Russia as well as the United States.

Yevtushenko claims as his masters Hemingway (to whom he had dedicated one of his finest poems, "Encounter"), Esenin, Mayakovsky, and Pasternak, whom he knew personally and who offered friendly criticism of his early verse. The influence of Esenin and Mayakovsky is not always evident in his style, although at first glance he seems to be an avid disciple of Mayakovsky. Yevtushenko uses the "step lines" of Mayakovsky, but the verbal brilliance, bold speech, and innovation of the older poet are rarely evident. Yevtushenko employs a colloquial style, with many words borrowed from foreign languages. His poetry is filled with vivid twentieth century speech, with frequent sound effects, internal rhymes, and wordplay not always evident in English translations. He uses a wide variety of rhymes and rhythms, as well as free verse. His earlier poems tend to be freer than the poems of the late 1970's and early 1980's, which make use of regular meters and indulge in much less verbal experimentation. At all times he seems to write with ease and facility, although his poems frequently give the impression of too great haste. He is a prolific, spontaneous poet who writes without looking back and sometimes produces profound and startling insights.

Yevtushenko is a poet who wishes to be accessible to as many people as possible. He refuses poetic isolation and an elitist concept of art. In fact, he has chosen photography as a medium because its meaning is immediately obvious and it does not become obscure in translation. Above all, he is an apostle of human brotherhood. He believes in kindness and mutual understanding. *Invisible Threads* captures this theme dramatically . He is satirical, disarmingly frank, yet idealistic and trusting. Images of Christ, the sea, African jungles, and neon lights all serve to highlight his essential optimism and hope for the future.

Yevtushenko's poetry falls into distinct periods. The first, from 1952 to 1960, contains poems of youthful enthusiasm and is extremely autobiographical, as in "Zima Junction," "The Visit," and "Weddings." Memories of war and the child's inability to grasp its impact appear in "Weddings," "Party Card," and "A Companion." Since Yevtushenko had not begun his travels at this time, his inspiration was limited to Russia, centering especially on Moscow, Siberia, and Georgia. Although Yevtushenko was born long after the Revolution and did not know it at first hand, he manifests amazing conviction and enthusiasm for its ideals. "Lies" and "Knights" are among the many typical examples. Lyricism, love, and, above all, human sympathy characterize this early period.

"ZIMA JUNCTION"

Perhaps the best and most important poem of this period is "Zima Junction," first published in the journal *Oktyabr* in 1956. It refers to a visit to his native village in 1953, after the death of Stalin, the Doctors' Plot, and the deposition of Lavrenti Beria. Relatives and friends in far-off Siberia are anxious to learn all the news at first hand from this Moscow visitor, who, they expect, has all the information and has known Stalin personally. He accepts their naïveté with humor and respect for their simple lives, while at the same time noticing how both he and they have changed, and how they too have anxieties beneath the apparent simplicity of their ways.

The return to Zima Junction is the occasion for a retrospective glance at his own past and the past of his ancestors, as he recalls his great-grandfather's trip to Siberia from his peasant village in the Ukraine, and his grandfather's revolutionary idealism. Yevtushenko returns to the place where he was born not only for the past but also for the future, to seek "strength and courage." He realizes that he, like the people of the village, has changed, and that it is difficult to decide wisely on a course of action. He personifies

Zima Junction, which speaks to him through the forest and the wheat, in some of his best nature images. The section "Berry-Picking" has frequently been reprinted separately.

Throughout the poem, local color abounds, and Yevtushenko's narrative quality emerges through images of such people as the barefoot berry picker, the garrulous fisherman, and the disappointed wife in the hayloft who complains of her ungrateful and inattentive husband. Yevtushenko's family such as Uncle Volodya and Uncle Andrei, simple laborers, contrast with Pankratov, "the ponderous didactic president." The wheat and the village speak to young Zhenya, who is on the uncertain threshold of manhood, urging him to explore the world over and to love people.

Although the poem consists of many isolated incidents, they are obviously linked by the village and its message of courage and hope. The style is simple and colloquial, interspersed with local Siberian and Ukrainian expressions. The dialogue is suited to the speaker, and the nature imagery is among Yevtushenko's best. Belief in revolutionary ideals is evident, and party ideology, although present, is sincere and unaffected. Yevtushenko began to acquire fame after publishing this poem, where the personal note becomes universal.

"Babii Yar"

Yevheny's second distinct period—the poems of the 1970's—shows a broader scope and is mainly influenced by travel. Yevtushenko writes especially of the United States, Latin America, Cuba, Alaska, Hawaii, and Rome. He speaks out more freely against hypocrisy and loss of freedom, and he addresses social and political abuses, of which "Babii Yar" is the most significant example. At the same time, he professes strong patriotism, as evidenced in the lengthy *Bratsk Station, and Other New Poems*. The North, especially Siberia, is an inspiration for his work, especially *Kachka*. The personal and autobiographical theme returns in poems about love and loss of love. A more serious note is expressed in images of guilt, suffering, and repentance. Poems such as "Twist on Nails" and "Torments of Conscience" (published in English in *Stolen Apples*) express these themes through religious and dramatic imagery, of which one of the most striking examples is that of the pierced hands of the crucified Christ. These are poems of maturity and of considerable depth and sensitivity in both the personal and the social order.

"Babii Yar" was first published in the *Literaturnaya gazeta* in 1961. It is a poetic meditation on the tragic fate of the Jews in Eastern Europe, thirty-three thousand of whom were killed by the Germans in 1941 at Babii Yar, a ravine near the city of Kiev. As an attack on Soviet anti-Semitism, the poem stimulated controversy in the Soviet press and provoked counterattacks from leading journalists, but Yevtushenko continued to publish. In the poem, Yevtushenko deplores the absence of a monument at Babii Yar. One has subsequently been erected, without reference to the specific massacre of 1941.

The poem is not confined to Soviet anti-Semitism; it attacks prejudice against all peoples, but especially against Jews everywhere. In the poem, Yevtushenko, who is not Jewish himself, identifies with all the Jews of the past: those in ancient Egypt, Christ on the Cross, Alfred Dreyfus, and Anne Frank. Amid the harsh indictment of those who killed the Jews, Yevtushenko inserts delicate poetry: "transparent as a branch in April." He emphasizes the need for all people to look at one another and to recognize their responsibility and their brotherhood. By poetic transfer, Yevtushenko sees in himself each of these murderers and accepts responsibility for the terrible massacre. With characteristic optimism, he expresses trust in Russia's international soul, which will shine forth when anti-Semitism is dead.

"BRATSK STATION"

"Bratsk Station" was first published in the April, 1965, issue of *Yunost*. It is a long discursive poem of epic proportions: five thousand lines divided into thirty-five unequal and loosely connected parts. The main idea, as expressed by Yevtushenko himself, is a "controversy between two themes: the theme of disbelief expressed in the monologue of the Pyramid and the theme of faith, expressed by Bratsk Station." The Bratsk project was launched in 1958. It is a gigantic hydroelectric station, and it also contains lumber mills and plants for pulp, cardboard, wood by-products, and aluminum. Located in central Siberia along the Angara River, it is one of the largest hydroelectric plants in Russia. Yevtushenko sees it as a monument to free labor and considers the manpower that constructed it and keeps it in operation as a symbol of brotherhood, expressed in the word "bratsk," which means "brotherly."

The essential conflict is expressed in the recurring dialogue between the Egyptian Pyramid and Bratsk Station. Yevtushenko sees the Pyramid as a construction of slaves, and therefore it has no faith in itself. Moreover, it maintains that all men will ultimately turn to slavery and that freedom is only an illusory dream. This naïve interpretation of Egyptian history has provoked much criticism, notably from Andrei Sinyavsky in "In Defense of the Pyramid," where he maintains that Yevtushenko does not understand the significance of Egyptian society. The Bratsk Station, on the other hand, extols the free labor that built it, for it is the daughter of Russia who has attained freedom through centuries of suffering.

To illustrate the quest for freedom in the Russian soul, Yevtushenko evokes a number of events and heroes from Russian history, especially Stenka Razin, the Decembrists, and the followers of Mikhail Petrashevsky. To these he adds Russia's greatest writers; Alexander Pushkin, Tolstoy, Dostoevski, and the modern writers he so admires; Esenin and Mayakovsky, with a poem in the style of the latter. Finally, there are the unsung heroes of the people: Issy Kramer, the Light Controller, who still suffers from anti-Semitism; Sonka and Petka, the concrete pourers; and Nushka, the unwed mother. Yevtushenko relates that when he read his poem to the workers of Bratsk Station, mothers like Nushka held their children up to him, recognizing themselves in his poem.

Themes of socialism and patriotism abound in the poem, frequently exaggerated. Despite its loosely connected parts, the poem moves quickly, with dramatic and lively style and balladlike quality. There are echoes of "Babii Yar" in the Light Controller and of "Zima Junction" in the images of the taiga and the Simbirsk Fair, and the work is autobiographical as well as political and social. It begins and ends with poetry. In the "Prayer Before the Poem," Yevtushenko invokes Pushkin, Mikhail Lermontov, Nikolai Nekrasov, Blok, Pasternak, Esenin, and Mayakovsky and asks for their gifts (mutually exclusive, claims Sinyavsky). The final section, "The Night of Poetry," evokes the Siberian custom of improvising poetry and delivering it to musical accompaniment. In the moment of recitation, Yevtushenko sees before him the great Russian heroes and writers of the past and experiences with them the glory of freedom symbolized by Bratsk Station.

THE 1970'S

The years from 1970 to 1981 show both a return to basic structures in theme and composition and a broadening of scope into various genres: photography, the theater, the novel, and the essay. As the father of a child, Yevtushenko again writes about childhood, as in "Father and Son," "Walk with My Son," and "A Father's Ear." Now approaching middle age, he writes more of death ("A Child's Grave," "Come to My Tomb") and speaks of his desire to live in all lands and be all types of people possible, but to be buried in Russia. The travel theme is still uppermost, with an emphasis on the Far East, where Vietnam becomes an important social and political question. Yevtushenko, always against war, continues to make an appeal to human brotherhood in Northern Ireland, in South Africa, and between the United States and Russia.

IVANOVSKIYE SITSI

Still drawn to the epic theme, Yevtushenko published *Ivanovskiye sitsi* in the journal *Avrora* in 1976. The title means literally "calico from Ivanovo" and refers to Ivanovo-Voznesensk, a large textile center important for the labor movement. In 1905, there was a strike there that led to the establishment of one of the first Soviets of Workers' Deputies. Yevtushenko is always fond of wordplay and thus uses "Ivan" in several contexts. There is Ivan the Terrible, czar of Russia from 1533 to 1584, the symbol of autocracy in constant conflict with the people. Ivan the Fool is an important but composite character from folk epic and represents the growing popular consciousness. The poem glorifies the Revolution and the proletariat and expresses faith in the consciousness of the working class, bearers of the Russian soul. Yevtushenko maintains, however, that the Revolution extols heroes of all nations—Joan of Arc, John Brown, and Anne Frank—and aims for human brotherhood and a real International.

INVISIBLE THREADS

Invisible Threads, published in the United States and composed of poetry and photography, takes its inspiration from Edward Steichen's *Family of Man* exhibit and emphasizes the same theme. It contains poems from the late 1970's and addresses contemporary themes such as the threat of atomic warfare, the conflict in Northern Ireland, and the universal themes of birth and death, the former inspired by the birth of Yevtushenko's son in London. In the poem "Life and Death," a balladlike lyric, Life and Death exchange places. Death realizes that she is respected, if only because of fear, whereas Life is not. Yevtushenko pleads again for human dignity. Religious images are more evident than in the past, although Yevtushenko sees salvation among human beings on earth. He wishes to echo every voice in the world and "dance his Russian dance on the invisible threads that stretch between the hearts of men."

THE COLLECTED POEMS, 1952-1990

The Collected Poems, 1952-1990 reflects Yevtushenko's poetic career in microcosm: vast and ever astonishing in its variety. The title is somewhat misleading, since the volume offers only a selection from Yevtushenko's extensive career, and in addition, several long poems are represented in excerpts only. The translations by twenty-five translators vary in quality: A few are revisions of earlier versions, and because most of Yevtushenko's poems use slant rhyme relying heavily on assonance, few attempts were made to retain this feature in the English translations, or indeed to use rhyme at all.

Yevtushenko's characteristic political criticisms and commentary find a dominant place in this collection. He praises Chile's Salvador Allende and Cuba's Ché Guevara, condemns the Vietnam War, and deplores the situation in Northern Ireland. He also warns against Soviet political abuses, castigating militarists and dishonest bureaucrats. These critical poems range from "Stalin's Heirs" and "Babii Yar," from the early 1960's, to later poems, including "Momma and the Neutron Bomb" and poems about the dissident Andrei Sakharov and the Afghanistan war (with the Soviets) in the 1980's. When one considers that, due to censorship, many of Yevtushenko's poems were not published when they were written in the 1960's, his cynical critique of Soviet politics is understandable. Included in this collection are a number of his censored poems. Among them are verses to fellow Russian poets, "Russian Tanks in Prague," and "The Ballad of the Big," a bawdy tale about castration for the good of the party.

Another thread running through Yevtushenko's work is the importance of poetry and the responsibility of the poet to humankind. He constantly questions his own talent and mission, thus continuing the Russian tradition of meta-poetry. Likewise very Russian is the dialogue between writers living and dead that Yevtushenko carries on, in poems addressed to or evoking Pasternak, Pablo Neruda, and Jack London, along with numerous others. He also blasts modern writers in "The Incomprehensible Poets," in which he admits: "My guilt is my simplicity./ My crime is my clarity." In "I Would

Like," he notes: "I would like to belong to all times,/ shock all history so much/ that it would be amazed/ what a smart aleck I was."

Personal accounts, such as "On a Bicycle" and "Flowers for Grandmother," fill several pages in the collection. "Blue Fox" combines his concern for animals with an allegory of the collective state; "Monologue of an Actress" is a witty complaint by an aging actress that no worthwhile roles are left to play. His own experiences are represented here as well, contributing to his range of personal stories. His poetry is a kind of diary that details his extensive travels and especially his many love affairs. Remarkable love poems follow the poet from first love, to the birth of his sons, to the sadness of falling out of love again. The poems contain a rich fabric of quarrels, memories, farewells, and even a conversation with his dog, who shares the poet's grief that his woman has gone. The human breadth that he captures is perhaps the strongest aspect of this collection.

WALK ON THE LEDGE

Walk on the Ledge, despite the subtitle "A New Book of Poetry," contains both new and old poems, including "Babii Yar" and "Fears," which were written more than forty years earlier but appear in new translations alongside the original Russian. A few of the poems, such as "On the Grave of May the First" (1996) and "The City of Yes and the City of No" (1964), were also written earlier. However, the majority of the thirty-seven poems in this book are new and come from the early twenty-first century. Most of these poems were translated and edited by Gracie and Bill Davidson with help from Deborah Taggart. Yevtushenko has continued to tinker with his best-known poems long after they were first published. The 2005 version of "Babii Yar" differs from the 1961 version in significant ways, perhaps due to different translations and continued additions. Yevtushenko's postscript to "Fears" states that ever since Shostakovich based his thirteenth symphony on the poem, the poet had wanted to revise it because some stanzas seemed poetically weak. He attributes the flawed earlier version to his own hurried composition and the censorship standards of the Soviet magazine that first printed it. The predominant themes are by now familiar to Yevtushenko's readers: the expansiveness and generosity of youthful love, alienation from mother Russia, feelings of displacement in foreign countries, cultural conflict between western capitalism and idealistic socialism, Chechen separatists and their battles for ethnic identity, and the effects on people clinging to the failed Soviet socialist system.

Walk on the Ledge follows the modern trend towards bilingual publishing, printing English and Russian language versions on opposite pages. Perhaps Russia's increasing importance as a strategic partner of Western Europe and the United States has increased the attractiveness of Russian language study in schools and colleges.

The title poem, "Walk on the Ledge," describes Yevtushenko's tenuous relationship with his homeland during Stalin's 1950's repressions, when the poet felt as if he were balanced on a precipice with a glass of vodka in his hand, a metaphor for the political balancing act of creative expression in an authoritarian state. The poet confesses his joy of singing and climbing to the rooftops, playing at love and clamoring to escape through the Iron Curtain to the liberties beckoning from Rome or Paris. Much of the appeal of Yevtushenko's poetry comes through his exuberance and desire to thumb his nose at the humorless doctrine of Soviet socialism. Equally joyful are the poet's many effusions dedicated to love of women and relationships such as "My First Woman," "Eyelashes," and "Men Don't Give Themselves to Women." In "Old Photograph," Yevtushenko reflects on a youthful dalliance with a fellow intellectual, a young American woman who left the poet with a photo inscribed with her wish for his future success. As he holds the photo of his old girlfriend, the poet hears her voice admonishing him to keep producing, to keep loving, and to keep living zestfully.

Another of Yevtushenko's favorite themes is the idealism of the early Soviet vision for an egalitarian utopia versus the crumbled reality of a corrupt political system and severe restrictions against artistic freedom. "Tsunami" deals with the disastrous 2004 earthquake and resulting tsunami that claimed thousands of lives in Thailand and across Southeast Asia. The poet recalls hiding in San Francisco during the 1960's with his American girlfriend under the watchful eyes of the Central Intelligence Agency and the KGB. At this time, young people idolized Cuban revolutionary Ché Guevara and admired Fidel Castro's new socialist republic in Cuba, but the reality of Cold War politics became clear. Fashionable "socialists" in Hollywood did not care about the political message as long as profits from films and records kept flowing. Meanwhile, new oil-rich Muscovites cared nothing for political theory as long as they could wear shiny new clothes and ride around in chauffeur-driven stretch limousines. The intensity and loss of life of the tsunami that hit Thailand rendered political discussions meaningless. Political commentary continues in many poems such as "When Will a Man Come to Russia," "Gorbachev in Oklahoma," and "On the Grave of May the First."

In "School in Beslan," the poet reflects on the 2004 hostage crisis when Chechen rebels stormed a school and took children as hostages, demanding that Russia stop the war. Yevtushenko compares Beslan to a place of his youth much like in "Zima Junction" and finds abundant buried reminders of the unconscious powers that shaped his imagination. He feels the jumbled emotions of his expectations for greatness and early fame in his homeland mingled with his strange twenty-first century irrelevance in midwestern America. Yevtushenko looks over the range of twentieth century history with the wreckage of Stalin's purges, dissidents, deportations to Kazakhstan, the war against Chechen rebels, and Yeltsin's egoism. The poet wonders whether the multinamed "gods" of Muhammad, Christ, or Vladimir Ilyich Lenin will together be able to save anyone in the ongoing war between religions, nations, and armies.

The final poem in this collection is "La Corrida" ("The Bullfight"). The long, discursive narrative poem employs a variety of stanza structures, voices, and tones ranging from talking horses to political commentary. The poet discusses seeing the spectacle of sport and savage animal sacrifice in Seville, Spain, which becomes a statement of universal suffering, human hypocrisy, and passions of the moment. The grandiose celebration of toreadors, street parades, and drunken revelry masks the brutality of primitive religion and blood sacrifice. Animals are enslaved for human entertainment much in the same way that power politics views individuals as expendable pawns in a game of conquest. The public spectacle renders brutality into grand theater for the benefit of those in power, the bullfighters or politicians. Murderers are viewed as heroes by the frenzied crowd as blood flows through the streets of Seville, Berlin, or Moscow.

YEVTUSHENKO: SELECTED POEMS

This work pays homage to the importance of Yevtushenko in the revival of the traditional lyric poem in the Soviet Union/Russia of the twentieth century. Translated by British scholars Robin Milner-Gulland and Peter Levi, *Yevtushenko: Selected Poems* is a reissue of the original 1963 Penguin Classic that wound up on many shelves of politically aware college students in the United States and Europe. When first published, *Yevtushenko: Selected Poems* outsold every book of foreign poetry in translation except E. V. Rieu's *Odyssey*. It contains many of Yevtushenko's strongest works, such as "Babii Yar," "Zima Junction," and "Fears," and an assortment of amorous and politically inspired short poems. Levi writes that the appeal of Yevtushenko has to do with the poet's personal sensibilities and his concept of what are acceptable topics, which are far outside the Westerner's experience. The core of Yevtushenko's message is found in honesty, acceptance of what life brings, and a hopefulness about human nature that transcends politics. It destroys the common image of Soviet society as being hostile, impenetrable, and cold-blooded.

OTHER MAJOR WORKS

LONG FICTION: *Yagodnye mesta*, 1981 (*Wild Berries*, 1984); *Ne umirai prezhde smerti*, 1993 (*Don't Die Before You're Dead*, 1995).

PLAY: *Pod kozhey statuey sbobody*, pr. 1972.

NONFICTION: *Primechaniya k avtobiografii*, 1963 (*A Precocious Autobiography*, 1963); *Talant est' chudo nesluchainoe: Kniga statei*, 1980; *Fatal Half Measures: The Culture of Democracy in the Soviet Union*, 1991.

BIBLIOGRAPHY

Brown, Deming. *The Last Years of Soviet Russian Literature: Prose Fiction, 1975-1991*. New York: Cam bridge University Press, 1993. History and criticism of late Soviet-era Russian literature. Includes bibliographical references and index.
Brown, Edward J. *Russian Literature Since the Revolution*. Rev. ed. Cambridge, Mass.: Harvard University Press, 1982. A survey and critical analysis of Soviet literature. Includes bibliographic references.

The Economist. "Past, Implacable." 306, no. 7535 (January 30, 1988): 75-76. Draws parallels between Yevtushenko's poetic themes and glasnost, concentrating on "Bukharin's Widow" and "Monuments Not Yet Erected."

Emerson, Caryl. *The Cambridge Introduction to Russian Literature.* New York: Cambridge University Press, 2008. Comprehensive historical essays that cover the range of Russian poetry and prose. Includes thematic essays and index.

Hingley, Ronald. *Russian Writers and Soviet Society, 1917-1978.* New York: Random House, 1979. A history of Russian literature of the Soviet era. Includes a bibliography and index.

Kinzer, Stephen. "A Russian Poet Steeped in America." *The New York Times,* December 11, 2003, p. E1. Deals with the poet's beliefs and his interactions with students.

Milne, Ira Mark, ed. *Poetry for Students.* Vol. 29. Detroit: Thomson/Gale Group, 2009. Contains an analysis of "Babii Yar."

Slonim, Mark. *Soviet Russian Literature.* 2d ed. New York: Oxford University Press, 1977. A historical and critical study of Russian literature.

Vanden Heuvel, Katrina. "Yevtushenko Feels a Fresh Wind Blowing." *Progressive* 24 (April, 1987): 24-31. Addresses Yevtushenko's views on Russian politics, poetry's public service, glasnost, and relations with the West.

Yevtushenko, Yevgeny. "September 11th as Teacher of Teachers." *South Central Review* 19 (Summer/Autumn, 2002): 11-22. Reflective essay by the poet about the emotional reaction to flying on the day of the terrorist attacks in New York city.

Irma M. Kashuba; Sarah Hilbert
Updated by Jonathan Thorndike

CHECKLIST FOR EXPLICATING A POEM

A. Before reading the poem, the reader should:
1. Notice its form and length.
2. Consider the title, determining, if possible, whether it might function as an allusion, symbol, or poetic image.
3. Notice the date of composition or publication, and identify the general era of the poet.

B. The poem should be read intuitively and emotionally and be allowed to "happen" as much as possible.

C. In order to establish the rhythmic flow, the poem should be reread. A note should be made as to where the irregular spots (if any) are located.

II. Explicating the Poem

A. *Dramatic situation.* Studying the poem line by line helps the reader discover the dramatic situation. All elements of the dramatic situation are interrelated and should be viewed as reflecting and affecting one another. The dramatic situation serves a particular function in the poem, adding realism, surrealism, or absurdity; drawing attention to certain parts of the poem; and changing to reinforce other aspects of the poem. All points should be considered. The following questions are particularly helpful to ask in determining dramatic situation:
1. What, if any, is the narrative action in the poem?
2. How many personae appear in the poem? What part do they take in the action?
3. What is the relationship between characters?
4. What is the setting (time and location) of the poem?

B. *Point of view.* An understanding of the poem's point of view is a major step toward comprehending the poet's intended meaning. The reader should ask:
1. Who is the speaker? Is he or she addressing someone else or the reader?
2. Is the narrator able to understand or see everything happening to him or her, or does the reader know things that the narrator does not?
3. Is the narrator reliable?
4. Do point of view and dramatic situation seem consistent? If not, the inconsistencies may provide clues to the poem's meaning.

C. *Images and metaphors*. Images and metaphors are often the most intricately crafted vehicles of the poem for relaying the poet's message. Realizing that the images and metaphors work in harmony with the dramatic situation and point of view will help the reader to see the poem as a whole, rather than as disassociated elements.

1. The reader should identify the concrete images (that is, those that are formed from objects that can be touched, smelled, seen, felt, or tasted). Is the image projected by the poet consistent with the physical object?
2. If the image is abstract, or so different from natural imagery that it cannot be associated with a real object, then what are the properties of the image?
3. To what extent is the reader asked to form his or her own images?
4. Is any image repeated in the poem? If so, how has it been changed? Is there a controlling image?
5. Are any images compared to each other? Do they reinforce one another?
6. Is there any difference between the way the reader perceives the image and the way the narrator sees it?
7. What seems to be the narrator's or persona's attitude toward the image?

D. *Words*. Every substantial word in a poem may have more than one intended meaning, as used by the author. Because of this, the reader should look up many of these words in the dictionary and:

1. Note all definitions that have the slightest connection with the poem.
2. Note any changes in syntactical patterns in the poem.
3. In particular, note those words that could possibly function as symbols or allusions, and refer to any appropriate sources for further information.

E. *Meter, rhyme, structure, and tone*. In scanning the poem, all elements of prosody should be noted by the reader. These elements are often used by a poet to manipulate the reader's emotions, and therefore they should be examined closely to arrive at the poet's specific intention.

1. Does the basic meter follow a traditional pattern such as those found in nursery rhymes or folk songs?
2. Are there any variations in the base meter? Such changes or substitutions are important thematically and should be identified.
3. Are the rhyme schemes traditional or innovative, and what might their form mean to the poem?
4. What devices has the poet used to create sound patterns (such as assonance and alliteration)?
5. Is the stanza form a traditional or innovative one?
6. If the poem is composed of verse paragraphs rather than stanzas, how do they affect the progression of the poem?

7. After examining the above elements, is the resultant tone of the poem casual or formal, pleasant, harsh, emotional, authoritative?

F. *Historical context.* The reader should attempt to place the poem into historical context, checking on events at the time of composition. Archaic language, expressions, images, or symbols should also be looked up.

G. *Themes and motifs.* By seeing the poem as a composite of emotion, intellect, craftsmanship, and tradition, the reader should be able to determine the themes and motifs (smaller recurring ideas) presented in the work. He or she should ask the following questions to help pinpoint these main ideas:
1. Is the poet trying to advocate social, moral, or religious change?
2. Does the poet seem sure of his or her position?
3. Does the poem appeal primarily to the emotions, to the intellect, or to both?
4. Is the poem relying on any particular devices for effect (such as imagery, allusion, paradox, hyperbole, or irony)?

BIBLIOGRAPHY

Gᴇɴᴇʀᴀʟ ʀᴇꜰᴇʀᴇɴᴄᴇ ꜱᴏᴜʀᴄᴇꜱ

Bɪᴏɢʀᴀᴘʜɪᴄᴀʟ ꜱᴏᴜʀᴄᴇꜱ

Jackson, William T. H., ed. *European Writers*. 14 vols. New York: Scribner, 1983-1991.

Kunitz, Stanley, and Vineta Colby, eds. *European Authors, 1000-1900: A Biographical Dictionary of European Literature*. New York: Wilson, 1967.

Magill, Frank N., ed. *Critical Survey of Poetry: Foreign Language Series*. 5 vols. Englewood Cliffs, N.J.: Salem Press, 1984.

_____. *Critical Survey of Poetry: Supplement*. Englewood Cliffs, N.J.: Salem Press, 1987.

Serafin, Steven, ed. *Encyclopedia of World Literature in the Twentieth Century*. 3d ed. 4 vols. Detroit: St. James Press, 1999.

_____. *Twentieth-Century Eastern European Writers: First Series*. Dictionary of Literary Biography 215. Detroit: Gale Group, 1999.

_____. *Twentieth-Century Eastern European Writers: Second Series*. Dictionary of Literary Biography 220. Detroit: Gale Group, 2000.

_____. *Twentieth-Century Eastern European Writers: Third Series*. Dictionary of Literary Biography 232. Detroit: Gale Group, 2001.

Cʀɪᴛɪᴄɪꜱᴍ

Coleman, Arthur. *A Checklist of Interpretation, 1940-1973, of Classical and Continental Epics and Metrical Romances*. Vol. 2 in *Epic and Romance Criticism*. 2 vols. New York: Watermill, 1974.

Jason, Philip K., ed. *Masterplots II: Poetry Series, Revised Edition*. 8 vols. Pasadena, Calif.: Salem Press, 2002.

The Year's Work in Modern Language Studies. London: Oxford University Press, 1931.

Dɪᴄᴛɪᴏɴᴀʀɪᴇꜱ, ʜɪꜱᴛᴏʀɪᴇꜱ, ᴀɴᴅ ʜᴀɴᴅʙᴏᴏᴋꜱ

Auty, Robert, et al. *Traditions of Heroic and Epic Poetry*. 2 vols. Vol. 1, *The Traditions*; Vol. 2, *Characteristics and Techniques*. Publications of the Modern Humanities Research Association 9, 13. London: Modern Humanities Research Association, 1980, 1989.

Bede, Jean-Albert, and William B. Edgerton, eds. *Columbia Dictionary of Modern European Literature*. 2d ed. New York: Columbia University Press, 1980.

France, Peter, ed. *The Oxford Guide to Literature in English Translation*. New York: Oxford University Press, 2000.

Henderson, Lesley, ed. *Reference Guide to World Literature.* 2d ed. 2 vols. New York: St. James Press, 1995.

Oinas, Felix, ed. *Heroic Epic and Saga: An Introduction to the World's Great Folk Epics.* Bloomington: Indiana University Press, 1978.

Pynsent, Robert B., ed. *Reader's Encyclopedia of Eastern European Literature.* New York: HarperCollins, 1993.

Weber, Harry B., George Gutsche, and P. Rollberg, eds. *The Modern Encyclopedia of East Slavic, Baltic, and Eurasian Literatures.* 10 vols. Gulf Breeze, Fla.: Academic International Press, 1977.

INDEX OF PRIMARY WORKS

Hoffman, Herbert H. *Hoffman's Index to Poetry: European and Latin American Poetry in Anthologies.* Metuchen, N.J.: Scarecrow Press, 1985.

POETICS

Gasparov, M. L. *A History of European Versification.* Translated by G. S. Smith and Marina Tarlinskaja. New York: Oxford University Press, 1996.

Wimsatt, William K., ed. *Versification: Major Language Types: Sixteen Essays.* New York: Modern Language Association, 1972.

RUSSIAN POETRY

Blok, Aleksandr. *Us Four Plus Four: Eight Russian Poets Conversing.* New Orleans, La.: UNO Press, 2008.

Bunimovitch, Evgeny, and J. Kates, eds. *Contemporary Russian Poetry: An Anthology.* Translated by Kates. Champaign: Dalkey Archive Press, University of Illinois, 2008.

Cornwell, Neil, ed. *Reference Guide to Russian Literature.* Chicago: Fitzroy Dearborn, 1998.

Kates, J., ed. *In the Grip of Strange Thoughts: Russian Poetry in a New Era.* Brookline, Mass.: Zephyr Press, 2000.

Nabokov, Vladimir Vladimirovich, comp. and trans. *Verses and Versions: Three Centuries of Russian Poetry.* Edited by Brian Boyd and Stanislav Shvabrin. Orlando, Fla.: Harcourt, 2008.

Poggioli, Renato. *The Poets of Russia, 1890-1930.* Cambridge, Mass.: Harvard University Press, 1960.

Polukhina, Valentina, and Daniel Weissbort, eds. *An Anthology of Contemporary Russian Women Poets.* Iowa City: University of Iowa Press, 2005.

Rydel, Christine A., ed. *Russian Literature in the Age of Pushkin and Gogol: Poetry and Drama.* Dictionary of Literary Biography 205. Detroit: Gale Group, 1999.

Tschizewskij, Dmitrij. *History of Nineteenth-Century Russian Literature.* Translated

by Richard Noel Porter. Edited by Serge A. Zenkovsky. Nashville, Tenn.: Greenwood Press, 1974.

Wachtel, Michael. *The Cambridge Introduction to Russian Poetry*. New York: Cambridge University Press, 2004.

_____. *The Development of Russian Verse: Meter and Its Meanings*. New York:
Cambridge University Press, 1998.

Maura Ives
Updated by Tracy Irons-Georges

GUIDE TO ONLINE RESOURCES

Web Sites

The following sites were visited by the editors of Salem Press in 2010. Because URLs frequently change, the accuracy of these addresses cannot be guaranteed; however, long-standing sites, such as those of colleges and universities, national organizations, and government agencies, generally maintain links when their sites are moved.

LitWeb
http://litweb.net

LitWeb provides biographies of hundreds of world authors throughout history that can be accessed through an alphabetical listing. The pages about each writer contain a list of his or her works, suggestions for further reading, and illustrations. The site also offers information about past and present winners of major literary prizes.

The Modern Word: Authors of the Libyrinth
http://www.themodernword.com/authors.html

The Modern Word site, although somewhat haphazard in its organization, provides a great deal of critical information about writers. The "Authors of the Libyrinth" page is very useful, linking author names to essays about them and other resources. The section of the page headed "The Scriptorium" presents "an index of pages featuring writers who have pushed the edges of their medium, combining literary talent with a sense of experimentation to produce some remarkable works of modern literature."

Poetry Foundation
http://www.poetryfoundation.org

The Poetry Foundation, publisher of *Poetry* magazine, is an independent literary organization. Its Web site offers links to essays; news; events; online poetry resources, such as blogs, organizations, publications, and references and research; a glossary of literary terms; and a Learning Lab that includes poem guides and essays on poetics.

Poetry in Translation
http://poetryintranslation.com

This independent resource provides modern translations of classic texts by famous poets and also provides original poetry and critical works. Visitors can choose from several languages, including English, Spanish, Chinese, Russian, Italian, and Greek. Original text is available as well. Also includes links to further literary resources.

Poetry International Web

http://international.poetryinternationalweb.org

Poetry International Web features information on poets from countries such as Indonesia, Zimbabwe, Iceland, India, Slovenia, Morocco, Albania, Afghanistan, Russia, and Brazil. The site offers news, essays, interviews and discussion, and hundreds of poems, both in their original languages and in English translation.

Poet's Corner

http://theotherpages.org/poems

The Poet's Corner, one of the oldest text resources on the Web, provides access to about seven thousand works of poetry by several hundred different poets from around the world. Indexes are arranged and searchable by title, name of poet, or subject. The site also offers its own resources, including "Faces of the Poets"—a gallery of portraits—and "Lives of the Poets"—a growing collection of biographies.

Western European Studies

http://wess.lib.byu.edu

The Western European Studies Section of the Association of College and Research Libraries maintains this collection of resources useful to students of Western European history and culture. It also is a good place to find information about non-English-language literature. The site includes separate pages about the literatures and languages of the Netherlands, France, Germany, Iberia, Italy, and Scandinavia, in which users can find links to electronic texts, association Web sites, journals, and other materials, the majority of which are written in the languages of the respective countries.

ELECTRONIC DATABASES

Electronic databases usually do not have their own URLs. Instead, public, college, and university libraries subscribe to these databases, provide links to them on their Web sites, and make them available to library card holders or other specified patrons. Readers can visit library Web sites or ask reference librarians to check on availability.

Canadian Literary Centre

Produced by EBSCO, the Canadian Literary Centre database contains full-text content from ECW Press, a Toronto-based publisher, including the titles in the publisher's Canadian fiction studies, Canadian biography, and Canadian writers and their works series; *ECW's Biographical Guide to Canadian Novelists*; and *George Woodcock's Introduction to Canadian Fiction*. Author biographies, essays and literary criticism, and book reviews are among the database's offerings.

Literary Reference Center

EBSCO's Literary Reference Center (LRC) is a comprehensive full-text database designed primarily to help high school and undergraduate students in English and the humanities with homework and research assignments about literature. The database contains massive amounts of information from reference works, books, literary journals, and other materials, including more than 31,000 plot summaries, synopses, and overviews of literary works; almost 100,000 essays and articles of literary criticism; about 140,000 author biographies; more than 605,000 book reviews; and more than 5,200 author interviews. It contains the entire contents of Salem Press's MagillOnLiterature Plus. Users can retrieve information by browsing a list of authors' names or titles of literary works; they can also use an advanced search engine to access information by numerous categories, including author name, gender, cultural identity, national identity, and the years in which he or she lived, or by literary title, character, locale, genre, and publication date. The Literary Reference Center also features a literary-historical time line, an encyclopedia of literature, and a glossary of literary terms.

MagillOnLiterature Plus

MagillOnLiterature Plus is a comprehensive, integrated literature database produced by Salem Press and available on the EBSCOhost platform. The database contains the full text of essays in Salem's many literature-related reference works, including *Masterplots, Cyclopedia of World Authors, Cyclopedia of Literary Characters, Cyclopedia of Literary Places, Critical Survey of Poetry, Critical Survey of Long Fiction, Critical Survey of Short Fiction, World Philosophers and Their Works, Magill's Literary Annual,* and *Magill's Book Reviews.* Among its contents are articles on more than 35,000 literary works and more than 8,500 poets, writers, dramatists, essayists, and philosophers; more than 1,000 images; and a glossary of more than 1,300 literary terms. The biographical essays include lists of authors' works and secondary bibliographies, and hundreds of overview essays examine and discuss literary genres, time periods, and national literatures.

Rebecca Kuzins; updated by Desiree Dreeuws

CATEGORY INDEX

SUBJECT INDEX